CW00767147

Land Rover Series I Restoration Manual

Theo Ford-Sagers and Benjamin Stowe

Land Rover Series I Restoration Manual

Theo Ford-Sagers and Benjamin Stowe

THE CROWOOD PRESS

First published in 2022 by
The Crowood Press Ltd
Ramsbury, Marlborough
Wiltshire SN8 2HR

enquiries@crowood.com

www.crowood.com

© Theo Ford-Sagers and Benjamin Stowe 2022

All rights reserved. No part of this publication may be reproduced or transmitted in any form
or by any means, electronic or mechanical, including photocopy, recording, or any information
storage and retrieval system, without permission in writing from the publishers.

British Library Cataloguing-in-Publication Data
A catalogue record for this book is available from the British Library.

ISBN 978 0 7198 4058 6

Disclaimer
Safety is of the utmost importance in every aspect of an automotive workshop. The practical
procedures and the tools and equipment used in automotive workshops are potentially
dangerous. Tools should be used in strict accordance with the manufacturer's recommended
procedures and current health and safety regulations. The author and publisher cannot accept
responsibility for any accident or injury caused by following the advice given in this book.

Typeset by Jean Cussons Typesetting, Diss, Norfolk
Cover design by Blue Sunflower Creative
Printed and bound in India by Parksons Graphics

Contents

Acknowledgements

We are extremely grateful for the guidance and encouragement of many Series I owners and specialists while writing this book. Particular thanks go to Rob Sargeant and Martin Plewes for their help with the stripdown of our demonstration vehicle, to Series I parts supplier CKD Shop for answering our questions and allowing us to take some photos on their premises, and to Charlesworth Mouldings for doing the same.

1

Introduction

This restoration manual is for anyone considering restorative work on a Series I Land Rover, whether rebuilding from the ground up, or taking a more phased approach with a rolling restoration.

For illustrative purposes, the book follows the refurbishment of a 1957 109in petrol Series I. The chapters will guide you through all the procedures involved, describe how to achieve a prize-winning result, and show you how to save money by refurbishing components rather than replacing them outright.

As any experienced enthusiast will know, it is beyond the scope of any one book to describe the myriad changes and variations that the Series I underwent during its ten years of production, but we hope the reader will find it useful to follow the restoration of one particular Series I, as a source of ideas, reference, context and inspiration.

There are some limitations on the depths we can go to in these pages, so you won't find much guidance about (for example) the intricacies of welding, or how to fully rebuild an engine – procedures that require considerable skills or investment in machinery. We will, however, show how the corroded chassis and bulkhead were repaired, and how to recommission an engine that has been laid up, including the restoration of certain ancillaries, and we will provide an introduction to the gearbox and demonstrate why it may require an overhaul. In each chapter we endeavour to describe the overall function of each system and its components – but we must also assume that the reader has some basic knowledge of how vehicles essentially work.

The chapters are structured according to subject area, and take a broadly chronological approach – although the reader will occasionally be invited to look to a different chapter for the completion of a particular system. Therefore the precise order of events as they appear in this book need not be followed too slavishly.

In addition to this book, you will benefit from owning Rover's Series I workshop manual and parts catalogues. They will outline certain repair procedures, help you understand how components fit together, and provide part numbers that will be useful for any components you need to order – both for the vehicle itself and for optional equipment.

A SHORT HISTORY LESSON

The Series I is the original Land Rover. Rising from the ashes of World War II, it is the purest and most basic iteration of what later evolved into the widely adored Defender.

Old Land Rovers are rarely considered mere tools, despite their humble simplicity and emphasis on function over form. For anyone who has owned one or relied on one, they represent a way of life – an uncomplicated and authentic way of engaging with our increasingly hyperconnected, fast-paced world. Buy a Series I today and you are joining a worldwide community of people who appreciate those original values that made the Land Rover special. You are also buying a machine that has developed its own unique character: now that more than sixty years have passed since the last Series I was built, each survivor is a veteran of decades of toil and adventure. Inevitably, therefore, almost all have either been restored, or need restoring.

According to legend, it all began with an outline traced in the sands of Anglesey, off the north-west coast of Wales. Maurice Wilks, later to become Rover's managing director, had been inspired to create a new four-wheel-drive utility vehicle to replace his old Willys Jeep that had been left over from the war. It seemed to be a good idea, and the export potential was strong, so in April 1948 the first Series Is were unveiled to the world at the Amsterdam Motor Show. The motoring press loved them, orders flooded in, and the legend was born. After forty-eight pre-production models, production began that summer, even though the design of those first 1,500 vehicles built up to Christmas 1948 (chassis numbers 860001 to 861500) was in a constant state of flux – a nightmare for restorers seeking to make their vehicle 'correct' today.

The original Land-Rover (the name lost its hyphen later on) had been intended as a mere stopgap to see Rover through the difficult years of post-war austerity, but by 1949 the Solihull factory on Lode Lane was already making about eighty Land Rovers a day, and by 1951 they were outselling all Rover's other models by a factor of two to one. Production would ramp up even further for Series II production as vehicles were sent all round the world, many in 'CKD' kit form for assembly overseas.

Much of the appeal of the Series I derives from its boxy design and construction, which couldn't be simpler – and that is part of the key to its enduring success as an all-terrain, utilitarian beast of burden. For decades, Series Is were among the cheapest Land Rovers you could buy, and plenty of today's car enthusiasts had their first introduction to automotive engineering by stripping, modifying or generally 'hacking about' with an old Series Land Rover. Sometimes that meant playing with their dad's workhorse on the farm, sometimes it meant going trialling in an old heap – perhaps sticking a Rover V8 under the bonnet. Sometimes it meant smacking their heads on the roof on the way home from school, and later peering underneath to find out why old Land Rovers are so bouncy.

The very first production-model Land Rovers at Solihull in late June 1948. BRITISH MOTOR INDUSTRY HERITAGE TRUST

All this rugged simplicity means that restoring a Series I may be relatively straightforward, compared to many other classic vehicles. Most of the mechanical components are easy to understand, and there are virtually no extra systems other than what is necessary to get from A to B – no brake servo, no power steering, no anti-roll bar, no superfluous upholstery or air conditioning, and certainly no ABS. There's hardly any trim to worry about, and the electrics are the 'knife and fork' variety – as simple as they come.

One convenient result of the vehicle's off-road design is that most mechanical components are easy to access: the high ground clearance means that it's easy to get underneath, and the large wheel arches – built to accommodate suspension articulation when clambering over rough ground – can easily accommodate a mechanic's arms, and his head, too, if needs be.

Another strength of the Series I is that, in various ways, they were better built than the Series IIs, IIAs and IIIs that followed. In these later years, the profits generated by Land Rover sales tended to be syphoned off to other areas of the business rather than being reinvested back into Solihull. Obvious examples of the Series I's superior quality include the bonnet and door frames, which are galvanized on Series Is, but non-galvanized and rust prone from the Series II onwards.

Series Is undoubtedly have their complications, ranging from high cost and poor availability of certain parts, to the difficulty in determining the correct specification, particularly of the very early models. But if you have never restored a vehicle before, they offer a deeply rewarding and manageable place to start.

WHICH MODEL IS WHICH

Although all Series Is share much in common, there were some important mechanical changes throughout the ten-year production run from 1948 to 1958. There are also obvious structural differences between long and short wheelbases, and the main body styles: hard top, soft top, truck cab (aka 'regular') and Station Wagon.

In mid-1953 the wheelbase (the distance between the centres of the front and rear wheel hubs) was increased from 80in to 86in, and a long-wheelbase 107in model was introduced. During 1956 both wheelbases were lengthened, the short wheelbase becoming 88in and the 107in becoming 109in, although the long-wheelbase Station Wagon retained its 107in wheelbase. The extra 2in were added between the bulkhead and the front crossmember, effectively enlarging the engine bay in order to accommodate a new 2.0-litre diesel engine – a powerplant that did not gain much popularity and is very rare today. In many ways, all these later Series Is share more in common with each other than they do with 80in Series Is built up to 1953.

Demand is generally greatest for early 80in Series Is, which have an extra layer of difficulty for the restorer as certain parts are very expensive and difficult to obtain. On the other hand, some parts are now made for 80s and not for later Series Is, due to the extra demand and the higher budgets of those restoring them. Rarer derivatives may also attract a premium, including the long-wheelbase Station Wagons. As always, the best restorations are defined by a high degree of originality.

RESTORING TODAY

The days of finding a cheap Series I in every farmyard are long gone. These are now collectible classic vehicles in their own right, and are appreciated by petrolheads worldwide, not just within diehard Land Rover enthusiast circles. During the 2010s values boomed, particularly around the time of the original Defender's demise in 2016. The surge in interest inevitably caused a growing incentive to restore, resulting in a dwindling supply of new-old stock spares, and rising prices for those parts that were left. ('New-old stock' refers to parts that were originally built by Land Rover and have been sitting unused since, as opposed to modern aftermarket or remanufactured parts.)

It is extremely rare for a Series I to retain its original chassis, bulkhead and drivetrain, partly due to corrosion having ruined so many structural components, and partly due to the large range of engines that can be installed in a Series I to improve its performance – especially later Series engines and Rover V8s. Many Series Is have also become donors for each other, and it has been common for Minervas to be used as donor vehicles. Minervas (built from 1951 to 1954) were left-hand-drive Series Is, built in Belgium for the Belgian military using steel bodywork and a Belgian-made chassis (without the capability of running a PTO) but using the same engine, gearbox and axles as the regular 80in models – this made them ideal donors, especially in decades when breaking a Series I was less frowned upon than it would be today.

Nevertheless, the Series I restoration scene has never reached the maturity of some other areas of the classic car world. At the UK's main classic vehicle shows you will find multiple suppliers of complete new bodyshells for a wide range of classics, whereas not all Series I bodywork is available to buy 'off the shelf'. Rover made large reserves of spares, and the British military hoarded much of it for decades, but the larger repositories have mostly been sold, and it's fair to say that we are now scraping the barrel when it comes to new-old stock.

Certain hard-to-find parts are provided by various small businesses – often comprised of a single individual creating work of a very high standard, and operating mainly by word of mouth. Other parts will be impossible to find in unused condition, in which case a second-hand item or a later spec alternative may have to suffice. Sometimes the main governing factor behind these decisions will be your budget, and we will discuss some of them throughout the following chapters.

HOW MUCH WILL IT COST?

First you need to consider the current values of Series Is. At the time of writing (2021), Series I projects range from around £5k for a ropey 88in, to perhaps £15k for a tired but solid and original 107in Station Wagon. Once restored to top condition, the 88in could be worth at least £20k, and a concours 107in Station Wagon will fetch up to £40k.

At the top of the spectrum, a restoration by Land Rover's Reborn division will typically cost over £100k, while restorations carried out by CKD Shop (which specializes in the earliest models up to Christmas 1948) are typically on behalf of customers with at least £150k to spend.

Ultimately there are five main factors that will determine the total cost of your restoration:

◆ Which model will you choose?
◆ Which areas of the vehicle are deteriorated, and how badly?
◆ How much of the work will you do yourself, and how much will you rely on specialists?
◆ What level of perfection are you aiming for? (Are you happy to keep some patina?)
◆ Are you striving for 'factory correct' specification, or not?

If you're collaborating with a specialist, it is important to discuss clearly all these points in advance, and to put them in writing (along with a time scale), to make sure you are all on the same page.

If you are doing all the work yourself, expect the minimum cost for a total restoration to be around £15k–20k. This is for an 88in Series I that does not require a new chassis, or its engine or gearbox rebuilding – just a strip-down with recommissioning of ancillary parts along the way, a retrim and fresh paint, applied by you. A specialist would need to charge a minimum of £30k–35k for this work.

Bear in mind that an accurate budget will be very difficult to forecast in advance, due to the large prices now paid for certain small sundry parts, and many of these nasty surprises will catch you out if this is your first Series I restoration. Meanwhile the true condition of the chassis and the engine is unlikely to be gauged accurately on the first inspection, and each of these could require thousands of pounds to put right or replace. The total cost will also fluctuate as parts sell out and new parts come on the market.

AUSTRALIAN SERIES IS

Imported Series Is from Australia have become a popular option for restoration, as the supply of decent 'barn finds' in the UK has almost completely dried up. In recent years it has been estimated that around 100 Series Is per year have been arriving in the UK from Australia, and supplies haven't run out. Australia is still a good source of weather-beaten workhorses that have lived in the arid outback, and a small network of specialists in both countries specialize in sourcing them. The paintwork tends to be heavily patinated and bleached by the sun, and you will often find that the region of Australia where the vehicle was initially based is painted on to a wing, adding to the car's patina and individuality.

Australian Series Is typically have much less corrosion than those that have lived in the UK. This can make them more cost effective to restore, considering the price of replacing or repairing a rusty chassis and bulkhead. As a general rule, most Series Is in the UK were ready to expire from corrosion after only ten to fifteen years. In Australia they have tended to soldier on until mechanical fatigue eventually gets the better of them. Some say the old tradition of repairing rather than replacing parts lives on in Australia more than in the UK, perhaps due to poorer availability of parts (especially for 80in models) than in the Land Rover's home territory.

A pair of battered but solid Australian Series Is awaiting restoration in the UK.

Even when sourcing from a dry climate, it's important not to expect a perfectly preserved vehicle. Some degree of rust is still likely, and many have taken a huge amount of mechanical punishment from heavy use. They may have received 'bushcraft' maintenance in regions where spare parts are hard to come by, and possibly been laid up for a long while before coming back to the UK.

Australian Series Is are essentially the same as those sold in the UK, with the exception of a few minor details. Many have also received Holden engine swaps to gain more power or to replace a worn Rover 2.0-litre engine. Generally they use the original gearbox, with an adaptor plate, and the front crossmember usually has a notch cut out – sometimes crudely done – to give enough room for the engine, so this will need repairing or replacing.

RESTORING RARITIES

The Land Rover has never been only the 'farmer's friend'. In the words of one early brochure, the Land Rover was 'For the farmer, the countryman and general industrial use', but even that didn't cover the diverse range of applications that Series Is were adapted for – some built under licence by approved businesses, some by Solihull. One of the pleasures of Series Land Rovers is in learning more about these exotic derivatives, which can generate major interest at shows and in some cases will attract a premium at auction. However, these models usually demand many hours of careful research. Certain parts may not be available and will have to be made bespoke, pushing up the overall cost.

For example, the first station wagons used coach-built bodies made by Tickford on 80in chassis, using aluminium bodywork over an ash frame, with sideways seating for four in the rear plus three up front. The Tickford has a full-width tailgate and no rear bulkhead, and its doors, rear bodywork, roof and windscreen are all unique to the model. To restore an ash frame is highly specialist work requiring the services of a coachbuilder, and the interior trim will need to be made bespoke.

Other rare variants include the Swedish made 'Grip-Kaross'. Like the Tickford, its bodywork was built under licence using aluminium panels over a wooden frame, but with extra insulation and a larger heater for cold climates, and in either truck cab or estate form.

Solihull offered fire engines in 80, 86 and 88in guises. Instead of carrying their own water tank they would pump water from a separate source, and use a PTO-driven water pump mounted on the front or rear. Specification varied considerably, and many received changes during service, making it difficult to determine each vehicle's original specification today.

The many military variants include 86in Series Is built for the SAS with 24-volt electrics for radio gear, 88in two-wheel-drive models with no front differential, and the steel-bodied Minerva mentioned earlier.

Thirty-three 81in prototypes were built for evaluation by the British Army, incorporating the 2.8-litre Rolls-

A 1949 Tickford Station Wagon, with rare and challenging bodywork. JAGUAR LAND ROVER

Restored 80in fire engine, complete with period equipment. LEN WRIGHT

Minerva Series I, with distinctive steel bodywork. STEVE GLOVER

Royce B40 engine as used in the Austin Champ. The conversion, carried out by Hudson Motors Ltd, required significant changes to the chassis (including moving the rear spring mounts to create the extra wheelbase), and it is believed that only two survive with their original engine. Other rarities include 'Royal Review' vehicles, welders and radio vehicles, but this is by no means an exhaustive list of the wide range of interesting conversions – not to mention the large selection of Rover-approved accessories.

Some of the best known include winches (hydraulic drum or mechanical capstan), power take-off units (PTOs), and 15cwt Brockhouse trailers. Built by Brockhouse & Co. Ltd and available from 1949, these were designed specifically for use with the Land Rover, with an identical axle track. Less conspicuous options included a propshaft guard, while certain models were able to include an auxiliary tank mounted opposite the main tank. Possible creature comforts ranged from a Smiths heater in the cab, floor mats, an addi-

tional windscreen wiper or a water-temperature gauge, capillary-fed from the thermostat housing.

Some accessories that have been commonly fitted to Series Is would not be introduced until Series II/IIA/III production; a notable example is the Fairey overdrive, which was not introduced until the 1970s, but can easily be added to a Series I to create extra gearing for more relaxed cruising.

Again, this list is far from comprehensive, but hopefully gives a flavour of the range of possibilities.

2

Assessing the Project

This chapter will outline how to gauge the overall condition of a project vehicle, focusing on inspections that can be made without raising the vehicle off the ground, and without any major dismantling.

THE DEMO VEHICLE

Most of the images in this book show Ben's restoration of this long-wheelbase 109in Series I, which came to us via UK-based Land Rover importer Jonathan Holmes (Cross Channel Classics).

This is a 'trayback' body style, popular in Australia but never originally offered by Rover. It would have started life as a CKD ('complete knocked down') pickup or 'Regular', with a rear tub that was separate from the cab. The underpinnings of a 109in Series I are very similar to a 107in from the bulkhead back, and the tray is a simple construction, very easy to fit and remove. It arrived in our yard mechanically standard and essentially complete – lacking just a few pipes, cables, fuel sedimenter… and one or two other parts that would not become obvious until later.

Clearly this vehicle had had a tough life. The intensity of its abuse became increasingly clear the more it was stripped down, and we found everything from stress fractures around the chassis to broken gears. Ben has rebuilt many Australian Series Is, and can confirm that this level of mechanical fatigue is quite common.

The plan was to retain and repair parts where possible, rather than replace them. When replacement of parts was the best course of action, second-hand parts would be sourced if they could be found in good condition, to help keep costs under control. Our purpose is to present the reader with an 'attainable' restoration, resulting in a smart and usable vehicle with a high degree of originality, rather than a high-budget 'trailer queen'.

Bodywork would be straightened out and mended wherever possible,

The 109in trayback, as it arrived at the workshop.

The bulkhead plaque tells us that this vehicle was assembled by Pressed Metal Corporation Ltd, Sydney.

and the original chassis and bulkhead would both be repaired, with the aim of illustrating what can be realistically achieved if you are willing to be hands on and to put in the effort. When a choice had to be made between achieving a perfect finish or retaining historic authenticity, the latter would be prioritized.

The result is a sympathetic and attainable renovation, rather than a prize-winning restoration. It makes the process take longer, but it tends to reduce the overall cost. Whereas a more 'perfect' Series I might be considered too precious to be taken out of the garage, a restoration of this type can be put to use and enjoyed as its creators intended.

These decisions also extend to the mechanicals. For this restoration, areas that were best restored by a specially equipped workshop (such as the radiator and gearbox) were sent away for recommissioning, but the chapters guide you through all the more achievable tasks, and show you how to make important assessments for yourself.

Factory-fresh perfection is obviously a perfectly valid target. In some ways this will make the restoration simpler, because to achieve an immaculate

This rear tray is probably a couple of decades newer than the rest of the vehicle.

finish typically requires a higher proportion of brand new components. A new chassis and bulkhead should reduce the likelihood of alignment issues or internal corrosion, which are difficult to address when restoring old metal.

At various points in the following chapters there are descriptions of how to create a more 'perfect' finish than is appropriate for this 109in, sometimes using examples from other Series Is that Ben has restored previously.

YOUR FIRST INSPECTION

Always inspect a vehicle before committing to buy it, or have an inspection carried out on your behalf. The opinion of an independent expert may be more valuable than your own, depending on your level of knowledge and theirs. Even an honest seller can be unaware of the vehicle's true condition. Make it your own responsibility – not theirs – to determine how much work the vehicle needs. During the course of your restoration you will get to know it far better than the seller does.

To carry out a thorough inspection you will need to have a few things with you, and you should consider taking the following:

◆ Overalls
◆ A foam mat to lie on
◆ Rubber gloves and/or heavy duty wipes
◆ A small torch
◆ A starting handle (in case you need to manually check if the engine is seized)
◆ Coolant and oil (in case the engine is too dry to run)
◆ Gallon of fuel (to enable a test drive)
◆ Small hammer (to check for rust)
◆ Basic toolkit containing spanners and screwdrivers

Series Is use a smaller range of materials than can be found on later vehicles. Plastics were not yet in common usage during this period, and Bakelite (an early type of plastic) can be found in only a few places – primarily the fusebox, regulator box, switch gear, inside the fuel pump, and the steering-wheel rim (which is built round a steel frame).

DETERMINING ORIGINALITY

Ideally the chassis number and engine number will correlate with each other. (Lists of serial numbers can be found in an original workshop manual.) The engine number should be stamped into the machined upward-angled face that the exhaust manifold is mounted to, visible from above. The chassis number was always stamped into the chassis, but its precise location varied according to the model type. For 107in Station Wagons it will be stamped on the inside leg of the front dumb-iron on the right-hand side. For 86s, 107 regulars, 109s and 88s it is always on the rear left spring hanger, and for 80s

Series Is it will be found on the left-hand engine mount.

The location of the chassis number is less predictable on CKD cars; this 109's chassis number is on a rear spring shackle, but they are also sometimes found on the front dumb-irons. The gearbox number will be on the right-hand side of the gearbox casing, and the axle numbers will be on the upper part of the casing on the left-hand side.

Elsewhere around the vehicle, deciphering the level of originality can be a deeply complex endeavour, and will require you to obtain at least some basic knowledge of how the Series I evolved during its

The engine number of the 109 on a rear spring shackle hanger, after painting. This was difficult to make out before cleaning off the surface rust.

The chassis number of an extremely early 80, beside the front left engine mount.

production. The most significant differences are between 80in models and those that followed, and even between 80in models there was a great deal of variation, particularly in the first few months of production up to Christmas 1948 while the final details were yet to be finalized by Solihull. Of these first 1,500 examples, it has been estimated that changes were made roughly every hundred vehicles. Although the design stabilized somewhat when the 86 and 107 replaced the 80 for the 1954 model year (mid-1953), the subtle evolution still continued.

Whatever the wheelbase, tell-tale clues will help you determine whether the vehicle's various parts originally belonged together. These clues can be found in all areas of the vehicle – from small details such as rivets and electrical components, to more structural aspects such as the design of the chassis and bulkhead. For example:

One example of the many subtle variances in spec. The box-sectioned crossmember is from a pre-1957 107in Station Wagon; the double C-shaped version is post-1957.

- Before Christmas 1948, the pressed-steel bulkhead was not ready for production, so the first 1,500 vehicles left Solihull with fabricated bulkheads comprising many separate parts and fixings.
- Production 80s up to 1950 can be identified by a 'fishplate' bumper mounting at the front of the chassis, so called because of its resemblance to a fish tail. During 1950 this was replaced by a bracket welded to the bumper rather than the chassis.
- An 80's chassis has straight outriggers for the bulkhead; they are curved on all later Series Is.
- External door handles were introduced to the 80 during 1952.
- 107in Station Wagons up to 1956 have a panel on the B pillar with four rivets in a diamond pattern; this was lost on later models.
- 107in Station Wagons up to 1957 have box-section rear crossmembers; thereafter the crossmember was made from two C-shaped sections.
- Headlamps up to 1950 were 5½in in diameter and were mounted behind the grille. These were followed by 7in lights-through-the-grille headlamps (with the grille encircling the lamps), followed by the upside-down T-shaped grille.

- Steel panels were initially made of aluminium, but this changed to steel for the 88/109. The arrangement of the holes also differed: 88s and 109s have a single hole, and three different designs were fitted to 80s.
- Early 86in Station Wagons have two vents in the roof; this increased to four during 1955.
- A fully floating rear axle (identifiable by the dust caps on the rear wheel hubs) replaced the standard semi-floating design in spring 1957 for 88s, and in 1958 for 109s.

This is just a small selection of the most easily identifiable changes. A helpful mine of information on the topic is James Taylor's book, *Original Land-Rover Series I*. Where these differences affect the restoration procedure, many will be pointed out in the following chapters.

THE ENGINE

If the engine has been inactive for some time, be prepared that it will be reluctant to start without new spark plugs, HT leads, condenser, points, rotor arm and ignition coil, and of course a healthy battery. Don't forget also to check the coolant and oil levels, and top these up if required. You may

encounter problems with stale fuel, leaking or blocked fuel lines, or a non-functioning fuel pump. Fuel blockages can be caused by rust filling the carburettor's float chamber, or by the degradation of old rubber fuel pipes due to the use of modern fuels, resulting in loose fibres blocking the sediment bowl's gauze filter or the carburettor jets (more on this in Chapter 9).

After a prolonged dormancy, you will need to make sure that the pistons have not seized into the bores. If so, the block will need to be sent to a specialist for the bores to be re-honed. To find out, turn the crankshaft either by using a starting handle or by rotating the fan. As you rotate the engine you should feel the resistance build and drop with each stroke.

If the engine initially turns but can then be felt to lock up, it is likely that a valve is stuck open – a problem that is usually exclusive to the exhaust valves because of their upward angle. When an exhaust valve is open, its combustion chamber is open to the atmosphere, and any moisture or condensation that may form on the valve is able to run down the valve stem, where it collects and causes corrosion. The inlet valves (and all the valves in ohv engines) are above the combustion chamber and positioned vertically, so the valve stem is less prone to collect-

Assessing the engine: the 109's engine bay is not a pretty sight.

ing moisture in this way. A stuck valve can usually be freed off, but you will need to take the head off first.

If you discover a crack in the block around the bores, then the engine is likely to be scrap, and replacing it will add significantly to the cost of your restoration.

An engine that has not been run for a long time will suffer from extra internal wear when fired up for the first time, because its lubricating oil will have drained into the sump, and will not be fully circulated until the engine has passed through a few rotations. You can minimize this effect on the cylinder bores by removing the spark plugs and squirting a very small amount of light oil such as WD40 into each cylinder. It is important to squirt only a very small amount, and not enough to pool – too much will introduce the risk of 'hydraulic lock' when the engine is turned over.

It is also wise to remove the top rocker cover and lubricate the inlet valve gear with oil, and ideally the exhaust valves and timing chain too, inside the timing chest. Prepare for these tasks by having spare gaskets or gasket compound ready.

THE TRANSMISSION

Try to select all the gears, even if the engine doesn't run. This will highlight whether the gearbox selectors are corroded. If you are able to drive the vehicle, ensure that all the gears select cleanly without excessive scrunching, and that there are no excessive chattering, grumbling or whining noises. It is also important to check that the gearbox does not jump out of gear, by driving at fairly high revs and sharply backing off the accelerator – repeat this process in each of the forward gears. If you encounter any of these issues, we advise removing the gearbox and sending it away for a rebuild by a specialist (*see* Chapter 8).

Early Series Is have permanent 4WD, with a ring-pull mechanism in the driver's footwell that enables the front axle to disconnect automatically on over-run. It is very difficult to assess whether there are any faults with this system without driving the vehicle. Later transfer boxes with selectable 4WD are easier to diagnose, as you have the option to jack up the front axle and see if it is free to turn or not;

if the transfer box is in 4WD, the front and rear propshafts should effectively be locked together.

Further 'downstream', the best way to assess the propshafts is with them still attached to the vehicle. Check for play in their universal joints (UJs) by manually rotating the propshaft side to side, and looking for any play in the cups that sit on the spider section within the yokes; these can be cost-effectively replaced. To check for wear in the propshaft splines, grab the shaft and push it up and down in the middle; if you detect any movement in the spline then it will need reconditioning by a specialist, although it is usually cheaper to find a replacement propshaft. (Incidentally, the 86in Series I is the only Land Rover that has identical propshafts front and rear – more on this in Chapter 12.)

While pushing the propshaft up and down, check for play at the nose of each of the differentials. Movement here is likely to indicate wear in the bearings that the pinion shaft runs in. Replacement is ideally carried out by a specialist, because the preload in the pinion bearings will need to be precisely calibrated

The transmission inspection: make sure all the gears engage.

BELOW: *This 109 is missing gaiters, and has no handbrake!*

The 4WD knob is missing, and the gear-lever base has the wrong bolt.

against the crownwheel. The carriers for the bearings at either side of the differential can also be wound in and out, adjusting the left/right position of the differential inside its casing – but again, we would recommend you find a specialist who can perform this work for you, and budget accordingly.

SUSPENSION

The suspension on all Series Land Rovers is extremely sturdy and simple, with leaf springs on all four corners. These springs will continue functioning, albeit poorly, even when extremely worn and rusty, which is partly why old Land Rovers have a reputation for being quite rough to ride in. The truth is, however, that a well set-up example with fresh springs should feel safe and handle predictably.

Leaf springs can last for decades, but corrosion between the leaves prevents them from sliding against each other, increasing the spring's stiffness. This can be improved by dismantling the leaves, grinding out the rust and rebuilding with grease, but if the spring has sagged it will need retempering –

in which case, buying new springs and looking after them well (with frequent lubrication) is typically a better course of action.

There are many different possible springs, determined by the wheelbase, body style, engine, and position on the vehicle, so it is worth counting the number of leaves on each one, and checking that the correct springs are fitted.

The width of the springs also changed: 80in Land Rovers originally had 1¾in wide springs all round. In 1951 they moved to 2½in springs on the front, giving slightly more controlled handling thanks to the weight of the engine. The wider springs give the same articulation as the older, narrower front springs, due to there being a different number of leaves. The narrow front springs have spring shackles at the front of the spring; the introduction of the wider springs saw the shackle move to the rear. All later model Series Is use 2½in wide springs front and rear, with rear-mounted shackles.

The shock absorbers for the 80in are different to later Series Is, with a 1½in eye rather than the 1¾in eye used in

later Series Is. Shock absorbers will typically be renewed as part of the restoration.

BRAKES

Take a look at the brake fluid, which should be clean and translucent. A hand-held brake-fluid tester can be used to assess the moisture content of the fluid, which absorbs water from the atmosphere over time, accelerating corrosion within the braking system. Any moisture content above 4 per cent can be considered high. In the case of a large-scale rebuild project such as this 109, this level of assessment is arguably less relevant, as all the major brake components will be replaced anyway; however, in less dilapidated vehicles a test such as this will give you an idea of how well looked after the vehicle really is, and how corroded the system is likely to be. In most cases it is wise to renew or recondition all the wheel cylinders and master cylinder, along with the complete set of brake lines.

Leaks are more common from brake pipes and hoses than wheel cylinders, which are more likely to seize than leak.

Check the leaf springs for cracks, splaying and sagging.

The handbrake expander can stick due to corrosion, and the ratchet mechanism can seize inside the handle if the vehicle has been left out in the open without a roof, allowing moisture to run down the handbrake lever. If the lever is seized, you can remove the pin connecting it to the expander, allowing the expander to relax so the vehicle can be moved.

The handbrake shoes may also stick against the drum, as a result of corrosion on the drum's inner surface. You can try backing off the shoe adjuster on the back of the drum, but if this fails, tapping the drum with a soft hammer will sometimes free off the shoes. If oil is leaking out through the back of the transfer box into the handbrake drum, the shoe linings will be contaminated and must be replaced, after the leak has been fixed (*see* Chapter 8).

Bear in mind that the handbrake is a transmission brake and should never be used to bring the vehicle to a halt: doing so can cause severe damage. Only ever engage the handbrake when the Land Rover is stationary.

STEERING SYSTEM

The steering system ought to be assessed for wear in its many joints and, more importantly, in the steering box and relay. (The steering box shouldn't be confused with the steering relay, which is mounted further 'downstream' in the front crossmember.)

The initial inspection consists of moving the steering wheel left and right and checking for play. It will help if you have an assistant to manipulate the steering wheel so you can check each component more closely. Play in the ball joints is a minor issue as these are cheap to replace; slackness inside the steering box may simply require tightening of the adjuster nut (on recirculating ball types) or more expensive intervention. If slackness is found within the steering relay, this has the potential to be highly problematic due to the potential difficulty of extracting it from the chassis. In many cases it will be rusted into place so tightly that extraction requires replacement of the entire front crossmember – a process that requires great care to avoid introducing chassis alignment issues. Hopefully you will find no play between the relay's top and bottom arms, so you can leave it in place.

The chrome-plated swivels are integral to the steering system. Surface pitting on the chrome surfaces is highly likely in vehicles that have been left standing, especially in a damp environment, and will require the swivels to be replaced. They also contain a bush and bearing that can wear, and most resto-rations will involve replacing all these components together. (The original splined peg arrangement for a Railko bush will be replaced in Chapter 6.) In some cases you may find the swivels to be enclosed within leather gaiters, which can be effective at preventing mud and road salt from increasing corrosion, but if they have accumulated water inside, then it is likely they will have had the opposite effect.

BODYWORK

Non-structural panels are all made from Birmabright, an alloy comprised primarily of aluminium. It is important to check for areas of galvanic corrosion (also known as bi-metal corrosion) wherever aluminium alloy and steel meet, causing the aluminium to corrode into a fine white powder. Fortunately this problem is less severe than on later Series Land Rovers, in particular around the seat box, which is more likely to have stress fractures than major corrosion (especially in Australian Series Is) – but galvanic corrosion can still be an issue.

Birmabright also loses its malleability with age, increasing the likelihood of fractures forming, especially around stress points where the panel meets a mounting point. It cannot realistically be welded, so repairing damage

Seat-box corrosion is less likely on Series Is than later Land Rovers, but check anyway.

typically involves either attempting to return it to its original shape and perhaps introducing some filler (the cheaper option), or replacing the panel altogether (which is more expensive). Depending on the type of restoration you're aiming for, you may choose to retain damaged panels to preserve the vehicle's character – provided the metal is safe and free from jagged protrusions. This will be discussed in more depth in Chapter 10. New body-work sections range in availability and affordability, so it is worth researching and budgeting for this carefully before you begin your project.

The Birmabright panels are built around steel frames (body cappings, windscreen surround, door frames, bonnet frame), which were all galvanized to a high quality. If the galvanized coating has deteriorated and rust is showing through from underneath, these parts can be sent away for hot-dip regalvanizing. However, regalvanizing just one piece will cause it to stand out awkwardly, with a much brighter finish than the other galvanized parts, so it is best either to galvanize all the exposed areas, or not at all.

Check the alignment of the doors. If a door is drooping, this can be a sign of structural problems where the body is mounted to the chassis, particularly where the tub mounts to the outriggers behind the seat box – a common spot for corrosion. But you may need to think more broadly to reach an effective diagnosis: for example, a sagging door may be the result of a notch that has worn into the hinge (sometimes repairable with a drop of weld), or simply due to poor assembly. Such issues are best diagnosed before the vehicle is stripped.

All rubber seals perish and go hard with age, and it is likely that you will need to replace all of them. Their designs are different from later Series Land Rover designs; some are fiddly to install, especially the door seals, but in many cases they are longer lasting. As for the rear glazing rubbers, on Series Is and IIs the seal's filler strip is exposed on the outside of the vehicle; on later Series Land Rovers it was concealed on the inside to prevent thieves from easily removing it to gain access.

The wipers can wear a sweep pattern on the windscreen due to grit or

The Birmabright in the rear corner of this 80 is well past saving, but the badge, capping and grab handle should be salvaged. Note the steel angle from a previous 'repair' holding it together.

the deterioration of the (often poor quality) blade or blades. Delamination of the windscreen can also sometimes be a problem, so look out for air bubbles appearing, and if you find any, budget for new glazing.

THE BULKHEAD

The main bulkhead between the engine and the cab needs to be strong enough to withstand considerable forces when driving, and its structural integrity is extremely important. There are essentially two main types, and both are susceptible to corrosion.

The first was used on 80in Series Is from Christmas 1948. Its main section is made from one piece of steel, pressed into shape, with smooth edges around the footwells. The sidelights in these bulkheads were deleted in 1952, and thereafter the door hinges comprised just a single lower pivot.

The second category of Series I bulkheads was introduced in 1953 when the 80 was replaced by the 86/107. This saw a change to a fabricated steel design, made from separate sections of steel sheet that were spotwelded together, with the addition of a full-width interior shelf. The bulkhead is similar on 88/109in models – part of which is taken up by a larger instrument panel. The stiffener on the front face of the bulkhead between the footwells is a single pressed piece instead of two welded plates.

The rare exceptions to these two main categories are the first 1,500

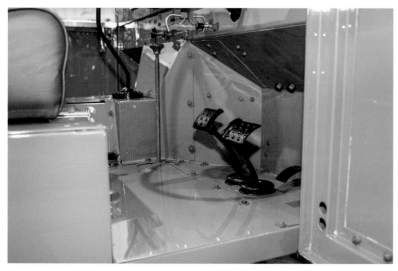

An early footwell. This is the driver's footwell of a 1948 Series I with a fabricated bulkhead, restored by the CKD Shop.

A pressed-steel 80in bulkhead, restored by Ben Stowe. Note the curved edges round the footwell corners.

A rare 1952 aluminium bulkhead, freshly restored by Ben. Note the angular edges round the footwell corners.

hand-fabricated bulkheads built up to Christmas 1948; these have a removable centre section, which enables good access to the back of the engine, and no rainwater gutter beneath the bonnet level.

Aluminium alloy bulkheads were also used sporadically throughout 80in production, with a steel frame for the door pillars, the top rail and the mount for the steering box, but the panels are Birmabright. Exactly why this was the case has been the subject of some debate, and there has been speculation that the press broke in 1952, and hand-made aluminium bulkheads were a stopgap – but it may also have been due to material shortages in the post-war years. Even these versions are not entirely aluminium: the door pillars, top rail and bulkhead stay brackets are all steel. This frame is then clad in aluminium panels, which are riveted to the frame using rivets – both pop rivets and solid rivets.

Repairs are generally easier to perform on the later steel bulkheads, as they are made of mostly straight sheets and lack the compound curves of the earlier type, which are very difficult to replicate. However, the extra folds and spotwelds of the later type can allow moisture ingress, so they are more prone to creating rust traps.

Suppliers of restored 80in bulkheads will typically start with a bulkhead whose central, curved sections are complete, and will weld in new sections where required. The original curved instrument binnacle is also usually retrieved – sliced out and welded into brand new metal. Completely new pressed bulkheads have also recently become available.

On the front of 80in bulkheads you will find two horseshoe-shaped brackets that mount the bulkhead to the chassis. Moisture accumulates behind

This very rotten 80in bulkhead shows where rust can take hold on the early type. It is barely salvageable, and only because the curved areas round both sides of the footwells have escaped corrosion. Rust in these areas would mean that the bulkhead was a write-off.

Severe and typical corrosion round the horseshoe-shaped mounting bracket on an 80 bulkhead.

them, causing rust in both the bracket and the footwell. This is repairable, but awkward to achieve because of the multiple layers of steel. The area in front of the lower door pillar also tends to rust badly – another location where repairs here can be difficult, depending on the severity of the corrosion.

With both types of bulkhead, the horizontal top rail that sits beneath the windscreen needs to be assessed carefully for corrosion. On a soft-top, it is advisable to fold the windscreen down and check beneath the windscreen seal; on a hardtop this will not be possible without removing the roof first, so for your initial inspection you will need to attempt to feel hidden areas around the top rail with your hand. It rusts in a similar way to the later style bulkhead: the top surface corrodes, as do the supporting pillars beneath it. New top rails can be bought and welded into place, but it is not a simple process and you will need to have solid metal to weld on to.

With the windscreen still in situ, it was clear that the top rail of the 109's bulkhead needed replacing. This area, to which the hinge bolts, has two layers, hollow inside, and is particularly vulnerable to rust.

Along with the top rail, the corroded front section of the bulkhead will also need replacing.

Corrosion in the lower door pillar of an 80in bulkhead – another common weak spot.

The dismantled 80in bulkhead showing typical corrosion along the top rail – with the windscreen in situ this can't be seen.

The lower areas of the door pillars also corrode, and the footwells tend to rust along their seams, mainly along the lower edges due to road spray from underneath. Pre-formed footwells can be bought and welded into place, by drilling out the spotwelds of the original footwells, and adding a small puddle of weld in their place.

Pre-formed footwells can be bought and welded into place, by drilling out the spotwelds of the original, and adding a small puddle of weld in their place when welding in the new material. Alternatively you can fabricate your own smaller sections – *see* Chapter 5. (In our case the rust was mainly to be found in the upper areas of the footwell.)

THE CHASSIS

The condition of the chassis is arguably the single most important component to check, due to the cost of buying a replacement, or the labour involved in the restoration of the original. All Series

Land Rovers (and Defenders up until 2016) used an ungalvanized, painted steel chassis, on to which the engine, transmission, running gear and bodywork are all bolted. The chassis is vital to the strength and safety of the entire vehicle, and any holes or weak areas must be repaired to a high standard.

Once corrosion sets in, it will be difficult to keep on top of it, partly because the metal deteriorates from the inside out. In some cases, the chassis might have received an injection of wax to prevent corrosion, but this is rarely a perfect solution. In practice it is unlikely that a completely thorough coating can be made throughout the inside of the chassis, and an efficient seal is only possible on metal that is perfectly clean and dry. Underseal applied to the outside of the chassis is also no guarantee against corrosion, especially if it has been applied to metal that was already weak or poorly prepared.

The entirety of the chassis needs to be checked thoroughly, but there are a few common weak spots. These are the rear crossmember, the front dumb-irons (where the main chassis rails extend forwards to the bumper), the bulkhead outriggers, and the areas around the spring hangers. The shape of the hangers makes them very difficult to weld, and they tend to be weakest on 107in Station Wagons, which – unlike our chassis – have the springs mounted on outriggers extending either side of the chassis. You should also expect to find weak metal between the bump stops and the chassis, as it's a perfect trap for mud and moisture.

Along the whole length of the chassis there is a tendency for mud to sit along the top and cause rust. The top of the chassis is difficult to see in most places, so you will need to get a hand up there and press down firmly to test the metal. However, the worst rust is usually along the chassis rails' lower areas, where mud that has accumulated inside causes it to rust from the inside out. All areas of the chassis ought to give a reassuring 'ting' when tapped with a hammer.

Incidentally, although the front bumper is rarely thought of as a crossmember, some early publications refer to the bumper as being Crossmember 1, and the front chassis crossmember

Check for signs of repair such as this, especially if it has been done poorly. This shackle sleeve is completely loose in the chassis rail.

The rear shock-absorber mount had partially torn the socket out of the chassis rail.

The rear crossmember, often a weak spot, was reasonably solid on this vehicle; however, on removing the towplate later, rust was revealed behind it.

The top of the chassis seemed solid at this stage, although rust became evident after blasting. This shows where one of the tray's feet mounts to the chassis, attached with U-bolts.

as being Crossmember 2. This makes more sense in light of the fact that early Series Is had the bumper welded to the chassis.

Finally, be alert to any signs of poor alignment in the chassis. Unfortunately this is difficult to gauge accurately while the bodywork is still on the vehicle. If the vehicle is roadworthy, your best option is to ask someone to drive the vehicle while you follow along behind, watching to see if the Land Rover is crabbing (this is when the rear wheels follow a slightly different line from the one taken by the front). If it is clearly doing so, the chassis could effectively be scrap. These complications will be discussed in Chapter 4.

WHAT ARE WE DEALING WITH?

The steel panel needs repair, but is salvageable.

The non-original seating is worn and needs replacing.

These late-type instruments are usually easier to salvage than 80in versions.

The chassis and trayback's underlying structure are mostly solid.

THE VERDICT ON THE PROJECT VEHICLE

The initial inspection of the project 109 revealed that it was in a very bad way, but not beyond restoring. Clearly it had not been used on the road in many years, and had seen some severe off-road abuse.

The engine was initially empty of oil and coolant, but with some encouragement and a replacement fuel pipe, it was persuaded to run. The age of its internal components was unknown to us, so it required a partial stripdown to determine whether anything would need to be sent away for machining. One element that definitely did require the attention of a specialist was the gearbox, as one of the gears could not be selected.

The bulkhead's top rail was badly corroded and some smaller repairs were needed lower down, but these are quite common issues, and overall it was worth saving. The chassis had some visible corrosion in common places, which would need repairing, but the rust did not seem excessive. Of more concern were the stress fractures and broken suspension mounts – features that are often seen in Australian examples. Restoring the chassis was clearly going to be a big job.

Some of the bodywork was badly battered, especially the front wings, but Ben has experience of returning Series I bodywork back into its original shape, so these flaws were considered to be within acceptable limits. The rear tray, however, was so badly misshapen that it was decided to fabricate a new one from scratch. In the vehicle's favour were its relative completeness and originality, and the fact that it could at least be made to run.

Ben therefore drew up a plan to restore the vehicle while retaining the original chassis, bulkhead and running gear, with the aim of creating an unusual and practical Series I with plenty of originality and period character. When finished, it would make an attractive working vehicle, well suited to a farm or other commercial usage.

The steel tray is rusted and battered so it will be used as the basis for making a new one.

Illegal, dangerous, and useless off-road – these tyres are only fit for trundling round a yard.

The engine bay is mostly complete; exceptions include the air-inlet hose and the coolant manifold for the inlet manifold.

The door trim is totally past saving, but this vehicle can do without it anyway.

3

Stripping the Vehicle

Taking apart a Series I can be a reasonably quick process, thanks to the lack of trim and the vehicle's simple construction. It can also be satisfying if time isn't against you, so long as you are prepared for a likely encounter with hidden horrors – especially rust related. Much of the work is self-explanatory, but this chapter offers an overview of the process, and includes some key pieces of safety advice.

Trying to reduce every assembly to its smallest components at this early stage would be unnecessary. For example, the axles and bodywork sections – once detached – should remain complete. They can then be dismantled and rebuilt when required, and you may choose to leave these stages until after the chassis has been restored. The structure of this book follows the same principle, so some of the more complex assemblies will be dismantled in the relevant chapters, while this one will focus on the initial breakdown.

The project Land Rover has chassis number 123800267, stamped into the left-hand rear spring shackle. Land Rover's *Workshop Manual for Series I* contains a comprehensive breakdown of which numbers were assigned to which vehicles, and it confirms that this vehicle left Solihull in 1957 in CKD form, as a right-hand-drive 109in petrol model.

TOOLS, WORKSPACE AND GETTING READY

Although you don't need a workshop, a full restoration is much harder without one. What you can't do without is enough space for the chassis, axles, bulkhead, engine, gearbox and body sections when they are all separate from each other. Dismantling a vehicle means creating chaos from order, so your working environment has to be prepared for this. You will need to keep it under control to prevent being overwhelmed with parts everywhere. Don't rush, and stay organized. Invest time in keeping related components together and categorized; ice-cream tubs, boxes and ziploc bags labelled with permanent marker will all help. This will pay dividends later.

The vast majority of the work featured in this book can be achieved with a small range of basic tools. You will need a complete set of spanners and sockets in Whitworth and Imperial AF sizes, as well as metric tools for any non-original fixings that have been added to the vehicle in more recent decades. A torque wrench will be required when reassembling certain fixings to the tightness specified by Rover.

You will also need some method of raising the engine and gearbox out of the chassis, using either a forklift (as we do in this book) or an engine crane, which will require a flat, level floor to run on. A ramp is a luxury that many restorers are able to do without.

Good lighting will make the job much easier, and will extend your ability to work during winter evenings. Ideally you will have a combination of free-standing lights, and one or two hand-held worklights with magnetic bases, enabling them to stick to the vehicle and illuminate awkward crevices. A headtorch can also be useful.

A large, strong workbench with a heavy vice will be useful (almost essential) for dismantling some components. A parts washer is a non-essential but useful addition, so you can submerge whole components in a flow of degreaser. Large quantities of penetrating oil, degreaser and mechanics' soap such as Swarfega are essential.

As for power tools, you will require a strong drill, and an angle grinder with cutting discs and grinding wheels. A cordless electric impact wrench will also save you much time and effort, although it isn't essential.

Safety gear should be considered essential, rather than optional. The most important item is a pair of safety glasses to protect against dirt, sparks or splashed fluid. Disposable rubber gloves are vital for protecting your skin against the long-term damaging effects of paints, oils and hydraulic fluids, and also help prevent cuts and scrapes. Overalls or old clothes will be needed, and these must not be allowed to accumulate too much old

Making a picture record of the chassis number.

oil before being cleaned, or they can become a fire hazard. Your feet should be protected at all times by steel toe-capped work boots. Extra safety gear is required for welding: this will be covered in Chapter 4.

A blowtorch can help with freeing off stuck nuts, and a breaker bar will give you a lot more leverage. Some mechanics swear by induction heaters, which wrap round the offending nut and super-heat it to extreme temperatures, but these are expensive. In many cases you'll have no choice but to cut off bolts with an angle-grinder and cutting disc.

We will introduce more specialist tools throughout the following chapters, as and when they are required. You could easily spend large sums of money on a wide array of specialist

A blowtorch will enable you to super-heat rusty fixings to help free them off.

Have plenty of hands-free light available, some of it pointing down from above.

Running a wire wheel is one of the many uses of a strong drill.

Use a drift for driving out pins.

A brass-headed hammer reduces the risk of fracturing harder metals.

tools, but whether it is best to buy, borrow, hire or simply make do without, will depend on how often you expect to use them.

Soak every visible nut and bolt in penetrating oil as soon as you begin to plan your rebuild, and reapply it whenever you can. This can relieve some of the effort involved in releasing seized fixings, but you will still find plenty. In most cases, cutting them off with an angle grinder is the most efficient way to deal with them, while taking great care not to damage any of the surrounding metal.

If the body panels have any tears in them, this is the moment to stop them

creeping further. Do this by drilling a $^1/_8$in (3mm) hole at the tip of the tear. You can fix it later with filler, and the hole will stop the tear from getting any worse in the meantime.

Before you dismantle anything, make a written and/or photographic record of what works and what doesn't, what lines up properly and what doesn't, and what is original and what isn't. It is far easier to plan the job when the vehicle is still intact, and relying on memory alone is unwise – especially if you are sharing the work with other people. Photographs and written notes help everyone stay on the same page.

You will need a large quantity of penetrating oil when dismantling.

UNDERSTANDING WHITWORTH, BSF, UNF, UNC

If you are not used to working on vehicles from this era, the names used to describe the dimensions of fixings are likely to cause confusion. Whitworth fixings – known as BSW, or British Standard Whitworth to give them their full name – were used by Solihull throughout Series I production. Devised in 1841 by Charles Whitworth, an engineer from Cheshire, this was the first standardized screw thread in the world. Whitworth is an 'imperial' unit, one of a series of standardized weights and measures used across the British Empire.

The 'W' suffix denotes that this is a Whitworth spanner.

You will also find BSF (British Standard Fine) threads in Series Is. Both Whitworth and BSF fixings have thread angles of 55 degrees, but BSF threads are finer than Whitworth; this creates a higher surface area, which can withstand higher torque.

UNF and UNC (Unified Fine or Coarse) threads were developed in the United States and Canada after World War II. Although they were not widely used in Series Is, some can be found on late models – for example on steering boxes from 1957 onwards.

Whitworth and UNC threads are not compatible, due to the pitch and shape of the thread. Whitworth bolts also have smaller heads than UNF or UNC, so they require a dedicated set of tools. Whitworth tools may seem unusual because the stated size of the tool relates to the diameter of the thread, not the distance from one flat side of the hexagon to another (the latter being A/F, or 'across flats'); they can be distinguished by the W prefix after the fraction.

Some parts (such as the vertical bolts that secure the upper sides to the tub – or the rear bulkhead in our case) are interchangeable with later Series II or III parts, but these will be UNF rather than BSF, so you will lose a degree of originality.

The drivetrain of Series Land Rovers continued using Whitworth threads until the gradual transition to metric during the 1970s. Bodywork fixings are all BSF on Series Is, and moved to UNF from Series II onwards. Metric fixings started being introduced to the Series III from 1980. (Propshaft nuts and bolts remained UNF even up to the end of Defender production in 2016.) Any metric fixings you find will date from this period onwards, and will not be original to the vehicle.

Collection of new sherardized fixings – important for a high quality restoration.

All Series I fixings are sherardized, meaning they have a highly rust-resistant zinc coating with a dull grey texture. BSF fixings are more expensive and harder to come by, especially sherardized, so UNF fixings can make a viable alternative if you are prepared to sacrifice a little originality. However, it is good practice to minimize crossover between measurement systems wherever possible, for obvious reasons.

You will also find a small number of Acme threads. These are very coarse threads, found on screws for spire nuts around the footwell. Other applications include the spire clips that hold the control panel on to the front of the bulkhead (in 86in Series Is onwards), and also the levers that operate the vent flaps.

THE ORDER OF EVENTS

Our initial objective is to remove all components from the bulkhead and chassis, so they can be repaired and painted. These two comprise the structural backbone of the vehicle, so getting them restored early on in the process provides a firm foundation for the reassembly of the remaining components.

Removing and reinstalling the cappings adds quite a lot of work that may be difficult to justify if you do not intend to have them regalvanized.

When you come to paint the bodywork later, an acceptable result can be achieved simply by masking over the cappings – the decision is up to you. For this 109's rebuild we have chosen to detach certain components (such as the spare-wheel mount and bonnet hinges) but to leave some of the larger, more complex parts in place.

If you have detected any wear in the steering relay, you should attempt to remove it before too much weight has been removed from the chassis, with the drivetrain, axles and bulkhead still in place. Hopefully the relay will simply pull out of the chassis once you have removed the attached linkages and undone its mounting bolts. If it is seized, the best method of removal is to jack up the front of the vehicle by exerting upward pressure on the relay itself, with the weight of the vehicle resting on it – which is why it will help if the drivetrain is still in place. *Please note that great care is needed while doing this, or serious damage may occur.* Ensure that the relay cannot collide with any components above it when it finally pushes above the crossmember. You will also need to make sure that the chassis, when it falls, does not collide with the jack.

An alternative method is to fabricate a cradle that holds a hydraulic jack underneath the steering relay, and clamps round the top face of the crossmember. If the steering relay still won't move, the front crossmember will have to be cut out and replaced, making this potentially one of the biggest possible jobs when refurbishing a Land Rover.

Unfortunately no Series Is were ever fitted with an unboltable gearbox crossmember, as later military Series vehicles were. The gearbox cannot therefore be removed from underneath the vehicle, so it has to come out from above. If you are not performing a complete rebuild, and are leaving the bodywork in place, the gearbox is removed by first extracting the seat box and then lifting the gearbox out through the passenger door using an engine crane. When performing a complete restoration, as we are, it makes more sense to strip off the whole body first.

You will need assistance and/or lifting gear for lifting the following items:

◆ The rear tub
◆ The bulkhead
◆ The roof
◆ The seat box
◆ The windscreen
◆ The bonnet
◆ The engine
◆ The gearbox

Standard Land Rover tubs are much easier to lift by hand (being composed primarily of lightweight Birmabright). If you don't have a forklift, you will need at least two people to lift a short-wheelbase rear tub, three for a long-wheelbase, and at least four or five to lift a heavy steel trayback such as this one.

REMOVING THE BODYWORK AND THE REAR TRAY

To begin, any sections that do not require unbolting are removed: the doors, bonnet and seats all simply lift out. Then the roof and cab wall are removed, and so on downwards.

There is one bolt at the top of each corner of the windscreen, and bolts on each side where the base of the truck

Undoing the front corners of the roof.

Undoing the cab wall from the bulkhead.

The roof and rear wall being removed – they remain attached for now.

cab meets the rear bulkhead next to the door opening, plus two smaller nuts along the back edge. Undoing the windscreen at this point gives a little flexibility to jiggle the roof free (you may need a breaker bar to free it off). The windscreen and rear wall of the cab can then be lifted together and removed.

Unbolting the roof from the rear section of the cab.

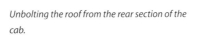

All the original perspex glazing and the window channels in the doors and the rear of the cab will also be removed, in preparation for painting later on. New sliders will be fitted all round, together with new seals for the doors, and all the glazing will be replaced – some of it with glass rather than rubber.

The wiring for the wiper motor was detached, then the motor was detached prior to removal of the windscreen.

The roof is separated from the rear cab (note the clouded old perspex).

The windows are removed by unscrewing their channels.

Undoing one of the wing nuts that secure the windscreen.

STRATEGIES FOR RUSTY FIXINGS

The front windscreen bolts of this project 109 provide a good example of threads that required multiple methods of attack. After leaving them to soak in penetrating fluid, the exposed threads were cleaned of dirt and corrosion with a wire wheel, to help them to turn once past the initial phase of getting them moving.

If you have a firm grip on a seized fixing, increase the pressure in small increments, and each time you make a small amount of progress, reverse the direction of rotation and add a little more penetrating oil before unwinding again. This back-and-forth motion helps the rust particles inside the thread to work their way out. Super-heating the thread using a blowtorch will also help, but take care to avoid damaging any nearby glass or rubber components – and obviously this must never be attempted anywhere near the fuel tank or fuel pipes.

In some cases, applying enough brute force to break the fixings free is the most efficient way to make progress – but this only applies to easily replaced bolts that screw into nuts. A breaker bar will do the trick. However, there are times when a more subtle approach is needed, and applying a large force should be an absolute last resort – for example:

◆ Bolts that screw into housings, which may crack if too much force is exerted on them.
◆ Unusual bolts that may be expensive to replace.
◆ Bolts with long shanks, which are more likely to sheer because the shaft can twist and snap before the torsion is transmitted to the threads.
◆ Partially rounded-off nuts, which are liable to slip and become even smoother.

You will need a back-up plan for those fixings that can't be undone.

The easiest method is to cut off the fixing using a slitting disc on an angle grinder.

Seized nuts can be removed by carefully slicing into an outside face with a slitting disc, making sure you don't cut through to the thread, then attacking the groove with a cold chisel and mallet. A section of the nut should split off, revealing the thread, and you will then be able to knock off the nut or undo it with a spanner. It is likely that both threads will be damaged with this technique, so you may prefer to use a nut splitter, which drives a wedge into the side of a nut to break it, using pressure generated by a spanner on the other end of the tool; this technique usually preserves the male thread.

To extract a broken stud, or a bolt whose head has sheered off, you will need an inexpensive bolt extractor tool, whose threads are in the opposite direction to a regular drill bit. The first step is to punch an indentation in the centre of the exposed part of the bolt, then increase its size with a small drill bit. This crater enables the extractor tool to bite into the shank of the bolt while turning anticlockwise, and then to unscrew the bolt.

You will not be able to salvage every single nut, and there is not much point in trying.

A wire wheel being used to clean the thread.

A breaker bar was needed to get this thread moving.

Although doing so will save you a little money and help retain the vehicle's historic character, shabby fixings can let down the appearance of your restoration, and new versions of all the original thread sizes are available with the original sherardized coatings. It is particularly important not to reuse critical fixings relating to brakes and suspension components, and these should be renewed even if the originals seem to be in good condition.

Heating with a blowtorch, being careful to avoid seals and glass.

Once the thread starts to move, a pair of Whitworth spanners can finish it off.

A sheered bolt: inevitably some fixings will not want to oblige.

The nuts securing the tow bracket were cut with a slitting disc, then broken off.

Once the windscreen was finally released from its fixings, it was removed in one piece. Reglazing the windscreen cab can be achieved quite simply, but in most cases it will not be necessary to remove the glass from the frame, so they can stay assembled.

The trayback of this 109in was held to the chassis with four U-bolts. The easiest way to free the trayback from the chassis was to cut through these bolts with an angle grinder, then rotate each section by 90 degrees. A forklift was then used to lift it into the air, with an extra pair of hands to make sure it didn't tip on its sling. If done carefully this is quite safe, as long as the chain and tackle have an appropriate strength rating.

With the rear tray removed, it became easier to access the body mounting tabs that the rear bulkhead is secured to. (In most Series Is you will also need to detach the rear bodywork from the tabs along the rear cross-member.) On an 86 or 88, the front of the tub incorporates the rear cab bulkhead – so essentially the rear bulkhead on this 109in is identical to the front section of a short-wheelbase tub.

The windscreen being lifted off.

Only with 107s and 109s is the rear tub entirely separate from the cab, with a small gap between the two.

New seats will be purchased for this vehicle, but the vertical brackets together with their securing pins and washers will need to be retained and transferred to the new items. Door cards are also available new, so there is no requirement to retain the originals.

80in Series I Land Rovers are similar to Series IIs and IIIs, in that the front floor is in three sections: two outer sections plus the transmission tunnel. However, 88s and 109s such as this vehicle have a single-piece floor. In either case, the floor fixes along the sills at the outer edges, and the front and rear are secured with coarse-threaded, hex-headed screws; they screw into spire nuts along the front of the seat box and bottom of the bulkhead (an

Cutting off the U-bolts that secured the rear tray.

A forklift is used to remove the tray.

Half way there…

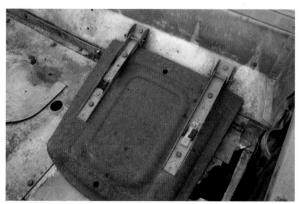

These brackets need to be retained.

The red knob broke off, but replacements are available.

Undoing the floor fixings.

Unbolting the front section of the transmission tunnel.

LEFT: *The floor sections and transmission tunnel being removed as one section.*

80in uses captive nuts rather than spire nuts). Before lifting it out you'll need to unscrew the red and yellow knobs of the transfer box and 4WD levers, and pull out any surviving gaiters.

Once the floor panels are removed, and the seat box is unbolted from the sills, the seat box and the rear bulkhead can then be removed as a single unit (and separated later), but you will need a second pair of hands when lifting. The fixings include an angular captive plate, tucked out of sight, which enables the bulkhead to be secured to the mount behind the fuel tank. It is only required on the driver's side because

the fuel tank impedes access to the body mount. Corrosion will probably hold it in place, so after removing its

nuts you may need to tap it free. These plates were also found on SWB Series Is but not 80s.

To remove the wings you will need to unbolt them from the front panel and the bulkhead. Don't forget to disconnect any wiring before trying to pull the panels away. If you are renewing the entire wiring loom, as we are, you might as well cut through the old wires.

Once the wings are off, the front panel will need to be unbolted from the front crossmember. The front panel can be lifted away complete with the

Tapping out the captive thread plate behind the fuel tank.

The captive thread plate removed. The captive thread plate is needed.

Undoing the rear bulkhead from the chassis tabs on the other side.

Rear bulkhead, seat box and sills being lifted off as one.

Unbolting the front of the right-hand sill.

The rear bulkhead and seat box can remain assembled for now.

Undoing the fixings that secure the front of the wings to the front panel.

Removing a wing… but remember to detach the wiring first.

radiator, cowl, bonnet stay and head-lamps all still connected. Obviously the radiator hoses need disconnecting first, the radiator needs draining, and the headlamp wiring needs discon-necting; this can be done at the six-way junction box on the bulkhead, or on the back of the lamps themselves.

SMALLER SUB-ASSEMBLIES

Dismantling the various sub-assem-blies of bodywork can mostly be left to a later phase, tackling each area when-ever you are ready to repair or repaint them. We'll focus on just one example here, the bonnet, as it combines rivets, bolts and small fittings in a relatively small area.

The rubber buffers are unbolted first. Some are often missing anyway, as the rubber becomes brittle in the heat and breaks away over time. The two hinges are also unbolted (four bolts, their nuts being accessed from underneath), and then the spare-wheel mount.

Spare-wheel mounts come in differ-ence sizes; for 80in Series Is they are shallower and have smaller diameter bolts than on later Series Is. (Series IIA onwards have an even larger diameter bolt.)

The bolt holes in the mount are threaded, and their two mounting

Unbolting the front panel.

Lifting off the front panel and radiator together.

Work begins on the bonnet, which was already missing a rubber buffer on which the spare wheel sits.

bolts have split pins rather than nuts on the ends of their shanks, to prevent them from unscrewing. These bolts often sheer when you try to undo them – as happened with this project 109. Ben had to resort to mole grips, penetrating oil and a blowtorch to work them free. Then came the task of drilling out the rivets that secure the mounting plate to the bonnet.

When these rivets have been drilled out, the mount can be pulled away. Although these rivets securing the bonnet mount need to be drilled out, note that we don't touch any of the dome rivets securing the bonnet skin to the steel frame.

The frames of Series I bonnets are galvanized, like the doors, and do not usually rust – a welcome relief if you are used to the rust-prone frames of later Series Land Rovers.

The 'zig-zag'-shaped clamps that secure the spare wheel to the bon-net were made in two different sizes, determined by the offset of the rim; long-wheelbase Series Land Rovers have a deeper offset, requiring the larger-sized clamps.

LINKAGE REMOVAL

Before the bulkhead can be removed, the pedals will need disconnecting from the arms that form the pedal link-age beneath the bulkhead. You will need to keep track of the large number of small components. Both the brake and clutch mechanisms use threaded adjuster rods, and the threads need to be assessed for corrosion.

In our project 109 there was a lot of surface rust on these components, but they were in serviceable condition and

The spare-wheel mount is removed by drilling out all its solid aluminium rivets.

With the rivets drilled out and the mount removed, you'll be looking at something like this.

The bonnet hinge being unbolted, which saves having to mask it for painting later.

worth restoring. This would include replacement of the phosphor bronze bushes that the linkages pivot around. (Everything would also be sanded and painted for protection.)

On both the clutch and brake pedals, undo the pinch bolt to remove the pedal from the arm, and use a flat screwdriver to prise the arm open enough to pull the pedal out. The brake pedal's bolt has a nut, whereas the clutch pedal's bolt hole is threaded. At the pivot, the outer circlip is removed, then the large washer. The bottom end of the brake arm should have a clevis pin, but on this vehicle it has been replaced with a nut and bolt. Pull the brake lever off the shaft, then remove the large washer behind it. Next, use pliers to remove the clutch spring, and remove the clutch arm.

The clutch arm connects to an adjustment rod, whose opposite end attaches to the clutch relay, which pivots inside phosphor-bronze bushes in the chassis, and emerges inboard of the chassis rail at the cross-shaft lever.

Both the clutch relay shaft and the pedal pivot shaft have grease nipples. As you can see, our pedal pivot shaft hasn't been greased, making the arms difficult to remove, and this increases wear on the bronze bushes. Compare it with the clutch relay shaft that has been lubricated. Easily overlooked lubrication points such as these are one reason why it is important for a

Prising the clutch relay out of the chassis, together with the adjuster rod and the connected arm.

The pedal shaft has clearly not been lubricated (right), but the clutch relay shaft (left) has.

A heavy-duty G-clamp extracting the pedal pivot from the chassis.

Extracting the pin that connects one of the collars on the clutch's cross-shaft to the relay that passes through the right-hand chassis rail.

Series I to be maintained by someone with detailed knowledge of the vehicle.

Undo the large nut on the inside of the chassis rail where the pedal pivot is mounted. It is common for these pivots to be seized into the chassis rail, in which case a hydraulic bottle jack can be used to push the shaft out of the mounting tube.

The pedal pivot may be seized into its tube in the chassis (which does not incorporate a bush). In this scenario, a heavy-duty G-clamp will be useful for forcing it through.

The brake-fluid reservoir is simply bolted to the chassis on a bracket. In the project 109 the feed pipe connecting it to the master cylinder was in reasonable condition, but we replaced it anyway. (On 80in Series Is, the brake master cylinder is mounted inboard of the chassis rail; on all later Series Is it is mounted outboard.) To remove,

disconnect the brake pipes from their unions, and drain the fluid. Undo the three securing bolts that mount it to the chassis. Once it's unbolted, it can be pulled backwards through a dedicated hole in the chassis. On an 80in there is no restriction, as it sits above the gearbox mount.

The throttle pedal and mechanical linkage that connects it to the carb also need unbolting from the bulkhead, taking care not to lose the multiple small components. With the exception of the springs, these components rarely wear out, but they will benefit from being painted.

THE BULKHEAD

The bulkhead is still mounted to the chassis, and the surrounding bodywork has now been removed, together with the pedal linkages. We are now ready to strip most of the remaining components from the bulkhead so that it can be lifted out and inspected fully.

First we need to remove the steering wheel, and the horn arm attached to the steering column, and then detach the column from the bulkhead, so the bulkhead can be pulled up over the column. You could also choose to separate the steering column and box from the vehicle first, if you prefer.

This vehicle has the later-type 'recirculating ball' steering box, as opposed to the 'worm and nut' design found on earlier models. With a design such as this, you may need a drift to knock out the almost vertical bolt that clamps the wheel to the steering column (use an aluminium drift with a brass hammer, to minimize the risk of damage). Penetrating oil may also be required to help remove the wheel from the column: remove the wheel's centre cap and apply the fluid to the splines, and gravity will help it creep down.

The earlier 'worm and nut' design found in 80s, 86s and 107s incorporates wiring down the centre of the column in a stator tube, and has no dipswitch on the floor. To remove the steering wheel you will need to undo the bolt at the bottom of the steering box, releasing the stator tube. The wiring for the dipswitch and horn needs disconnecting from the junction box, and then the stator tube can be withdrawn through the steering box. Be prepared to catch the oil that will come out of the hole in the steering box that the tube passes through. Once removed, the steering wheel's pinch bolt can be undone, then a drift can be used – as above.

Before removing the arm containing the horn button, the bearing cap needs to be tapped off the top of the shaft. The horn arm is secured by a nut underneath, which is undone so the arm can slide off the shaft.

This example has a non-original Foxton indicator arm that isn't a Land Rover part and looks out of place, so it will be removed. Indicator stalks were not introduced until the 1960s, and the indicator switch ought to be on an auxiliary panel on the bulkhead – this is what will be fitted later.

The mounting for the steering column consists of a clamp that goes round the column and secures it to the

The exposed bulkhead.

In this instance, soft metals are required for the drift and hammer.

The headlamp dipswitch was long gone.

front face of the bulkhead. This needs undoing.

The instrument panel is secured by visible screws. Just like a Series II/IIA, they go into captive nuts along the top, but along the bottom regular nuts are used so a small ring spanner is required on the back of them. Our instrument panel had acquired a large amount of Australian dirt inside. As the wiring loom was too old to salvage, we cut all the wires to free the panel.

Alongside the instrument panel are two non-original ash trays – characteristic of their era perhaps, but out of place today. One of them will be kept for originality's sake, and the other deleted.

In the engine bay, the starter solenoid is detached from the bulkhead, as well as the mounting plinth that includes the fuel pump, voltage regulator and fuse holder; this was removed with all the components attached for dismantling later. (We will be refurbishing and installing a correct SU fuel pump in place of the non-original type.) Care has to be taken at this stage to make

Exposing the wiring behind the instrument panel. Note the non-standard ashtrays – one will be kept and refurbished, but not two.

Unscrewing the mounting plinth from the bulkhead.

Undoing the left footwell from the slotted holes on the front bracket.

A nut in a similar position, on the driver's side, tucked under the steering box.

Undoing the left bulkhead mount; notice that the left nut is smooth.

Bulkhead bracket, kept together with its fixings.

ing rigidity and also help with calibrating the alignment of the bulkhead during reassembly.

Each bracket has bolts at the top going through the bulkhead, and three at the bottom going through the chassis. Note that the upper boltholes are slightly slotted to aid calibration, and that the foremost of these lower bolts has a domed head to prevent snagging a tyre (in this vehicle that would never happen, but it can for 80in vehicles). You will also need to undo the threaded stay bar at the top of the bulkhead, which is likely to require clamping with grips to prevent it from turning. The bracket on the driver's side, which also mounts the steering box, can be left in place temporarily, and removed together with the steering components as one assembly.

The cable connecting the starter motor to the bulkhead-mounted solenoid also needs to be removed. The final stage is to undo the long bolts that secure the bulkhead to the outriggers on the chassis. It then requires two people to lift it off the chassis.

Once the bulkhead is removed, the battery tray and air-filter bracket are detached next. These are a combined unit, held in place by four bolts round the base of the battery tray. Removal gives access to the drop arm coming off the steering box's output shaft, which can be detached after first bending the locking washer, then undoing the large BSF nut (take care not to lose it). With the nut released, a puller is used to remove the arm from the splined shaft. The supposedly easier method of simply knocking it off with a hammer risks causing damage to the thread or splines.

Undoing the bulkhead's top stay on the left-hand side.

sure that all wires, cables and linkages are detached from the bulkhead – failing to do so can result in damage when the bulkhead is lifted away.

The front of the bulkhead is attached to two large brackets that mount to the chassis, one at either side of the engine. These are essential for provid-

Unbolting the bulkhead from the chassis outrigger.

Battery and air filter mount.

The column and the steering box can remain attached to each other – you may wish to separate them later.

REMOVING THE DRIVETRAIN

The exhaust needs to be unbolted from the manifold and from its mounting brackets along the chassis. The engine is detached from its rubber mounts by undoing the top bolt (the bottom ones can be left alone for now). The procedure is similar for the gearbox mounts, but they use a bolt to secure the mountings through the chassis, and the nut is inside a hole in the gearbox crossmember.

Before lifting the engine and gearbox, we have three more jobs. First we need to remove the horizontal clutch arm (known as the 'cross-shaft lever') going into the right-hand side of the gearbox. It is secured with split pins and a clevis pin. Once removed, withdraw it from the connecting tube. Second, the propshafts need to be removed from both ends of the transfer box. And third, the pins securing the handbrake

Removing a gearbox mount with a Whitworth spanner and an impact driver.

pivot to the side of the transfer box need to be removed. (On the project vehicle, this has been replaced with a nut and bolt, which is incorrect.)

The rear propshaft is secured by four bolts at each end. At its rear end you

can use a socket, but access is tight for the bolts at the front end. We use a ring spanner that has been ground thin so it fits in the gap, and is kept just for this purpose.

As we have the use of a forklift, we lift the engine and gearbox together using this, but if you are using an engine crane, you will need to separate the engine from the gearbox first: this is achieved by undoing the twelve nuts and one bolt securing the bellhousing to the flywheel adapter plate. Once these are removed the gearbox will need some gentle persuasion to pull it off the studs, so either the engine or gearbox will still need to be attached to the chassis. It is slightly easier to lift the engine out first because the gearbox has less room behind it due to the crossmember, making it slightly more awkward to pull backwards off the studs. Separating the engine and gearbox will expose the clutch assembly and flywheel.

As you can see from the photo, we initially forgot to detach the front

Engine and transmission mounts sag with age. These will be replaced with new ones.

If you forget to remove either the clutch shaft or the front prop, the two will collide when you try to lift the drivetrain.

Unbolting the rear propshaft from the handbrake drum.

Unbolting the rear propshaft at the nose of the rear diff.

A ring spanner such as this comes into its own for certain propshaft bolts. This one has been ground thinner, to aid access to the propshaft bolts on 80in Series 1s.

propshaft from the transfer box. This wasn't critical, but it did add the extra complication of having to prevent the propshaft from colliding with the horizontal clutch rod as the drivetrain assembly was lifted.

The fuel tank is next to be removed. First it is important to undo the drain bung on the bottom of the tank and leave it to drain any residual fuel into a container. (This should be disposed of responsibly at your local recycling depot.) Then the bung is refitted and the fuel pipe is disconnected from the top of the tank, along with the wire to the sender. The fuel tank is secured to the chassis by six bolts. You might want to put a tyre beneath the tank to break its fall in case you lose grip, as dropping it could cause damage.

The engine, gearbox and transfer box are lifted out as one unit for later separation.

The engine and gearbox as removed, awaiting further disassembly.

Dropping the fuel tank could damage it or cause dangerous sparks.

Unbolting the fuel tank.

DEALING WITH STUDS

Studs require a different approach to regular bolts, otherwise the nut can tighten on to the stud before the stud is able to tighten into the receiving female thread. Whether unscrewing or screwing in, you'll get the control you need by winding two nuts together on to the stud. When one nut tightens against the other, you will be able to screw or unscrew the opposite end of the stud in the receiving thread, as if it were a bolt. To wind a thread in, apply the spanner to the top nut, which winds down against the lower nut; to unwind, apply the spanner to the lower nut, which pulls up against the nut above it. The nuts can then be withdrawn individually. Resist the temptation to grip any stud with mole grips, as this will damage its threads, and it is not necessary.

Turning this nut clockwise will screw the stud in clockwise.

Turning this nut anticlockwise will unscrew the stud anticlockwise.

REMOVING AXLES AND RUNNING GEAR

The steering components, axles and suspension also need to be removed. This phase begins by removing the brake pipes, and taking photos of them along their full length: this will be a valuable reference when installing new brake lines, especially if making them from scratch (as we will be doing). The original items would have been steel, but many nowadays are copper. Try to remove them without damaging them, so they can be used as templates for making new replacements. Ours are extremely corroded, so most of the unions had to be cut off.

There are important safety considerations when working on the suspension – especially when removing springs or shock absorbers. The springs can be under very high tension, and removing a critical part without making sure the weight of the chassis is correctly supported can cause these forces to be released suddenly, without warning. *Never attempt to release a spring when the vehicle is standing on its wheels.*

The sleeve for this shackle bolt has completely broken free and worn a hole in the chassis – which must have created a noisy and very unpredictable driving experience. This kind of damage will require extensive and creative repair work.

The front axle and suspension assembly is removed in one piece. First, the steering ball joint on the relay's drop arm is detached, leaving the arms attached to the swivel housings, and the drop arm is also separated from the relay. The brake flexi-hoses are unscrewed from the backs of the wheel cylinders and from their brackets on the chassis, and the front propshaft is unbolted from the flange at the back of the front differential.

The chassis is then securely raised (by jacking or, in our case, using a fork-lift) to take the weight off the axles until the tyres are just about to lift off the ground. Then the springs and shock absorbers can be detached.

The front shock absorbers are left bolted to the chassis while their lower mounts are detached from the axles: this involves extracting the large split pins and washers and pulling the shock absorbers off the mount-

Unbolting a front leaf spring using a breaker bar.

The four-way joint under the driver's floor that needed to be unbolted from the chassis.

Separating the drop arm from the ball joint and the relay.

Non-standard steering damper bracket.

The shackle pin being removed.

Rolling the front axle away, complete with leaf springs.

The front axle is turned upside down to aid removal of the springs.

An air-powered impact driver helps release a rear shock absorber's top bolt.

ing peg. Then comes the heavier task of releasing the spring shackles, best done with a breaker bar or impact driver. Each of the main bolts securing the leaf springs is secured by a locknut. The shackle plates are threaded only on the inside plate, which means the pins need unwinding and can't simply be knocked through. Have a blowtorch ready to help release any pins that are seized.

For some reason our vehicle's chassis was fitted with a non-standard bracket for mounting a steering damper, but no steering damper. The bracket was removed and discarded.

Obviously the chassis must be securely supported before the shackle pins are removed. Once the springs are fully unbolted, the axle can be rolled away from the chassis, and you will be left with a front axle, complete with steering components and leaf springs. Flipping it upside down gives better access to the nuts holding the U-bolts, which need to be removed so the springs can detach from the axles. U-bolts corrode and can stretch over time, so it is advisable to replace them each time a spring is removed from the axle.

FINAL STRIPPING AND CHASSIS INSPECTION

The chassis must be stripped so that the only items remaining are the front-to-back section of the wiring loom running down the inside of the chassis (this will help us install its replacement later) and the shackle bushes in their tubes. After shotblasting, a blowtorch will be used to burn the rubber out of these bushes, then the centre tubes will be driven out (this process will be covered in more detail in Chapter 4.) Aside from these items, everything needs to be removed from the chassis in preparation for shotblasting.

The axle check straps are unbolted, along with the rear grab handles and the tow-hitch mount. The front bumper is removed by undoing two bolts at each end, where the bumper meets the dumb-irons. Their nuts are tucked up underneath. This is a rust trap – dirt and moisture has collected inside the front of the chassis, rotting the front plate and destroying the bumper securing bolts.

We did not detect any signs of play in our steering relay, so thankfully it can remain in the front crossmember.

The rear crossmember had a couple of end caps with prongs on their insides to hold them in place. We believe they are unique to certain export-market Land Rovers, and were intended to keep mud or sand out of the chassis.

Other 'hangers-on' included the engine mounts, brake-fluid reservoir, the old brake-light switch, which disintegrated as we tried to remove it from the chassis, and the old brake master cylinder – an obsolete part so we wished to have it restored if possible. Parts such as these tend to be easily overlooked when calculating your initial budget, but replacement or renovation is often more expensive than you might expect, causing the overall cost of your project to inflate, one step at a time.

Removing the old check straps.

Burning the bushes out of the chassis.

Grip these mounts to prevent them turning as their nuts are undone.

Steering relay mounted in the chassis.

Unbolting the rusty brake-fluid reservoir.

RIGHT: *These metal bungs are rarely seen on Series Is.*

LEFT: *The old brake master cylinder being extracted from the chassis.*

ABOVE: *The brake switch was corroded beyond repair and had to be cut from the chassis.*

BELOW: *The chassis completely stripped and in the blast cabinet.*

LEFT: *The chassis securely raised to working height to aid final stripping.*

4

Repairing the Chassis

The full extent of any problems will not be revealed until the chassis has been thoroughly shotblasted, so you should expect the prognosis to become more severe after this has been done. The blasting process is best achieved using a large compressor in a sealed environment, and protective clothing is essential, so consider outsourcing this task to a professional.

As discussed in Chapter 2, if the Land Rover has spent its life in the UK, the chassis is likely to be severely compromised by rust, and it will probably have been repaired before. Vehicles sourced from Australia are more likely to suffer from stress fractures, though you should still expect to find some degree of corrosion – just not as much as on a Series I from the UK. The demo vehicle has plenty of everything: rust and damage.

You will have to decide whether your chassis is worth repairing, or whether it will be more worthwhile to buy a new replacement. In many cases it is not cost-effective to ask a specialist to restore a severely deteriorated chassis, due to the large amount of time required. Fortunately, however, many repair sections are available, and the cost of raw materials and paint is quite low, so if you are competent at welding, then repairing your chassis may be a viable and rewarding way forwards. You will also have the satisfaction of preserving a key element of the original vehicle.

Initial checks also need to determine whether there are any misalignment issues. A large setsquare can be set in each of the right-angles where the main chassis rails meet the crossmembers, to ensure that each angle is 90 degrees.

Another technique is to use a length of string to measure the distances between the mounts where the fronts of each leaf spring mount to the chassis, measuring diagonally in the shape of a cross (front right spring to rear left spring, and front left spring to rear right spring). A plumb bob is used to mark the spot directly beneath each of the measuring points, then the chassis is moved away so the distance between the marks can be measured. A useful reference manual, which lists the precise dimensions of the chassis, is included in Section K of the *Land Rover 1948–1958 Workshop Manual* published by Brooklands Technical Books.

Ideally the margin of error should be zero. Any major discrepancy in these measurements suggests that not enough care has been taken when repairing sections of the chassis, or that it has taken a heavy whack (or many whacks).

Replacement crossmembers and outriggers are available to buy, and this can be a sensible way of repairing weak areas. Some of these sections can be quite expensive, but the alternative is to spend considerably more on a new chassis, or attempt to fabricate the new sections yourself – not easy. At the time of writing, a complete new Series I chassis ranges from around £3,700 to £5,550 from Richards Chassis, depending on the wheelbase. The cheapest chassis are for 88s, with 107 Station Wagons being the most expensive.

The biggest upside is that you can have your new chassis galvanized (costing around £250 extra), theo-

Ben shotblasting the 109's chassis.

A clearly bent chassis rail, but only noticeable once the wing was removed.

retically enabling you to forget about chassis corrosion for the foreseeable future. You can also be sure that it will be perfectly aligned, reducing the likelihood of complications when aligning the bulkhead and bodywork during reassembly – intricacies that are discussed in Chapter 15.

As much of this vehicle as possible will be repaired, for maximum originality and to prevent costs spiralling, so we opted to repair the chassis instead of replacing it. All the new metal was fabricated from scratch, rather than using bought sections, so this was a major undertaking that took around forty to sixty hours to complete. If this time were billed by the hour, the total cost would have been comparable to that of buying a new chassis – but retaining the original chassis of a historic vehicle is obviously preferable, and helps add to the overall authenticity of the finished result.

REPAIRING RUST AND FRACTURES

As we have seen from Chapter 3, the project vehicle's chassis had had brutal damage, and some of its suspension mounts had been damaged. It had an old fracture near the front right-hand spring mount, which had previously been very poorly repaired. Not only had the chassis cracked, but the bush tube for the spring mount had also come loose and worn an oval hole in the chassis rail. This must have caused an absolutely horrible drive and was obviously dangerous.

A lot of care was needed to make sure the tube could be welded back into precisely the correct position, and

---

ABOUT WELDING

Welding is a complex skill, worthy of prolonged study and practice. Any novice should consult the many available books, articles and online resources on the topic, and consider attending a training course. Mistakes are always made when learning, and scrap metal should be used for practice, rather than anything important.

Any form of welding can be extremely dangerous, so it is vital that the proper safety precautions are taken into account and that the correct protective clothing is worn.

Metal inert gas welding, or MIG welding, is the most common form of welding when it comes to automotive repairs in steel. However, it is a relatively modern technique, and arc welding was originally used for building the chassis of Series Is. According to a 1950 article in *Welding* magazine, the sections of chassis were manually passed between a series of operatives who would tack each section together using 10- and 12-gauge electrodes, with a multi-operator arc welder enabling 300amps per user. A large number of clamps were used in combination with a system of electro-magnets to hold the sections in the correct shape. The tack-welded chassis would then be transferred to a spit for final welding. Solihull at the time was experimenting with more automated systems, but in these early phases the production was entirely by hand – labour intensive, but systematized and apparently efficient.

MIG welding is easier than arc welding, and runs less risk of blowing holes in the metal, provided the machine is kept on a low enough setting, with the wire being fed at sufficient speed. However, arc welding does enable better access to tight corners. We recommend using a MIG welder of reasonable quality, rated to at least 180amps and feeding 0.8mm wire. This will be capable of easily welding the 3–4mm plate steel that you should use for most chassis repairs, and generally it will need to be turned down to 25–30amps.

A clean weld requires clean metal to weld to. Any rust or other impurities will cause untidy spatter and make it more difficult to achieve a strong bond between the old and the new metal, so use an angle grinder to create bare metal surfaces. Grind both sides if possible, but in the case of a box section, such as round a chassis, you often won't be able to do this.

---

perfectly horizontal with the cross-members. Ben therefore carefully sliced out the whole of the outer and lower (upward facing in these photos) section of the chassis rail, but left the inner spring hole in place so that its precise location was not lost.

The tube was held against the inside of the chassis, using an engineer's square to make sure it was perfectly aligned, then it was tack welded into position around the hole. A template was made from card to determine the correct shape for the new section of

Badly damaged spring mount. The chassis was turned upside down for this repair, and mounted on axle stands.

The damaged metal removed, leaving a hole on the inner face of the chassis rail as a reference point.

A step drill enables a wide range of hole sizes to be made.

A bolt ensured correct alignment and prevented the tube from distorting.

metal for the opposite (outer) face of the chassis, then the shape was transferred to a sheet of 3mm steel. This was offered up to the chassis, while the outline of the tube was traced around it.

The new section was removed and a step drill was used to drill out the traced hole to the correct size – then it was welded to the chassis, and to the tube. The tube had to be securely welded round both ends, at both sides of the outer faces, then the lower section of the chassis rail (upward-facing) final section was prepared using a cardboard template, and welded into place. Finally the weld was ground back to create a smooth surface.

Another repair had to be made to the upper mount for one of the rear shock absorbers, which had been partially ripped out of the chassis. This had to be bent back into position, with its alignment determined by passing a long bolt all the way through the chassis. The crack was then welded up, with the bolt remaining in position to ensure the tube did not distort from the heat of welding.

One of the simpler repairs was to the rear crossmember, where the mount-

The rear crossmember's mounting plate for the drawbar was damaged.

Using a blowtorch makes the metal more malleable and easier to bend back into position.

Welding the original spring bushing tube back into the hole in the inner face. This gave us the location of the hole in the new plate.

The repaired section welded into place.

Watch out for a cracked engine mount such as this one.

A new crossmember tube in an 86in chassis, before being welded into position.

The finished tube in position, ready to receive paint and the steering relay.

ing plate for a drawbar had been bashed at one end. The section was heated with a blowtorch to make it more malleable, then bent back into position; however, the metal was too badly damaged for this to be sufficient, so a new section had to be made and welded into place. As this corner is simply a mirror image of the other side of the mounting plate, the shape could be determined by copying the other side (including the bolt hole) and flipping it over.

Later in this restoration we also discovered a crack in one of the engine mounts – perhaps not surprising, given the damage we had found on the chassis. In cases such as this, the weld can be easy as it doesn't require any metal to be cut away. Repairing this engine mount was simply a case of stripping away the surface rust, filling the crack with weld, grinding it smooth and then coating the mount with primer and paint.

Often you will need to use your own ingenuity. The pictures show the steering relay mounting tube, which had to be made bespoke in a different Series I chassis. Thanks to corrosion, the original tube became detached from the front crossmember when the relay was removed. At the time (a few years before writing), front crossmembers were not available to buy new, so replicating the tube was the most obvious thing to do. Today, you might find it easier to replace the whole crossmember, but creating a new tube will save money and avoid any risk of introducing chassis misalignment. The main complication is that this tube is a peculiar diameter and difficult to source; Ben has typically found it best to fabricate a new one from a sheet of steel.

The sheet will need to be rolled by an engineering firm so that it com-

fortably forms a tube. Then a length of it, slightly longer than the required circumference of the tube, is inserted into the chassis and tack welded to itself so it does not unravel when removed. Once pulled out of the chassis, the excess width is trimmed away, the join is welded along its length, and any protruding weld is ground away. The result should be a tube that is of the same dimensions as the original, fitting perfectly into the chassis. This is

added to the crossmember and welded round its full circumference, top and bottom, and then smoothed off with a flap disc on an angle grinder.

REPLACING CROSSMEMBERS, OUTRIGGERS AND FITTINGS

Fortunately our 109 did not require any replacement crossmembers, but this work is often required, and new crossmembers are available. Great

The chassis of an Australian 86in chassis, restored by Ben and painted Deep Bronze Green.

A 107in Station Wagon chassis, also restored by Ben.

The chassis was flipped over to complete the welding on this LHD 107.

A new front crossmember welded into a left-hand-drive 107in chassis, prior to the removal of the temporary brace across the front.

care needs to be taken when welding them into place to prevent introducing alignment problems.

It is common for the front crossmember to need replacing, either because the steering relay is firmly seized into it, or due to corrosion along its lower front section. Before slicing out the old crossmember, you will need to firmly brace the front of the chassis rails so that they retain their alignment throughout the procedure. The simplest and strongest way to do this is by tack-welding a length of angle-iron across the front; this remains in place until the new crossmember is fully welded into position.

To ensure the correct front/rear alignment of the new crossmember, the position of the original must be carefully measured before removal – in particular, the distance between it and the gearbox crossmember. This distance should be scored into each of the chassis rails to act as a visual aid, and must be accurately replicated when the new crossmember is welded into place. Precision here is very important, so if you find that the new crossmember is not aligning as perfectly as you had intended, do not be afraid of breaking your new welds and starting again.

All Series Is used identical gearbox

crossmembers. Do not be tempted to use a similar example from a later Series vehicle – it looks similar but is slightly deeper so it will sit too low.

When replacing a rear crossmember, a basic jig will be required to hold the new section while it is being welded into position. The jig should be made from box-section steel, with the old crossmember still in place. Holes are added across its rear section so that it can bolt on to the vertical tabs on the crossmember, and its forward-facing arms are tack-welded to the tabs that support the floor braces.

Care also needs to be taken to ensure it sits perfectly vertically. To do this, Ben takes measurements between the old crossmember and datum points on both the top and the

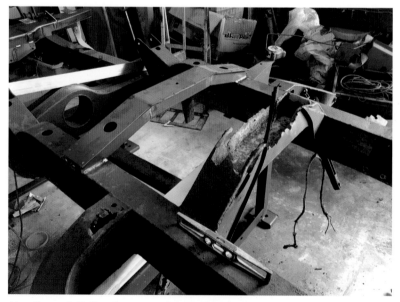

A heavily corroded bellhousing crossmember on an 86in chassis.

A heavily corroded gearbox crossmember (left) with a new replacement (middle) and a similar but incorrect Series II/III type (right).

bottom of the chassis, and replicates these when the new crossmember is added. Datum points are added to the underside of the chassis by lightly tack-welding a length of box section across the chassis rails; this gives a nearby fixed point of reference that can be measured against. The distance between the box section and the bottom of the new crossmember must be identical to the same measurement for the old crossmember. (You can do it without this added bar by measuring all the way back to the next crossmember, but shorter distances are easier to measure accurately.)

You may have seen Series Land Rovers with rear crossmembers that lean backwards or tuck under at the bottom – this is usually a sign that the crossmember has been replaced without a jig to ensure alignment (usually without removing the rear tub from the chassis), and without proper attention given to the measurements described above.

Once the jig and the lower horizontal rail are added, the jig is unbolted from the crossmember, which can now be cut off. The new crossmember is then lifted into position and its vertical tabs are bolted to the jig, holding it in exactly the same position as the original crossmember. Measurements are retaken between each new weld, and once the new crossmember is securely in place, the small welds securing the jig and the horizontal rail to the chassis are cut off.

Beneath an 80in crossmember is an optional drawbar. It can be bought as a kit supplied in four parts: the horizontal drawbar, and the three large brackets that attach it to the rear crossmember. Welding the middle bracket

A new rear crossmember being held in place by a simple jig.

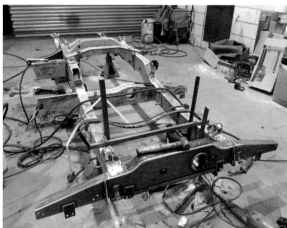

The bar welded to the bottom of this 1948 80in chassis gives datum points to measure from.

first on to the crossmember helps to ensure correct alignment, followed by the remaining brackets. All welds are tacked on first, then properly welded once the alignment of the brackets has been confirmed to be accurate. Finally, the drawbar itself is added.

If you need to replace a bulkhead outrigger, note that these were never originally welded all the way round by Solihull. This is true for all Series Is.

In severely deteriorated sections you may need to make multiple types of repair in close proximity, such as the rear of the 107in Station Wagon chassis

pictured, which was repaired using a combination of new parts and fabricated sections. The rear crossmember was supplied by Radford Bulkheads, while the bottom sections of the chassis rails were made from scratch using plate steel. The right-hand shackle mount had to be removed and rewelded back on to the chassis with new gussets. When replacing, a measurement was

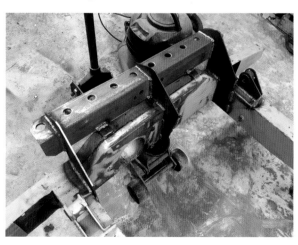

An early weld-on 80in remanufactured drawbar.

A new bulkhead outrigger on an 86in chassis. Note the welding pattern, which replicates the original.

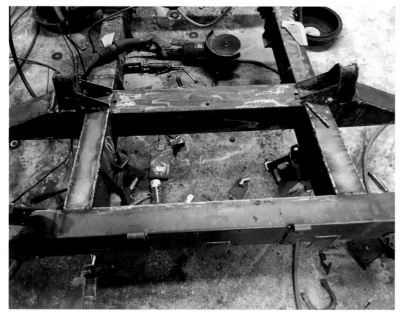

The new rear shackle mount from Radford Bulkheads, welded to an 80in chassis.

The rear of a 107in Station Wagon chassis (upturned) showing the new crossmember, new bottom sections of the chassis rail, and the repaired spring mount.

taken off the rear crossmember, and its alignment with the opposite mount was ensured by running a long tube between the two of them.

Once the main chassis rails, crossmembers and outriggers have been repaired or renewed, it's time to replace any damaged or corroded fittings. These are mostly available to buy new from UK suppliers such as Radford Bulkheads.

The precise position of any fitting should be carefully measured before the old metal is removed, to act as a reference when adding its replacement. Shackle mounts in particular must be perfectly square to the chassis, to prevent permanent twisting forces on the shackle pin and the bush.

Surface preparation and painting are the final stages. We cover these techniques in more detail when describing bodywork restoration in Chapter 10, but there are a few differences when it comes to the chassis. (Filler should never be used anywhere on a chassis.)

Various different colours were used for Series I chassis. Early types were silver, but Solihull changed to painting them light green during 1949. With early 86s and 107s the chassis was usually painted to match the colour of the body, but from 1955 onwards, all non-Station Wagons had a black chassis – so this was the colour chosen for our restoration.

After being shotblasted and repaired, the project chassis received two coats of epoxy resin primer followed by two coats of satin black. When painting a chassis to match the bodywork, Ben uses 2k etch primer, followed by two coats of high-build 2k primer, then two coats of 2k topcoat in the required colour.

A restored 1948 chassis painted silver, which is correct for the year. They were painted light green in mid-1949.

5

Repairing the Bulkhead

Along with the chassis, the bulkhead is one of the largest and most expensive structural elements of the vehicle. Most restorations will require at least some degree of welding, or complete replacement altogether. In this chapter some typical rust areas will be repaired, showing methods that are commonly required during a typical bulkhead restoration. Our project 109 provides an ideal demonstration as it has corroded in very typical places.

As discussed in Chapter 2, almost all Series I bulkheads are made entirely of steel, and there are various types that fall into two main categories: the earlier press-steel type fitted to 80in vehicles from Christmas 1948, and the later fabricated type, which is (usually) easier to repair. Replacing a bulkhead with one of precisely the correct specification requires forethought, as the design evolved continuously and sometimes subtly, affecting such things as the positions of the holes for lights, choke and strengthening pieces. If you have decided to replace your bulkhead, try to find an original example that dates from the same model year as the vehicle you are restoring.

The bulkhead has already been removed from the project chassis, so now it needs to be stripped, repaired and painted, ready for later addition to our rolling chassis. The two main areas where our bulkhead needs repair are the upper sections of the footwells, and the top rail, which will be cut off and replaced with a new, complete section.

FOOTWELLS

It is very common to find corrosion in the top outermost corner of each footwell. It happens where the corner of the strengthening gusset (with its curved edge) comes down and folds under the top section of the footwell. Moisture collects between the two sheets of metal, so they rot from the inside out.

Replacing the rusted metal involves making repair sections for both of these overlapping layers of steel. In this particular case we also had to cut out part of the bracket on the front side of the bulkhead, because its lower section butted up against the rust that we're attempting to fix.

It is possible to carry out this repair in situ on a complete vehicle, but as we are rebuilding the whole Land Rover we have obviously stripped the bulkhead already.

After scrubbing the metal clean with a wire wheel, the first step is to make a neat cut with an angle grinder round the section of the strengthening gusset that needs to be replaced. Use right-angles and straight lines where

Good lighting is important for intricate repairs such as these.

Corrored section in the footwell, awaiting repair.

Slicing through the top layer of corroded metal.

Drilling out the spotwelds.

Drill bit specially designed for removing spotwelds.

Spotwelds drilled, ready for separation of the layers.

Prising one layer off…

possible, as it makes it easier to create new sections that match perfectly.

The next step is to drill out the spotwelds that are holding the two sheets of steel together. You can buy dedicated drill bits for this purpose, or you can make do with an ordinary HSS bit. Don't drill all the way through – just enough to break each weld.

We are left with a rusty section of metal that can now be pulled away. Once they have been drilled out, what's left of these spotwelds can easily be broken off by prising the metal with a screwdriver. Because this section has already been cut away from the rest of the bulkhead with the angle grinder, it will now lift away. This piece will be used as a template to make a new piece, so it mustn't be discarded.

With the first layer removed, another area of corrosion can be seen behind it. This is the upper section, and it, too, needs to be cut out and repaired. Note that each layer is treated separately – we are not simply slicing through the whole lot.

Another neat slice is made around this rusted area, and the rust cleaned off the surrounding metal with a flap disc. It is preferable to hide the seam of the joint underneath the strengthening gusset so that it can't be seen. This is not always possible, depending how big the patch needs to be. If the weld can't be concealed, a full footwell replacement would make a neater job.

We have now revealed some perforations that weren't visible before the cuts were made. When you come across corrosion like this, in a spot that can't practically be cut out – somewhere that would look ugly if you tried

The corrosion behind is exposed and now needs to be cut out.

The corroded metal cleaned out and the edges ground back to bare metal, ready for welding.

The copper hammer stops the weld falling through the holes.

Holes filled with weld, prior to grinding smooth.

Outlining a replacement section on to a sheet of new metal.

Test fit…

to weld against it – the best solution is usually to fill the holes with weld. You'll need a copper backplate to weld against and to prevent the weld from dripping through. The copper won't melt or stick to the weld, and isn't damaged in the process. The head of a copper hammer can be used. Once there's a blob of weld in each of the holes they can be ground back to give a smooth finish.

The first new section welded into position, and the welds ground smooth.

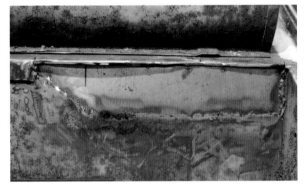

Next comes the task of making the first repair section. A template is first made using a piece of cardboard, trimmed until it exactly fits the space available. Then it is copied on to a sheet of steel that is welded in from the back, being careful not to blast through the surrounding good metal.

The gusset section comes next, using the original rusty strip to create an outline on a new sheet of steel. Instead of seam-welding all the way round this new section (which would look nasty) it is preferable to be as authentic as possible by replicating the look of the original spotwelds. Holes are therefore marked in the new section, in the same places as the original spotwelds, and then drilled out.

Once the new section is welded in

The old fragment is used as a template for the new piece.

along its top, where the original slice was made, the lower area is fixed down by using a little spot of weld in each of the holes, imitating the original spotwelds. Any excess weld is then ground smooth.

This repair is nearly done, but the vertical panel that had to be removed in the engine bay must still be fixed. Again, the original section is used as a template to make a new piece. The folds are replicated by marking

MIG welding the next layer of metal into position.

them with a pen, then each fold line is clamped in a vice and the metal pulled over by hand.

Manual sheet-folding machines are available to buy for relatively little outlay, but for small jobs such as this

The cut-away front section of the bulkhead, awaiting repair.

Folding the new section in a vice.

you will find this method perfectly sufficient. When creating a new section that includes a fold, it is tempting to simply trace round one face of the old metal, then roll it along the line of the fold and then trace the outline of the other surface; however, this will result in the new section being slightly too large, due to the original piece having stretched round the outside radius of its fold. The correct method is to closely measure the inside faces of the old piece, up to the *inside* radius of the fold, and to replicate these measurements on the new metal. This is easiest if you have a rule with zero at the very end, not starting a few millimetres in.

Once the metal is cut to shape, the new section can be MIG-welded into place, and the weld can be ground smooth.

This bulkhead bracket was scrubbed, cleaned and given a blast of black paint before being bolted back into the chassis, reusing the original long bolts through the chassis. Note those special bolts with the rounded heads.

New and original sections.

The repair section welded into place and ground smooth.

TOP RAIL

The project 109's top rail (the long horizontal section on which the windscreen sits) was very crispy and beyond repair. This is typical, due to the way that rainwater tends to collect along the bottom of the windscreen. New replacements are available, which have to be welded into position after cutting off the old metal.

This can be awkward, depending on where the rust is. It may be difficult to find secure metal to weld on to, because the new section will not come supplied with the vertical pillars that support it. These should be very carefully cut round with a slitting disc on an angle grinder.

If the pillars are also rusty, you will need to fabricate your own sections to repair them, but this is likely to be very difficult. Bear in mind that this is a prominent area, and poorly aligned repair sections may mean water ingress through the vent flaps, or other issues. Proceed with care, and wait until you have the new top panel in your possession before cutting the old metal off – especially if you have never done this before. This will help you work out exactly where the cuts need to be made, so you don't cut off too much metal. Good accuracy is critical.

Replacement of the top rail presents similar difficulties whether you are working on a fabricated bulkhead or the earlier pressed version.

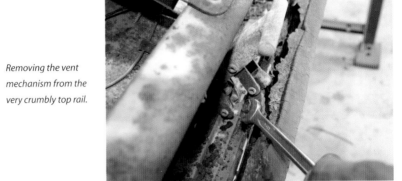

Removing the vent mechanism from the very crumbly top rail.

The rusty top rail and the centre pillar, which was carefully sliced round.

An 80in bulkhead, with its top rail and front face (they are the same piece) removed. The original steering-column brackets with their captive threads have been welded back on to the new steel.

New 80in top rail being fitted. The hinges and the rain gutter are the originals, transferred from the old metal and welded on to the new. This requires their position to be measured precisely before they are sliced off with an angle grinder. The hinges in particular require very careful alignment when refitting.

BELOW LEFT AND RIGHT: *Repaired footwell and front section, after smoothing and painting.*

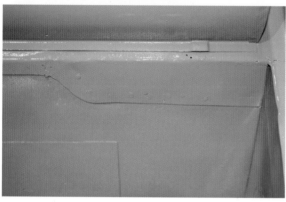
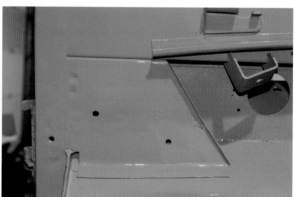

As we have seen earlier (*see* Chapter 2), there are other areas of potential rust you may encounter anywhere around a bulkhead. In particular you may find yourself having to make small repair sections into the pillars at each side of the footwell. For intricate cuts such as this, a small cutting disc on a drill or Dremel-type tool will give the most accurate results. You will need to cut your own repair sections out of new sheet as accurately as possible and carefully weld them in – following the same procedure as was used for the footwell repairs. It is unlikely that you will be able to create a perfect seam the whole way round any new section, but strength is more important; any messy excess weld can be ground smooth.

THE FINAL FINISH

In prominent places where a repair is going to be visible beneath the paintwork, it is acceptable to use a small smear of filler to smooth over the weld. If you have to build up a thick layer of filler, then you've done something wrong. Filler should never be used to mask major weaknesses, particularly in structural areas such as the bulkhead – it must be reserved for cosmetic purposes only.

Once the bulkhead is deemed to be entirely solid and as smooth as it can be, it's ready for paint. The painting process is described in Chapter 10.

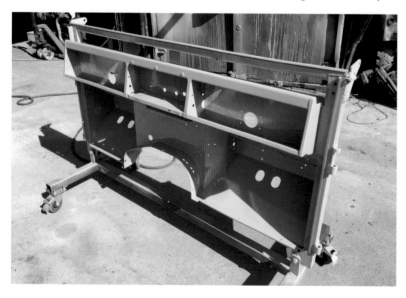

The fully restored bulkhead, with the new top rail, ready for installation.

6

Rebuilding the Axles

Our restoration will include rebuilding the wheel hubs front and rear, replacing a semi-floating rear hub with a fully floating hub, replacing the front axle's chrome swivels, installing Railko bushes, inspecting the differentials for wear, and replacing damaged components. (Braking components will be addressed separately in the next chapter.)

In this restoration, the axles were refurbished after being returned to the vehicle – a process we describe in Chapter 11 – but in most cases it is preferable to refurbish them while they are still separate from the vehicle. Supporting them on axle stands will make this work easier. Some oil will be spilled, so have a container and some rags ready.

OVERVIEW

Beam axles were used by all Land Rovers for half a century, until the first Freelander. (Range Rovers lost their beam axles with the third-generation L322, and the Discovery 3 went the same route, but they were a defining feature of the original Defender through to the end of its production in 2016.)

In a Series I, each axle houses a differential (or 'diff'), which is driven by a propshaft from the transfer box. The gears within the differential divide the power between the wheels at each end of the axle, while allowing each wheel to turn at different speeds.

The propshaft rotates the input pinion, which turns the crownwheel. Fixed inside the crownwheel, and rotating with it, is the carrier, which contains pinion gears and side gears (also called planet and sun gears) connected to the halfshafts.

Rover differentials throughout Series Land Rover production were designed for ten-spline halfshafts. Halfshafts pass through the axle tube, connecting each side of the differen-

tial to the drive flange at each wheel. The axle casing is partially filled with EP90 oil, which lubricates the differential and the shafts.

Towing and off-road driving put considerable extra strain on halfshafts, bearings and the gears inside the differential. Series Is are prone to snapping halfshafts when the abuse gets too much, especially when a fast-spinning wheel (perhaps raised in the air) meets sudden resistance (when it hits the ground). Wear also builds up between the splines and gears, causing backlash – a clunk when taking up drive – which can make a tired Land Rover quite unpleasant to drive. This wear is accelerated if the lubricating oil drains out or becomes contaminated with water.

The track of a Series I is narrower than a Series II because the axles are shorter. However, the suspension mounts (and the chassis rails) are the same width apart, which is why a Series II axle can be fitted to a Series I, creating a wider track.

Any restoration should involve removing the halfshafts for inspection, and examining the condition of the differential. Unless you are sure of their age, wheel bearings and braking components should also be replaced, in addition to the hubs' seals and bearings. Internal surfaces should also be checked for corrosion. We will address these areas in more detail.

SAFETY

Put the handbrake on and chock all the wheels before lifting the vehicle. The vehicle should always be thoroughly chocked front and rear, or safely raised off the ground using appropriately rated equipment. The handbrake operates on the transmission and holds the rear propshaft, so jacking up one rear corner will allow the vehicle to roll. The rolling motion of the opposite wheel will be transmitted through the diff, and cause the raised wheel to turn in the opposite direction.

AXLE CASINGS

The axle casings are very robust, but it's not unknown for them to corrode beyond repair if they have lived in damp conditions. The main weak points are the bottom of the diff casing where water droplets collect, and the dirt traps around where the U-bolts clamp to the axles.

In rare cases, if there is no oil in the axle and there has been water ingress, internal corrosion can also cause problems. In most cases though, the casings can simply be degreased, scrubbed down or shotblasted, then painted.

The valve in the axle breathers is a small but crucial component for the longevity of the axle oil.

Both front and rear, you will find brass breathers containing a small ball bearing acting as an air valve, screwed into the top of each axle casing. These are often overlooked, but they are important, as they allow the pressure inside and outside the axle casing to equalize. This prevents oil from being forced out under pressure through the hub seals or pinion seals. It also helps prevent moisture from being sucked in when the interior of the axle cools and contracts – for example, when a warm axle meets cool water. Therefore, when the breather becomes blocked with dirt, it can result in the axle oil becoming contaminated with water.

This breather valve was very blocked with dirt, but a few minutes with a small pick and penetrating oil got it working again.

THE TWO KINDS OF HUB

Two kinds of hubs were fitted to Series Is: semi-floating (which was only found on the rear) and fully floating. Semi-floating rear hubs are the earlier type. The fully floating design became optional on SWB models for export from 1956, and standard on LWBs from 1957.

Our Series I is unusual because its rear axle has a semi-floating hub on one side and fully floating on the other. Originally it would have been fully floating on both sides, but presumably one side was destroyed at some stage and was replaced with the semi-floating type from an earlier model. Replacing bearings on this later type is far easier, so this vehicle will be restored to the fully floating design on both sides.

The main difficulty of the semi-floating design is that the wheel bearing is pressed on to the halfshaft along with the retaining collar, which requires a

An assembled semi-floating hub, easily identified by its lack of a dust cap.

press to extract it, and the application of heat for reassembly. You will also need a long metal tube to fit the new bearing on to the halfshaft (a length of scaffolding pole can be used).

All this makes replacing a wheel bearing 'in the field' very difficult – although not impossible, if you are prepared to spend a long time hitting it hard with a hammer. The technique adopted by the 'First Overland' expedition from London to Singapore (and back) in the 1950s was to raise the halfshaft assembly in the air, and smash it down against a rock until the retaining collar was driven as far as the tapered section, allowing it to fall off. To reassemble, the collar had to be heated on a camping cooker until it expanded enough to slot on again – rarely on the first attempt. The expedi-

The long rear halfshaft and hub assembly are placed in the press.

The hub assembly is supported so that the bearing carrier takes the weight.

tion destroyed many wheel bearings, making this a frequent and frustrating process.

SEMI-FLOATING HUBS

Semi-floating hubs are more difficult to restore. The images in this section show part of the refurbishment of an 80in Land Rover, as our main feature vehicle received a fully floating hub in place of its semi-floating version.

To convert from semi-floating to fully floating hubs you will need the following:

◆ Stub axle
◆ Hub
◆ Bearing
◆ Flange
◆ Halfshaft (very difficult to find)

All other parts, including the backplate, axle tube and differential, are the same, whether semi-floating or fully floating.

The press is used to push the halfshaft through the bearing and collar. The drive flange with its five wheel

Left to right: The wheel bearing's retaining collar, the hub seal carrier, the wheel-bearing hub and the wheel bearing, after removal from the halfshaft (underneath).

The spacing ring ensures the wheel bearing isn't too close to the backplate: it is of imperative importance.

The old hub seal (left) with the new one sitting on its carrier, before being tapped in. The rear face of the seal is pointing up.

The wheel-bearing carrier, about to be pressed on to the driveshaft. Note the colourful tinge of the collar, still hot from the blowtorch.

Wheel-bearing hub with the new wheel bearing dropped in place, ready for the collar to be pressed in.

The final job: adding the hub seal and some grease for lubrication.

and wheel bearing are replaced with new items, and the other components are thoroughly cleaned and checked for any signs of damage – which is quite rare. The backplate also receives a fresh coat of paint. Note that the wheel bearing uses ball bearings, unlike the tapered roller bearings that are used in fully floating hubs.

The old hub seal is removed from the hub seal carrier by knocking it out with a drift, and a new one is tapped into place.

The halfshaft is returned to the press, and the wheel-bearing hub complete with its new bearing is dropped down over the shaft, along with the backplate. To push the bearing on to the halfshaft you will then need a long metal tube, longer than the halfshaft, to slot over it and push against the bearing. The tube is then removed, but will be needed again for the addition of the retaining collar.

Before the retaining collar can be added to the halfshaft, it will need to be expanded by heating it with a blowtorch. A bluish discoloration to the metal usually signifies that it has been heated sufficiently.

Once the collar has cooled down, the new hub seal and its retaining collar are tapped down over it. A little grease is added to the protruding part of the collar, and the assembly is then ready to be reinstalled on to the axle.

FULLY FLOATING HUBS

A fully floating hub has two bearings per hub – an inner and an outer roller bearing. Each bearing travels on a race, which is replaceable when worn. The inner bearing is slightly larger than the outer, and accessing it requires the hub to be removed from the stub axle. This is a simple process requiring only basic tools, but take careful note of the order in which the hub's inner components are fitted.

Here, the fully floating hub on the nearside rear is being dismantled. Begin by removing the brake drum, which is held in place using short screws requiring a large flat-head screwdriver. Whether you do this before or after removing the flange and halfshaft is up to you.

First, the six bolts securing the hub flange need to be removed. In our case this revealed a broken bolt in the hub,

studs is integral to the halfshaft, so this is not what needs to be pushed against. Instead, the assembly is supported on the six-holed flange bearing carrier, which sits in the backplate. This bearing carrier needs to take the strain as the halfshaft is pushed down through. A brake drum with the mounting face cut out to allow the centre to be pushed through can be used. The assembly is rested on strong metal bars, positioned as close to the centre of the hub as possible, to prevent the backplate from taking the strain.

Once disassembled, the hub seal

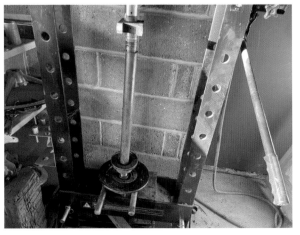

The scaffolding pole is slotted over the halfshaft, and pushes against the bearing.

A strong lever wedged between the bolts will fix the hub in place while you bolt the flange.

The outer wheel bearing, released from the hub.

which will need renewing. To stop the hub from rotating as you turn the nuts, you can use a strong prybar wedged between the studs (pictured) to give you something to lever against.

A soft hammer will help knock the flange off.

With the six bolts removed, put down a pan to catch the oil that's about to come out, then the flange can be pulled off complete with its halfshaft attached, and set to one side.

Inside the hub, bend back the tab that secures the hub nut in place. The tab forms part of a washer, part of which is bent forwards around the outer nut, while another part is bent backwards to secure another nut behind it. Once the tab is pushed back, you'll need a special hub-nut spanner (available from most Land Rover parts suppliers), or a 52mm socket, to undo the hub nut. Removing the nut will reveal the bent tab washer.

Remove the washer, then you'll need your 52mm socket again to undo the inner nut.

Next comes the thrust washer, which is the last piece before removing the bearings themselves. The pressure exerted on the bearings by the thrust

Extracting the locking washer.

washer is critical – we'll come to this later when reassembling. The hub can then be removed from the stub axle, complete with the outer wheel bearing, giving access to the inner wheel bearing and hub seal.

Setting the hub aside for a moment, we continue by unbolting the brake-wheel cylinder from the backplate, taking care not to damage it, as these are obsolete (more on that in the next chapter). Then the bolts around the middle of the backplate are undone, allowing both the backplate and stub axle to be removed from the axle casing. This enables us to inspect and clean the stub axle and backplate.

Now the hub, which still contains its rear seal, inner bearing and both races, needs to be dismantled. Turning the hub over and pulling out the rubber seal with a hook or lever will

This is a good quality, original Timken bearing, stamped 'Made in England', which you won't find on modern replacements.

This outer race is dark grey rather than bright and shiny, which means it is worn. Also note the lines on the shiny surface, where the rollers have been sitting. This race needs replacing.

Once the hub nut is released from the tab washer, it is undone with a 52mm socket.

The thrust washer sits between the inner nut and the hub's outer bearing.

The old inner race is knocked out of the back of the hub using a drift.

The cleaned hub receiving its new outer race.

give access to the inner bearing, which should just drop out.

Both bearing races can now be inspected. They should have a smooth, polished surface, totally free from any signs of corrosion or pitting, or dark discoloration – but if they are old then this is unlikely, so you will need to extract them from the hubs and replace them. Our races are showing wear, and also small vertical lines where the rollers have been resting, and causing pitting. Sometimes you might also find pitting on the bearing rollers, although we didn't in this case.

Unfortunately these are the kinds of hidden components that are easily ignored in a cost-cutting restoration, but it's not worth making false economies, especially if you want the finished vehicle to be able to cover significant mileages. Any wear in the race will reduce the lifespan of the bearing.

The old races need to be knocked out firmly, using a strong drift and a copper hammer to minimize risk of damaging the metal. Be very careful not to score the inner face of the hub as you do this. Once fully stripped, the hub then needs to be carefully cleaned before reassembly. Cleanliness is important from now on, as any contamination will

An old race is used to help exert even pressure around the new hub seal.

cause poorly fitting seals and increase wear in the bearings.

The new races are also tapped into position with a drift. (A hydraulic press can be used instead if your workshop has one.) As you tap them in, listen for a subtle change in the 'ting', which signifies that the race is seated all the way home. The new rear bearing is then packed thoroughly with grease and dropped into position, and the new hub seal is tapped into place behind it.

One of the new wheel studs, peened over in the groove in the back of the hub.

The old dust cap removed from the flange.

In some cases new wheel studs will need to be installed into the outer part of the hub, if the original threads are worn, or if the stud has become loose. To do this, the rear end of each stud needs to be peened over (crushed and splayed outwards), which stops them unscrewing with the wheel stud. First, tap the stud with a small chisel to distort the stud slightly, then use a fatter chisel to complete the job, making sure the stud is firmly held. Sometimes this won't work, in which case you might need to apply a small weld on the back to hold the stud in place.

The hub is now rebuilt and ready to receive its new bearings, but first there are some surrounding parts we need to assess: first the drive flange, then the stub axle and backplate. The drive flange is removed from the halfshaft by pulling off the dust cap, extracting the split pin, undoing the castle nut, then the washer. In our case, the star-shaped felt washer had failed.

Assess the condition of each drive flange by inspecting the splines. They become pointy as wear develops, and contribute to the overall backlash felt through the transmission. Most Series I flanges from UK vehicles rarely reach this condition unless the vehicle sees a lot of off-road action (the vehicle would typically expire from rust before severe mechanical wear such as this set in), but some of the flanges on our Australian import turned out to be severely worn.

Series I flanges are obsolete, so you have a choice between sourcing a second-hand item in good condition, or fitting a later-spec flange for a Series III; they look slightly different, but they do the job. We've opted for some good second-hand items, taken from a UK-based Series I. Use a new split pin when reassembling.

Check for pitting around the stub-axle flange, which could allow oil to escape from around the hub seal. In Series Is, no gaskets were originally fitted between the rear axle casing and the stub axle, although this did become standard for Series IIs.

We are also looking for signs of unlubricated hubs. In some cases this can cause the hub to become so hot that the bearing literally welds itself together. Once the hub assembly is removed, check for any colourful

Compare the worn and pointy splines on this worn drive flange…

Note the discoloration of the stub axle, either side of the thicker black band. (This was on the front stub axle.)

The new stub axle for the fully floating hob is offered up to the axle casing.

… with the squared-off splines on this replacement.

discoloration around the stub axle, indicating excessive heat.

The backplate is thoroughly cleaned, dried and painted prior to reassembly, and then bolted back on to the stub axle.

The hub can now be reassembled. You might choose to attach the brake components to the backplate before doing so (*see* Chapter 7), but it is not essential, and in this case we are proceeding without the brake parts.

A brand new stub axle will be fitted to the right-hand side, part of the process of restoring this axle to the correct spec, with fully floating hubs both sides. The stub axle is the same component found on Series II/IIAs. If you are concerned about oil leaks, a front-axle gasket can be fitted here, and/or some non-setting gasket compound applied – which is what is done in this case. It doesn't matter which way you orientate the stub axle, although it is common for the groove to be pointing upwards.

With the stub axle bolted in place, the backplate can be added to it. This is exactly the same plate that was used with the semi-floating arrangement. The semi-floating hub and bearing assembly is identical at the front and rear.

Apply some grease to the bearings and the threaded end of the stub axle, then push the hub on to the stub axle. The outer bearing is added next, then the thrust washer, and then the first nut is gently wound into place, but only finger tight.

The correct way to determine the tightness of this nut – as recommended by Rover – is by measuring the end float on the bearing using a dial test indicator (DTI), rather than adjusting the nut to a particular torque. The DTI is mounted on one of the wheel studs, with its finger touching the nut on the stub axle. The whole hub is then pushed in and out on the stub axle, to give a reading on the DTI, which needs to be between .004in (0.10mm) and .006in (0.15mm). If there is too much end float, the nut needs tightening. When the correct end float is obtained, the tab washer and lock nut are added.

Although the locking washers can usually be reused once or twice, it's good practice to renew them each time they are removed, as they do become weaker each time they are bent.

SWIVELS AND HOUSINGS

In most cases you should budget for rebuilding the front axle's swivel housings and installing new swivels. These are large chrome cups that rotate inside the swivel housings, enabling the wheels to pivot as the car steers. Over time the chromed surface becomes pitted, especially if the vehicle is under-used, and this roughness allows oil to escape from the housing past the rubber seal, which should sit tight against the clean, chromed surface. This corrosion is common, especially on old Land Rovers that have been left sitting. The swivels can be reconditioned but this is difficult to achieve properly, as an extremely smooth and durable surface is required to create a good seal. Replacement is usually the best course of action.

On the demo 109 each swivel hub and braking assembly will be stripped down into its component parts, including the chrome swivel. They'll be built

The left-hand front hub, brake and steering assembly, unrestored, ready for stripping.

Offside (right-hand) assembly, showing the correct bolts.

Nearside (left-hand) assembly, with oversized bolts.

back up using new parts where necessary, and the splined peg in the swivel will be converted to a Railko bush.

Compare the studs in the top of each of the swivel housings and you can see that one side isn't correct. In the left image, showing the left-hand assembly, the studs are clearly bodged; the opposite image, showing the right-hand assembly, has the correct 3/8 BSF fittings. Presumably the original studs on the left had stripped their threads, so someone drilled them out and tapped a larger thread in the housing. Both the swivel housing and the steering arm have been drilled through so the strength cannot be guaranteed, and they will therefore be replaced with second-hand parts in good condition. But to remove them, first the hubs, braking components, stub axle and halfshaft must be detached.

Although the braking components are different to the rear, the hubs and bearings are identical. The only practical difference is that you will not be able to extract the driveshaft and flange together, before removing the hub. We therefore begin by removing the drive flange and hub assembly, as described earlier in this chapter. The braking components are removed (described in Chapter 7), along with the backplate.

Pulling the stub axle off the driveshaft.

The full length of the nearside (left) front driveshaft. The universal joint sits inside the swivel and enables the vehicle to steer.

A poorly lubricated universal joint on a front halfshaft. Note the lack of rubber seals and grease nipple.

To remove the swivel housing, the stub-axle retaining bolts that pass through the backplate must be removed; the lock tabs (which are included in any swivel rebuild kit) will need bending back first. Then the backplate can be pulled away, the stub axle can be pulled off the driveshaft, then the driveshaft can be extracted through the swivel housing.

The universal joints in the swivels are slightly different from those on a propshaft; instead of having a grease nipple and rubber seals to hold the lubricating grease around the cup, these UJs have neither grease nipples nor seals, because the entire joint is submerged in oil. (80in Series Is have a different design using a Tracta joint, which we describe later in this chapter.)

It's now time to remove the swivel components. The four bolts securing the steering arm to the top of the housing come out first. The arm is then removed, complete with the splined peg, and the spring. The splined peg sits inside a tapered brass cone, which is pushed by the spring into the race on the top of the swivel. This preloads the movement of the swivel.

In the case of the demo 109, all these parts were badly rusted, including the

Clearly worn teeth receive the peg from the steering arm. This wear will cause slack steering, illustrating the weakness of this design compared with the Railko set-up.

Removing the incorrect, oversized bolts from the stop of the swivel housing.

The steering arm's splined peg, which slots into the cone.

The spring that creates the preload on the swivel.

A retaining ring holds the swivel seal against the swivel.

The race for the swivel's top bearing is very badly scored and rusted – this is definitely too far gone.

LEFT: *A severely worn lower bearing inside the swivel housing.*

RIGHT: *The swivel is unbolted from the axle casing.*

The roller bearing inside the back of the swivel.

The bearing race and retaining collar, on the halfshaft, prior to disassembly.

race in the top of the swivel, and the teeth inside the cone were very worn, which would result in a 'notchy' feel to the steering and a great deal of play. All these parts needed replacing.

The swivel is then unbolted from the axle casing to reveal the halfshaft's roller bearing in the back of the swivel, and the seal in the end of the axle. The axle seal pulls out (the halfshaft bearing is discarded with the swivel).

The last item to detach is the race on the halfshaft, which runs inside the bearing on the inboard side of the swivel. There is no way of pressing this collar off the shaft, so it has to be very carefully cut through with an angle grinder to release the bearing. When rebuilding, a new collar is driven on to the shaft with a press.

RAILKO BUSH CONVERSION

A Railko bush conversion kit will be installed into each front swivel housing of the demo 109. This conversion was offered by Land Rover in period (original part number 532268) and gives better steering feedback by reducing the number of points of contact. The Railko kit consists of new seals, lower bearing, upper bearing, fibre washer,

gasket, shims and top swivel pin. Land Rover also provided fitting instructions (with their own part number: 532269) but they are not very revealing, so we go into more detail in this chapter.

To access the swivel housings various braking components must be removed, so you will find it helpful to refer periodically to Chapter 7.

Whereas the older original design (with its cone and spring) relies on a splined peg, which can wear and cause play, the later Railko system uses a smooth peg that pushes inside a bush. Friction between the pin and the bush determines the stiffness of the steering, and the level of friction is determined by shims placed between the swivel housing and the steering arm. These shims adjust how firmly the pin is pushed into the bush (the preload). Unlike the original set-up, there is no spring involved, and there are no splines to wear out.

TOP: *The old toothed peg, together with the smooth new Railko pin. The wider part of the pin is slightly conical.*

MIDDLE: *A hydraulic press is used to push the new bush into the steering arm.*

BOTTOM: *The new Railko bush pressed into the steering arm.*

The bottom race is pushed into position in the new swivel.

The halfshaft bearing being pushed into the inboard side of the swivel ball, with a sheet of steel to spread the load.

The inboard side of the swivel ball, showing the indent where the bearing has been fully pushed in.

Using a seal pick to extract the old seal from the casing. Note the protrusion around the flange.

Depending on the manufacturer of your components, the Railko bush can be a very tight fit into the chrome ball. If so, use some fine sandpaper so you get the inner and outer diameters to match.

First a hydraulic press is needed to extract the old, splined pin from the steering arm, and replace it with the new pin for the Railko bush. The old part is often pinned in place, so driving it out is much easier with a press.

The new swivel then needs its bottom race pushed into it, followed by the top race. This part can be done with a copper hammer if you prefer, so long as you tap evenly around the circumference of the race. Lubricating the bush with a little oil will make it easier to drive home.

Then the new halfshaft bearing needs to be pushed into the back of the swivel ball. It has to be pressed all the way until it stops, so don't stop when it's flush with the face – keep going as far as it will go. This is because the axle casing's flange protrudes slightly, and it fits into this space.

The new rubber seal can then replace the old one in the end of the axle casing, and a new paper gasket can be placed around the end of the axle. Use a smear of grease to hold the new gasket in place, so you can have both hands free – or you can use gasket compound instead. (The rear axle technically should not have these paper gaskets at the ends of the casing, although they are sometimes fitted.)

The chrome swivel ball is now ready to be attached to the axle, along with the retaining ring and seal, which need to be placed over it first. Make sure you get them in the right order, and the right way round. Always use new locknuts and high tensile bolts of the correct rating when fixing the new swivel in place.

Don't worry if the design of the new rubber seal looks different to the original.

The swivel seal and retaining ring slot over the chrome ball like this.

The original swivel housing is given a thorough clean with brake cleaner inside and out, and its outer face is etch primed and given a coat of satin black. It then receives a new lower bearing, packed with bearing grease, and is then placed over the new chrome swivel ball.

Before we fit the top pin and steering arm, a fibre washer needs to be pushed into the top of the Railko bush. Theoretically, lubricant is supposed

The new lower bearing inside the swivel housing.

A fibre washer is added to the top of the swivel housing.

The arm and new pin, with shims, being added to the swivel housing.

to wick its way up to this washer, but it rarely does. The bush and the fibre washer should therefore be primed with 10w/40 oil before fitting, otherwise it can become extremely stiff. It's worth noting that these bushes also take a bit of bedding in, so they tend to feel stiff initially.

Now the steering arm and its new pin can be fitted to the swivel housing, with shims (from the new kit) sandwiched between them. Some calibration is needed here, as the number of shims determines the pressure of the pin in the housing. Too few shims means too much pressure, so the steering will be stiff; too many and there won't be enough pressure, causing play in the swivel – an MOT fail.

The correct stiffness is determined through trial and error, by using a spring balance. Start off by adding the complete pack of new shims to the housing, followed by the steering arm. One end of the balance is attached to the end of the arm, and a lateral pull is exerted on it – just enough for the housing to move round the swivel. The balance will give a reading at this point. This reading is known as the 'pre-load':

too high and the swivel will be too stiff, too low and it will be slack. The correct reading should be 8lb ft (10.85Nm).

To reduce stiffness, the arm is unbolted and the shims are removed, one at a time, until the spring balance gives the correct reading. (Removing each shim lowers the pin slightly into the cone.) Over time, the pin will wear inside its bush, and shims will need to be removed to maintain the right pre-load.

Finally the swivel seal is pushed on to

Gasket compound around the swivel seal helps prevent leaks.

the back of the housing, and the retaining ring is attached. There can be a tendency for oil to leak between the housing and the metal edge of the seal, but an even application of gasket compound will fix this.

It pays dividends to make sure that all these seals and bearings are a perfect fit, because having to redo this work will be time consuming.

The halfshaft can now be inserted through the swivel housing, and twisted until you feel it engage with the front diff. Before reinstalling the stub axle, check its bronze bush, which supports the front part of the driveshaft. If the bush is worn it can be cut out using an air hacksaw or punched out with a drift, and a new replacement would then be pressed in (hitting it in with a hammer could damage the bronze).

The stub axle slides over the end of the halfshaft, together with a new gasket, and is bolted up to the swivel housing with the brake backplate and new lock tabs. The fully floating hub and bearings are installed, following the same procedure described ear-

Adjusting the pre-load using a spring balance.

The fully assembled hub, viewed from inboard, with the swivel seal and retaining ring in place.

Secondhand flange being fitted with a new gasket. Note the new tab washer, bent in both directions.

Swivel housing being filled with 'one shot' grease.

Fitting the washer over a new felt/rubber seal.

Castellated nut and split pin in place, ready to receive the hub cab.

lier in this chapter. We then attach a second-hand drive flange (sourced from a UK vehicle) to replace our very worn Australian one. It's bolted to the assembly with a new paper gasket.

It is important to use a new felt/rubber seal on the end of the driveshaft to prevent leaks. The washer is pushed against the seal, then the castellated nut is tightened with a new split pin to secure it in place, and a new dust cap is tapped on.

The fully assembled swivel hub is now ready to receive its lubricant. The correct lubricant is EP90 or thicker, although in practice these oils are sometimes found to leak. 'One shot' grease became a common alternative a few decades after Series I production; originally developed for CV-jointed halfshafts (as used, for example, in

Range Rover Classics and Stage I V8s), it is much thicker, less likely to leak, and has become widely recognized as an acceptable replacement for the original oil – even though is it not technically 'correct'. Note that this is separate from the lubricant for the differential, which does need to be EP90.

'One shot' is available in packets that are designed to be the correct amount for one swivel. It is added through the filler hole on each swivel housing, stopping when the level just reaches the base of the hole – then the plug is inserted.

TRACTA JOINTS

If you are rebuilding an 80in Series I you will encounter Tracta joints at the each end of the front halfshafts, rather than universal joints. This type of joint was initially used by Citroen, and can also be found in the Austin Champ and Willys Jeep.

The Tracta joint is a simple kind of CV (constant velocity) joint. Whereas the universal joints on a 1954-onwards Series I connect the sections of a halfshaft together, the earlier Tracta joints mean the halfshaft sections are interlocked, but not attached. Instead, each one has a C-shaped jaw slotted round a two-part knuckle, which spins together with the driveshaft. While the jaws

An unused (and therefore extremely rare) 80in Tracta joint, with the jaws of the two halfshaft sections that have been separated from the central knuckle.

enable the shaft to pivot on one plane, the joint in the middle of the knuckle enables it to pivot on the perpendicular plane.

New parts are not available for Tracta joints, but they are durable and rarely wear out. In Series Is from the UK, they are usually in perfect condition – although they are occasionally found to be worn in vehicles from Australia. Wear occurs inside the knuckle joint rather than in the jaws on the driveshaft.

To disassemble this earlier design, the halfshaft's retaining collar has to be pressed off the shaft and its roller bearing, after warming the collar first using a blowtorch. The swivel is placed face-

The collar, which has to be pressed off the halfshaft.

This is the reverse of an 80in swivel, showing the different bearing.

down in the press, chocked slightly to make the driveshaft vertical, and the shaft is then pressed down through the collar – a similar process to the rear semi-floating halfshaft described earlier.

Unlike the roller bearings found on later Series I front halfshafts, an 80in front halfshaft uses ball bearings in a sealed unit.

DIFFERENTIALS

Rebuilding a differential from scratch is a very technical procedure – a task that a home-based restorer would be wise to entrust to a specialist. There are, however, some essential health checks to make, which we'll outline here. The halfshafts need to be extracted (at least partially) before the differentials can be removed or installed.

The first step is to drain the oil and check for fragments of broken metal, using a magnet. This should be done

Twisted, almost destroyed halfshaft.

routinely anyway, whenever the oil looks contaminated or dirty (Land Rover did not originally publish a service interval for transmission oil). You are likely to find small flecks of metal in the oil, but any large chunks of metal signify that something has been damaged.

We found broken gear teeth in the oil of this 109's rear axle, so it was obvious we were going to find problems when we came to inspect the differential itself. This is why it is a good idea to use magnetic drain plugs that capture fragments of metal, preventing them from being pulled back into the gears and causing additional wear.

You can also usually feel if something isn't right inside the axles, just by lifting both wheels clear of the ground

and rotating each wheel by hand. The rear axle of the demo 109 definitely felt wrong. When turning either wheel, a lot of backlash could be felt, and it seemed to be coming from the diff. (Backlash is the amount of free rotation that the wheel has before you feel the transmission components engage.) The offside wheel felt particularly odd – we later discovered that the inner end of the half-shaft was occasionally skipping teeth within the diff.

One of our halfshafts had severely twisted splines on its inboard end, suggesting it had nearly sheared altogether – probably during heavy use off-road.

The differential is exposed by removing a propshaft, then undoing the nuts from the studs around where the housing attaches to the axle casing. It is quite a heavy assembly, so be careful when you pull it off the studs.

Inside our differential, the crownwheel seems to be in good condition, but there are broken teeth on the planet and sun gears, so it would be very unwise to return it to the vehicle. Instead, we choose to replace it with a refurbished item, which can be obtained from specialists on an exchange basis (currently costing around £400). In some cases, the most cost-effective option is to replace the differential with a decent second-hand unit, if you can find one for the right price.

For a better understanding of the level of wear in the diff, you might also check for wear between the

Drain the diff oil first.

Large chunks of broken teeth in the oil – not a good sign.

Detaching the differential housing from the axle.

Inspecting the diff.

The arrow indicates one of the broken teeth that made this differential unviable.

crownwheel and the pinion gear. This involves cleaning away the old oil, then smearing 'engineer's blue' (a gear-marking compound) on the teeth of the crownwheel. The crownwheel is then passed through one full rotation so that some of the compound is worn off. Ideally you will then see long wear marks spanning the centre of each tooth; shorter marks near the edge of the teeth signify that the mechanism is worn and the mating faces of the gears have developed too much tolerance.

Although they can become noisy and develop backlash, these differentials tend to remain reliable, so (depending on your budget) you may choose to postpone replacing a less-than-perfect diff until minor wear becomes severe.

Various gear ratios are available, using standard Rover diffs from later Land Rovers, so you have the option of using a different ratio to suit your intended usage. If you have an unknown differential, you can calculate the ring- and pinion-gear ratio by counting the number of teeth on both the ring gear and the pinion gear. Divide the number of teeth on the ring gear by the number of teeth on the pinion gear: the answer is your diff ratio. A standard Series I diff ratio is 4.7:1, which is the same as later Series vehicles. Early 1948 Series Is have a diff ratio of 4.88:1, and are distinguished by a longer pinion drive flange, so they are known as 'long-nosed' diffs. These are only found in very early production vehicles. A lower final-drive ratio for more relaxed cruising can be achieved by installing 3.54:1 differentials from an early Range Rover Classic, Ninety or One Ten. Obviously differentials with the same ratio must be used in the front and rear axles.

Reattaching the diff to the axle is simply a case of thoroughly cleaning the mating surfaces, replacing the paper gasket (some added gasket compound is a good idea), and returning the diff housing to its studs. The nuts are added and progressively tightened in a star patten.

7

The Braking System

When rebuilding an axle, it is convenient to attach the braking components before adding the rebuilt hubs, so there is a little overlap between the order of events in this chapter and Chapter 6. For the sake of clarity, anything to do with the braking system will be addressed in this chapter.

Series Is have drum brakes front and rear, without servo assistance. It is extremely simple, but, being a single-line system – meaning that all four corners are connected by the same hydraulic circuit, rather than divided between two circuits – safety depends on it being built and calibrated properly.

When properly set up, Series I brakes should feel perfectly adequate and safe. However, even minor issues can result in weak performance. Also, because this is a single-line system, any loss of hydraulic fluid (resulting from damaged, perished or poorly fitted parts) will result in total loss of braking. Most of the components are affordable to replace, so any thorough restoration should include new parts all round. The only exception is certain handbrake components, and hard-to-replace wheel cylinders, which can be sent off for professional refurbishment.

There were different types of wheel-cylinder and brake-shoe arrangements used in Series Is, depending on the year, the wheelbase, and whether they were fitted to the front or rear. The front axle of the demo 109 has twin leading shoes, meaning that each piston pushes in the same direction as the wheel rotation when moving forwards. This is achieved by having both an upper and lower wheel cylinder, each pushing in the same direction. The other layout, found on the rear of this 109, is to have one leading shoe and one trailing shoe, pushed in opposite directions by a single wheel cylinder that pushes in two directions at once.

All wheel cylinders are available to buy 'off the shelf' and are quite cheap, with the exception of 80in front cylinders with their banjo fitting, and 107/109 rear cylinders, which have recently become available from a specialist UK supplier (Design & Development Engineering). However, they cost over £200 each, so it's worth salvaging the originals if possible. Ours were sent away for professional refurbishment, involving rehoning and the addition of new linings in the bores.

DRUMS

Short-wheelbase 86s and 88s have 10in drums front and rear (the measurement refers to the internal diameter), but the demo 109 has 11in drums.

If the screws that secure the brake drum are seized, they can be removed with an angled blow from a punch. You can also try using an impact screw-

A sideways blow with a punch is used to remove a seized brake-drum retaining screw.

ASBESTOS SAFETY

Thousands of people have died from asbestos exposure, and many more have suffered serious long-term illness. Asbestos is dangerous when broken or abraded, as minute airborne fragments are inhaled, and the resultant lung damage may take many decades to manifest. Extra care must be taken with any old brake lining dating from the Series I era.

Necessary considerations range from correct handling to workspace preparation, and the wearing of protective clothing. There are also laws governing how asbestos may be disposed of.

Full guidance on these matters can be found on the Health and Safety Executive section of the UK government website, which also has various free PDF downloads, available at www.hse.gov.uk.

(Incidentally, the Solihull factory is likely to have contained very dangerous levels of airborne asbestos during Series I production, as the welding booths in which chassis fabrication took place were separated by large asbestos curtains.)

driver, which applies a sharp twisting force when its end is struck with a heavy hammer. Once the shoes are unscrewed, they should pull off. If not, you will need to unwind the adjusters on the rear of the backplate.

When removing a drum from a vehicle that has been sitting for a long time, there is a high probability that the wheel cylinders will be seized. Backing off the adjusters will therefore have little effect, and the shoes will probably still hold the drum in place. Your only option is to bash the drum off firmly, using a copper hammer to prevent fracturing the cast steel of the drum.

Sometimes the braking surface is compromised by surface rust or scoring. Another potential problem is warping of the brake drum; this is usually the result of a shoe binding and overheating, caused by a seized or poorly adjusted wheel cylinder. The symptom of a warped drum will be 'hot spots' in the wheel's rotation where the shoes rub, and you will be able to feel for this later when you calibrate the shoe adjusters.

In most cases though, the drums are serviceable. They must be thoroughly cleaned round the inside using brake cleaner to remove any road grease – taking precautions against the risk of asbestos inhalation, as described earlier. They can then be cleaned and painted using heat-resistant black paint, while ensuring that the small drainage holes are clear of dirt, rust and paint. (Obviously the inside of the drum must remain unpainted.)

REAR BRAKES

Before removing the old shoes, take photos of the springs to show exactly where they attach. When you refit, the

Missing rear shoes, so the demo 109 had no rear brakes whatsoever!

Unbolting a rear wheel cylinder, bound up with wire.

Rear wheel cylinder removed. It is not in a bad state, but will need reconditioning.

springs must go into the correct holes on the shoes – sometimes this is done incorrectly.

Removing the rear drums revealed that the brake shoes were completely missing, and the wheel cylinder had been bound up with wire to prevent the pistons popping out when under pressure. This shows the level of 'care' that the project vehicle had received.

To remove shoes, use a pair of mole grips to hold on to the toe of the shoe (the end that touches the wheel cyl-

Brake-lining kit, for original shoes whose linings are riveted in place.

inder). Pull firmly to separate it from the piston, then pull it slightly sideways (towards you) and it should dislocate easily. The two shoes can then be removed together, joined together by the springs. To remove the springs from the shoes, you may need to use a punch to tap the little hooks out of the holes. The springs are long lasting, but they are also cheap, so it's good practice to replace them anyway.

Modern brake shoes have their linings bonded in place, and when they wear out, the whole shoe needs to be replaced. If your shoes are original, the linings will be riveted, and can therefore be replaced. This process is described for handbrake shoes later in this chapter.

The hose is now unbolted from the wheel cylinder, and the cylinder is unbolted from the backplate. This obsolete type of Girling was also used on 80s and 107s, and fitted to 109in Series Is with 11in drums from about 1957, lasting into Series II production to around 1959/1960. Unlike other Series I wheel cylinders, these feature a self-centring mechanism, and can be easily distinguished by the plate on the top

Applying heat was the only way to get this seized adjuster moving again.

with curved tabs. Don't be tempted to buy cylinders advertised as being compatible with the Rover P4 because although they are very similar, they have a different sized bore.

The demo 109's will be sent off to be professionally reconditioned by Suffolk-based specialist, Past Parts. This will involve reboring and the addition of a new stainless-steel sleeve (matching the bore of the original), so the same kind of rust damage will not happen again. The piston and seals will also be renewed with original-sized parts.

We also need to look after the little rear plate and the special spring washers.

The small adjusters for the rear brakes on the demo 109 are badly seized, but they are also obsolete, so they need to be salvaged. The backplate is unbolted and removed to a bench-mounted vice to make the job of freeing them off easier. After first cleaning the adjuster with a wire wheel, the adjuster is heated with a blowtorch, enabling the pistons to be tapped outwards from the middle using a drift and a brass hammer. Unlike the wheel cylinders, we don't have to worry about burning any brake fluid or rubber seals.

The backplates are given a scrub with a wire wheel and parts cleaner, then a spray of fresh black paint. Once dry, the backplate is bolted on to the

The adjuster has two of these pistons, which act on the bottom of the brake shoes.

The backplate is cleaned, painted and reattached.

stub axle and the brakes are ready for reassembly. The adjuster and wheel cylinder are added first.

The reconditioned wheel cylinder is fixed to the backplate using its special spring washers to allow for movement, together with the spreader plate and the correct locknuts. These are then tightened by feel, enough to grip the backplate but still slide. With this particular type of cylinder, it is important to avoid tightening these nuts too firmly; this would prevent the cylinder from self-centring, and cause difficulties when bleeding and balancing the

The rear brake cylinders on 109in Series Is (and IIs) use these BSF locknuts and tensioning washers.

Spreader plate and fixings, viewed from the reverse of the backplate.

brakes later. (Other types of wheel cylinder on Series Is should be tightened normally.)

Both springs need to be added to the correct holes in the shoes, before the shoes are offered up to the axle. Pay close attention to the photos that were taken of the old springs in position, and use this as a reference. If the hooks on the springs are difficult to insert, you may need to tap them in using a drift.

Pulling the shoes into their final position is awkward until you have done it once or twice, then it becomes easy.

The spreader plate, which is fitted to the rear face of the backplate.

Reconditioned Girling rear brake cylinder mounted in place.

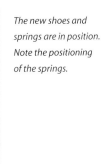

Force the shoes on to the bottom anchor using a mole grip. Don't grip the lining material itself.

The new shoes and springs are in position. Note the positioning of the springs.

This final order of events is different for the front axle, as described in the previous chapter.

FRONT BRAKES

As described in Chapter 6, accessing the swivel housing requires removal of all the braking components. The procedure is similar to the rear brakes, but the design of the cylinders and adjusters is a little different. As before, ensure the adjusters on the backplate are wound out fully for dismantling and reassembly.

The pipe unions for the wheel cylinders are often seized, but these cylinders are cheap to replace so the pipes can simply be cut off. Then the backplate and stub axle are removed, as described previously.

Once the new swivel housing, half-shaft and stub axle are reattached (as described in Chapter 6), the front brakes are ready to be rebuilt.

The two wheel cylinders are the same part number per side, but they are handed – so the two for the left-

Take care, because you need to exert quite a lot of force, and if the shoes slip out of position you can end up damaging components, or your hands. (Wearing gloves and safely goggles is advisable.) Always ensure that the springs are firmly attached before putting them under tension, and that the adjuster is fully retracted.

The best technique is to position one end of the brake shoe into position, and clamp a pair of mole grips on the other end – avoiding gripping the lining material as you do so. Check that the slot in the piston is aligned vertically (rotate it if necessary), and that the pistons are pushed all the way in. Once one end of the shoe is firmly located, use the mole grips to give you a firm hold as you pull the other end against the springs, far enough for it to engage. While you do this, be careful not to damage the rubber cover around the piston, which is crucial for preventing the ingress of moisture and dirt.

Finally the reassembled hub can be added to the stub axle, the driveshaft can be pushed into the axle, and the drive flange can be bolted to the hub.

The front brake assembly, prior to restoration.

Brakes and hub reassembled, ready for the drum.

These wheel cylinders were definitely not reusable.

Twin leading shoes and springs in place. Note the correct positioning of the springs.

Front brakes after the addition of the hub with new bearings, described in Chapter 6.

hand side are the same as each other, but are different from the two for the right-hand side. For the lower cylinder, the angled hole in the back receives a new bleed nipple, and the same hole in the upper cylinder takes a new brake hose. The other holes in the cylinders will receive the short length of pipe that runs round the front of the swivel housing, linking them together.

See our photo for the correct location of the springs: the front shoe's spring is attached to the lowest hole on the shoe, and the rear shoe's spring is attached to the highest hole.

Before attaching the hub to the stub axle, new wheel bearings and seals are installed. The process here is the same as for the rear.

The springs are slightly different from those at the rear, because each of them hooks on to its own anchor peg on the backplate. First attach the spring to the shoe, and attach the opposite end of the spring to the peg, and push the toe of the shoe into the piston of the wheel cylinder. Then use mole grips to stretch the spring, pulling the heel of the shoe outwards and far enough for it to marry up with the back of the other wheel cylinder. While you're doing this, make sure the rubber seals aren't getting pinched and damaged by the shoes.

For 10in drums with one leading and one trailing shoe (front and rear axles), the procedure is slightly different, because only one spring is attached to the backplate. First, the lower spring is fitted to the shoes, and the shoes are connected to the lower clamping plate – a feature that is absent in other types of shoe arrangement. The top spring is then hooked on to the peg at the back of the shoe, and pulled on to the peg

on the backplate using a pair of long-nosed pliers.

PIPES, HOSES AND JOINTS

All Series I brake pipes and flexible hoses can be bought ready-made off the shelf, but you will save some money if you can make the metal pipes yourself. This is a satisfying process, and a useful skill to have.

Early 80in Series Is had ¼in pipes, a larger diameter than the $^3/_{16}$in pipes that were fitted to all later Series Is. Components from ¼ and $^3/_{16}$ systems must not be mixed, because the pressure exerted on the pistons will be affected.

Solihull originally fitted brake pipes made of steel, so this is the only material that is technically correct. Copper is longer lasting and more malleable (it is easier to bend and form flared ends). However, for most of this vehicle we have chosen more expensive cunifer,

Copper (left) is a slightly brighter colour than cunifer (right).

a copper-nickel alloy that is closer to steel in colour, can be bent to a tighter radius than copper, and resists corrosion well.

Hopefully you took photos of the old brake pipes before taking them off, and you have retained any surviving lengths so you can replicate them. If you don't have a pipe to copy, you will need to get an accurate idea of how long the new pipe needs to be, accounting for all the curves along its length. The best way to do this is by using a length of stiff wire that you can manipulate into position and cut to length. You might find it useful to have some string or cable ties to hold it in position against the chassis while you do this. The wire can then be used as a template.

A hand-held pipe bender will help you make neat and uniform curves, and will greatly reduce the risk of introducing breaks or weaknesses. The tool will have angle markers to help you determine the degree of your curve.

Untidy pipework can ruin the aesthetic appeal of a vehicle, so this process is worth taking time over. Create straight lines and uniform curves wherever possible, running parallel

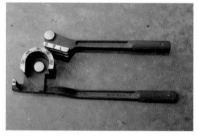

Hand-held pipe bender.

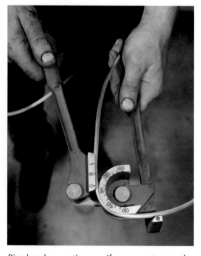

Pipe bender creating a uniform curve to exactly 90 degrees.

Original spec brake-pipe clip on the top of an 80in chassis.

An example of where care needs to be taken to prevent chafing against the leg of the battery tray. (From an 80in restoration.)

A flaring tool creates the required ends – don't forget to add the union first!

with the chassis rails and axles, and avoid unsightly meandering.

However, safety is more important than tidiness. Never allow pipes to take shortcuts through mid-air. Nor must they be allowed to chafe, so ensure there is enough clearance around any areas of protruding metal, and use pipe clips to anchor the pipes firmly to the chassis. To some extent, safety and aesthetics go hand in hand, because a strong pipe will typically be held securely and neatly tucked out of harm's way, straight where it needs to be, with any bends being smooth and even.

Use a dedicated pipe cutter so as to cut the metal without damaging the pipe or creating sharp edges. Doing this with snips will cause the metal to bend and fatigue, making it difficult to add the required flares to the ends.

Once your new pipe is cut to length,

A brake-pipe cutter is essential.

you will need to slot the correct unions over it. We are using $^3/_{16}$ UNF unions, which have an imperial thread, not to be confused with $^3/_{16}$ metric unions (which are for $^3/_{16}$ in pipes, but their threads are metric). Once the unions have been slid on to the pipe, it's time to flare the ends.

There are various types of flaring tool suitable for creating the two main types of flares required at the ends of the brake pipes. Here a vice-mounted version is used. The left-hand side clamps the end of the brake pipe in place, while the opposite side forces a die into the middle of the pipe, shaping the ends.

Like the metal brake pipes, all flexible brake hoses are available to buy

New rear brake hose connected to the three-way union above the rear diff.

off the shelf. Make sure you buy hoses with the correct UNF threads or they will be incompatible.

Finally the new pipes are screwed into the wheel cylinders. Be careful to ensure the union is properly aligned into the cylinder's female thread when you do this, as it is quite easy to get it cross-threaded and strip the thread in the cylinder. Get it finger tight first, before nipping it up with a spanner. When screwing and unscrewing unions, there is a risk of rounding them off. You can avoid this with a union spanner (or 'flare nut' spanner), which holds the union on more faces than a standard spanner will, but isn't hindered by the pipe protruding from the union in the way that a ring spanner would be.

On the front axle where there is a twin leading shoe arrangement, the small length of pipe that runs from the top wheel cylinder to the lower one should be run round the front of the axle, not the rear.

The junction pieces are readily available to buy (with UNF threads) if required, and the demo 109 uses two types. The first is a four-way junction mounted near the clutch pivot, to split the feed from the master cylinder in three directions: one pipe to each of the front wheels, and one pipe to the rear axle. The second type of junction is a T-piece on the rear axle, which splits the feed from the front into two directions, going to the left and right wheels.

80in Series Is have two T-pieces, and

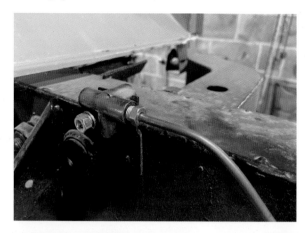

Four-way junction mounted to the chassis.

Joining piece that was only used on 80in vehicles.

The original, reconditioned brake master cylinder, added to the chassis.

also one connecting piece (similar in design to the T-pieces) fixed to the bulkhead steady bolt inside the chassis rail. This connector joins two lengths of pipe together, but was replaced with a single length of pipe when the 80in was superseded; unless you are aiming to recreate the original specification, you may choose to do the same.

MASTER CYLINDER

Certain aftermarket master cylinders are now available, but bear in mind that these are usually Series II master cylinders converted from a two-bolt fixing to a three-bolt fixing, rather than being cast as a whole unit, as the original item. Keeping the vehicle as original as possible therefore usually involves sending the master cylinder away to be honed and sleeved, together with any irreplaceable wheel cylinders – such as those at the back of the demo 109.

It is possible to convert an 80in from a ¼in system to a ³/₁₆in system, using imperial wheel cylinders from a later Series I vehicle and retaining the master cylinder from the 80. This requires a special union designed to receive ³/₁₆in pipe, with a ⁷/₁₆ BSF external thread to mate it to the master cylinder.

Master cylinders for 86/88s and 107/109s look the same, but the long-wheelbase version has a larger bore. A master cylinder for an 80 has a slightly different casting.

Once returned from being reconditioned by Past Parts, our master cylinder was bolted to the chassis.

ADJUSTMENTS AND BLEEDING

The final bleeding of the braking system takes place late in the restoration process when the pedal linkage and pivot assembly has been rebuilt, but the process will be described in this chapter to avoid confusion.

Before the brakes can be bled, the shoes need to be adjusted so that they are as close to the inner wall of the drum as possible, without rubbing when the wheel rotates. Having all the wheels off the vehicle will make access easier. If your transmission is fitted at this stage (the demo 109's is not) the

The rear adjuster for the brakes on the demo 109.

vehicle will need to be in neutral with the handbrake off.

Start with the adjusters fully backed off. For twin leading shoes with two adjusters (as on the front axle here) the front adjuster should be calibrated first, then the rear adjuster.

Spin the road wheel by hand, and slowly tighten the adjuster for the leading shoe, feeling carefully to detect when the shoe bites. For every few degrees on the adjuster, give the wheel another spin. As soon as you feel or hear the wheel being slowed by the brake shoe, back the adjuster off ¹/₈ of a turn (45 degrees), and spin the wheel again to make sure it's free. (This is where any warping in the drum will make itself known.) This adjuster should now be calibrated correctly, so you can repeat the process on the other adjusters.

This type of cam adjuster is sometimes found to be worn. They can be replaced, but avoid the very cheap and poor quality versions that are available. If in doubt, it may be best to replace the whole backplate with a good second-hand item.

For long-wheelbase rear brakes, you will need to readjust the shoes after bleeding the system, because the cylinder will centralize when the brake pedal is depressed.

Once all the pipes are connected and the shoes are adjusted, and you have double-checked that all the unions and bleed nipples are connected, you are ready to fill the master cylinder with Dot 4 brake fluid. Brake fluid is corrosive, so always wear safety glasses and gloves when dealing with it, and keep it off your paintwork.

Care must be taken to ensure the fluid reaches the entire braking system without leaving any air bubbles, so you will need to allow the air to escape from the bleed nipples on each wheel cylinder. This is done one at a time, starting with the cylinder furthest from the master cylinder, and working your way back. For a right-hand-drive vehicle such as this 109, the order is as follows: rear left, rear right, front left, front right.

You will need a length of clear tube to push over the end of the first bleed nipple, and a container to catch the fluid. With the tube attached, slacken the nipple using a ring spanner to pre-

Rear-wheel cylinder of a 109 Series I being bled. Clear hose is pushed over the bleed nipple, which is being slackened with a spanner to enable it to release fluid.

Original handbrake components. The expander is at the bottom; the adjuster is at the top.

Asbestos shoes, contaminated by oil, and worn down to the rivets: not good at all.

vent rounding it off, and slowly pump the brake pedal to build up pressure in the system, forcing the air out through the nipple. Eventually, fluid will flow. Wait until there are no longer any air bubbles, then tighten the nipple. Return to the master cylinder and top it up with fresh fluid. Any fluid you drain off must be considered contaminated and not reused.

This process is repeated for all the nipples, in the sequence above. When the job is complete, the brake pedal should feel firm and responsive. If it feels soft and spongey, there is probably still some air in the system, so you will need to repeat the procedure again. Note that poorly adjusted shoes will also prevent the pedal feeling firm, so these must be properly adjusted beforehand.

Pressure from the brake pedal should be enough to drive out all the air bubbles, but tools are available that force the fluid down from the master cylinder, using compressed air from a compressor or a tyre. This method is faster, and can be more effective at pushing stubborn bubbles out of the system. If air is lingering in the system, it is usually in the front upper cylinders on long-wheelbase models, because the bubble will resist being forced downwards and out of the lower cylinder.

HANDBRAKE REBUILD

The handbrake bolts on to the transfer box and acts on the transmission. Extreme wear inside the drum is rarely an issue, unlike the more common problem of oil contamination from a leaking seal on the back of the transfer box. In the case of the demo 109, we

BELOW: *Shoes detached from the assembly.*

have both. We also have the additional issue of the linings being made from hazardous asbestos, so they will need to be handled carefully and disposed of.

The complete shoes are obsolete, but you can buy non-asbestos linings that come supplied with new copper rivets. Our aim here is to strip the assembly, replace the linings, and clean, paint and reassemble it. The handbrake linkage and ratchet mechanism is described in Chapter 14.

The drum assembly is removed from the transfer box by first undoing the six nuts that secure the drum, removing the drum, then unbolting the flange. The expander also needs to be detached from the handbrake linkage.

The shoes can then be removed using a mole grip to pull them firmly against the springs, and out of contact with the adjuster and expander.

The shoes' linings and rivets (ten per shoe) now need to be replaced. First, the old shoes are held in a vice, and the old rivets are drilled out.

When fitting the new linings, the flat ends of the new rivets need to sit

Each shoe is clamped in a vice, and a 5mm drill bit removes its rivets.

A caliper pin from a One Ten is the right size for resting each rivet on as it is peened over.

Handbrake mechanism bolted to the back of the transfer box. Don't forget the central plate before adding the nuts.

below the outer surface of the brake lining, so you will need a drift or punch to push them in place while you peen over the other end. An ideal tool, if you have one, is a caliper pin; the bobble end is the ideal size for fitting in the holes of the lining.

The pin is clamped into the vice (bobble pointing up) and the new lining is held on the shoe, with one of the central rivets in place. This assembly is placed on to the pin, so the rivet takes the weight and the bobble sits inside the corresponding hole in the lining, and the rivet is struck from above using a large-diameter punch to peen it over. This is repeated with the remaining rivets, working progressively outwards from the middle.

The other stage to this process is cleaning the backplate and drum, using brake cleaner to remove the

Inner face of the shoe, showing the new rivets peened over.

The flange has been replaced, and the newly repainted drum is fitted to the six studs.

New lining, with the new rivets sitting below the surface.

oil deposits. It is important that this is done thoroughly, otherwise the new lining material will be contaminated and its braking potential will be severely reduced. Once all the components are clean, the backplate and drum are primed and painted, then put back together – including the new shoes. It is unlikely that you'll need to replace the springs, especially if they have been preserved from corrosion by oil seepage, as many have.

When refitting the shoes to the backplate, their notched ends marry up with the adjuster, and the smooth end meets the expander.

Once your gearbox and transfer box are deemed ready for installation (*see* Chapter 8) the assembly is returned to the back of the transfer box, together with the circular metal plate with its return lip – a feature designed to protect the oil seal from dirt. The flange is then slotted over the output shaft, and the drum is secured to it with six studs and locknuts.

With the handbrake drum in place, the shoes now need to be calibrated in a similar way to the brake shoes at the wheels. The drum is turned by hand to ensure it is moving freely, and the adjuster is slowly turned until the shoes are as close as possible to the drum without causing any rubbing.

8

Transmission Rebuild

Series I Land Rovers use LT76 gearboxes that were well built and tend to be reliable, but age and wear do eventually take their toll. Rebuilding a gearbox and transfer box is a major undertaking, and it is quite difficult to figure out how to do this on your first attempt – although they're simple enough to understand once you have grasped the fundamentals. The full subject is too complex for this book, but some of the common failure points for a Series I are described, and also what to expect when a gearbox is sent off to be rebuilt by a specialist.

It is theoretically possible to rebuild a Series I gearbox at home, as it can be achieved without some of the expensive tools (such as a press) that are required by more modern gearboxes. But there are many ways to get it wrong. Most people doing this for the first time will either face significant hold-ups, or will make mistakes that result in a finished gearbox that will need another rebuild before long. It is therefore recommended that you send your gearbox to a reputable specialist for a rebuild; this is the approach taken by Ben for all the Series Land Rovers he rebuilds, and for this restoration he chose Stephen A Brear Gearboxes Ltd in Leeds.

Series I gearboxes are all similar. The design originates from the 1930s, and they all have the same ratios and the same housing, regardless of the engine, although the lever mechanism was significantly different for the first 1,500 cars. The only significant change in the transmission system was when Land Rover abandoned the freewheel unit and ring-pull set-up during 1950, in favour of the more recognizable, selectable four-wheel-drive arrangement, with its yellow knob for high ratio – but these changes only applied to the transfer box; the gearbox remained the same.

The odometer is little help in deter-mining how many miles your gearbox has covered, because it might not be original to the vehicle, and if it is, it may have been rebuilt already. A properly rebuilt Series I gearbox should be good for about 50,000–80,000 miles (80,500–130,000km), but this figure is very variable. Some survive longer than this, especially if the oil is changed and the driver is capable of sympathetic double de-clutching.

CHOOSING A SPECIALIST

Find a specialist with experience of Series Land Rover gearboxes, ideally Series Is. A good specialist will know what complications to expect, and may have a stash of hard-to-find components – items that will sometimes be better quality than what is available to buy new, as modern remakes often aren't made to the same standards as the originals. If good quality replacements can't be found, a specialist should know whether modification or repair of certain parts may be appropriate, and they will have the means to do it.

Regarding lead time, bear in mind that the bread-and-butter work of some transmission specialists is not related to classic restorations with time horizons of weeks or months. Their schedule is usually occupied by work for more modern vehicles whose owners need them back on the road as soon as possible. They will usually appreciate a few weeks to rebuild your gearbox, allowing them to fit it in round more urgent jobs.

Parts supply for Series I gearboxes is generally good, but quality does vary. Decisions may have to be made about whether to use sub-optimal new parts, or good second-hand parts. Synchromesh rings are a case in point: Michael Brear advises that he'd sometimes rather install a good second-hand component than a new one, as the collar of new components tends to be tight.

Expect to pay around £650 to £850 (including parts and labour) for a simple rebuild such as the demo 109's, retaining parts where possible. Soda blasting will add to that price, as will any unforeseen complications. Alternatively, some specialists will charge over £2,000 for a more total stripdown, involving re-anodizing of bolts, and the renewal of every seal and bearing. You will also need to arrange and pay for palletized transport of the transmission to the specialist.

OVERVIEW

Michael Brear sent us photos of the demo 109's gearbox and transfer

---

MICHAEL BREAR

Michael Brear, who rebuilt the gearbox of the demo Series I, described the approach adopted by his business:

We treat each gearbox differently. After taking it apart and assessing its condition, we have a conversation with the customer about what we've found, and discuss what they'd like us to do. If it's beyond economical repair, there's no charge to the customer, and they can choose to receive the dismantled gearbox back from us. Generally we'd like about a month to work on a Series Land Rover gearbox, because customers with more modern vehicles tend to require a more urgent turnaround, but we can do it quicker if the customer wants us to.

box being assembled, and talked us through an overview of what a rebuild involves. Our purpose here is not to show how to rebuild the transmission yourself, but to offer an overview of how the transmission works, and to describe where some of its weaknesses lie.

The bearings do not wear out easily, and the quality of replacements is not always as good as the originals, so there's a case to be made for leaving them alone unless they are known to be worn. However, although they tend not to wear prematurely, corrosion can ruin bearings in vehicles that have sat unused for long periods in a damp environment.

Thorough steam-cleaning is the first step, to prevent any dirt from entering the gearbox during disassembly. Gearbox and transfer box are then parted; the top cover, selector and detent mechanism are detached from the casing; and the bellhousing is detached from the front of the gearbox.

Difficulties engaging a gear are usually due to a failure in the selector mechanism. This can be assessed with the gearbox still in the vehicle, after

The phosphor-bronze selector forks and their rods are checked for wear.

you remove the transmission tunnel, and unbolt the top cover that encloses the selector shafts.

The left-hand selector shaft operates third and fourth gears, middle operates first and second, and the right operates reverse. In other words, it's the opposite pattern to the motion of the gearknob, because the lever sits in a pivot so the lower ball moves in mirror image to the driver's hand. The shafts pass through horizontal channels that hold spring-loaded ball bearings and dowels; these comprise the detent mechanism, which holds the

shafts in the correct position for each gear by pushing the ball bearings (the middle two are elongated) into notches in the shafts.

Each of these shafts has a phosphor-bronze fork attached, passing down into the gearbox to move the gears on two shafts: the mainshaft (or first motion shaft) and the layshaft. The mainshaft contains the gears for first, second, third and fourth gears. The latter is part of the rear pinion gear, a 1:1 ratio that (unlike the other gears) does not involve the layshaft. The sole synchromesh unit fits over the mainshaft, and operates on third and fourth gear.

At the back of the gearbox, the mainshaft delivers power into the transfer box via a large gear. The widely spaced 'dog tooth' gear behind it drives a power take-off, if fitted, but if an overdrive is installed then the larger gear is removed altogether, replaced by a clutch sleeve that slots inside the main gear of the overdrive.

Clean gearbox and bell housing, minus the transfer box.

Selector and detent assembly, prior to adding springs at either side.

The front of the gearbox, minus the bellhousing, showing the brass synchromesh hub for third and fourth gears.

Inside the transfer box. At the bottom of the image is the output from the gearbox.

The synchro hub (not shown) has been pulled forwards off the mainshaft. The layshaft is alongside.

The transfer box contains the gears that determine whether the vehicle is in high or low range, and which send the drive to the front and rear of the vehicle. Drive is sent to the rear axle in both low and high range; drive to the front axle is selected by the mechanism inside the separate housing on the front of the transfer box. Wear may develop on the transfer box's thrust washers, bearings and seals, but the most common problem is oil leaking from the rear output seal on to the handbrake mechanism.

With the transfer box in neutral, power is no longer sent to either axle, which enables the Land Rover to power auxiliary equipment via a power take-off; in neutral, the gearbox's mainshaft can deliver power through the back of the transfer box to the rear take-off without simultaneously driving the wheels.

The low-range gears are cross-cut,

Clutch sleeve, required if fitting an overdrive.

Speedo cable housing, with shims.

and high-range gears are bevel-cut. There is some easily confused terminology here, as low range (used for low-speed driving) uses high-ratio gearing, whereas high range (for faster driving) uses low-ratio gearing. In other words, low ratio is not the

Mainshaft output, at the back of the gearbox. This gear sends drive to the transfer box.

The rear of the assembled transfer box, complete with speedo housing.

Selector mechanism for 4WD, partially dismantled, with the forward output shaft.

Housing replaced at the front of the transfer box, complete with output flange attached, and high-ratio 4WD selector linkage hanging down.

Don't forget to renew the O-ring on the gear-lever's ball joint.

output shaft can wear the bearing; if the preload is too slack (caused by too many shims) then the shaft will be out of true and will wear the seal. A poorly adjusted preload can result in a metal-lic whirring noise. Preload is deter-mined by measuring the end float, but problems here are rare. In most cases it is advisable to retain the same number of shims when rebuilding the gearbox, unless there is an obvious fault.

On the front of the transfer box, the four-wheel-drive (4WD) selector mechanism operates within its own casing. The spring on the upper arm is compressed when two-wheel-drive (2WD) is engaged, pushing against the dog-tooth collar on the driveshaft, and preventing the driveshaft from being engaged.

The 4WD system is slightly different in early Series Is up to 1950, compared with all later Land Rovers. These early models use a freewheel system at the front of the transfer box, which disen-gages the front propshaft on overrun. Pulling a ring-pull in the driver's foot-well locks the freewheel unit, provid-ing 4WD when required. Problems with this mechanism are fairly rare.

The demo 109's gear lever was sanded back and painted before reassembly, and the bottom mount was scrubbed with degreaser and a wire wheel to restore its shine. The shaft rarely needs removing from the mount, but the bottom O-ring does need replacing. This is an easily over-looked item that sits in the groove in the ball at the base of the gear lever. The gear lever will tend to clatter when this ring deteriorates, becomes hard, or falls off altogether.

COMMON FAULTS

Although there are many places where wear can develop, there are a few quite common issues.

Second and third gear spin round a bronze bush on the mainshaft, and it is extremely common for this bush to fail. The bushes should be anchored to the

same as low range. When discussing your gears with someone else, make sure that you are both using the same terminology!

At the back of the transfer box is the housing of the speedometer and its worm gear. The housing is mounted on shims, available in varying thicknesses, and they determine the preload on the bearing on the output side of the transfer box. If the preload is too tight (caused by not enough shims) then the

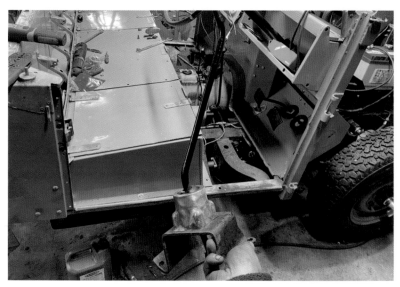

The gear lever after painting.

The most common Series I gearbox failure relates to this bronze bush, which is mounted on the mainshaft.

The synchro hub removed, with detached and broken springs.

mainshaft by small pins that prevent them from spinning, but these pins break, allowing the bush and the gear to spin together round the mainshaft, rather than the gear spinning round the static bush.

This doesn't cause immediate symptoms, but the problem intensifies because the oil channels are between the bush and the gear, and not between the bush and the mainshaft. The friction point is therefore poorly lubricated, so the bush wears prematurely (creating a yellowy tinge in the oil), and may eventually crack.

This was the case with the gearbox in the demo 109.

The equivalent component from a Series III gearbox can be machined down to fit, and the same is sometimes required of recently made versions that are supposedly the correct size for Series Is. A gearbox specialist is likely to outsource this particular task.

Another common failure is with the small leaf springs inside the synchro-mesh hub. These break or become dislodged, either jamming in the hub or falling into the oil, so look out for them when the gearbox oil is drained. The parts are cheap to replace, but accessing the synchro hub requires the mainshaft to be extracted from the gearbox.

Difficulty selecting 4WD is usually caused by wear in the selector mechanism (usually a fault with one of the springs). Hopping out of low range can have a similar cause, or this may also be due to excessive end float in the intermediate gear, requiring the transfer box to be stripped. The selector shafts that protrude out of the front of the casing can seize through lack of use, especially when mud is trapped between the cover and the rods, increasing corrosion.

Finally, a note about oil leaks. Note the thorough use of sealant around all the new gaskets and mating faces. Oil leaks are common in Series Land Rover transmissions, but they are not inevitable, and a properly rebuilt Series gearbox should not leak any oil. Although we tend to be more relaxed about oil leaks in the UK than in some other countries, we shouldn't be.

Leaks are sometimes due to poorly machined parts – for example, the transfer box's bottom cover plate, which often benefits from attention whether the transmission system is being rebuilt or not. This plate is not very rigid and is sometimes visibly warped, as you will see if you lay it on a flat surface. Make sure the studs are all properly buried into the casing by using the two-nut technique, plus a little thread-lock, and gasket compound around both sides of your new gasket.

9

Recommissioning the Engine

This chapter will guide you through the steps required to recommission an engine with an unknown history, but capable of being turned with the starting handle, proving that it is not seized. How to assess what specialist work may be required – particularly if the bores or bottom end are worn – will be discussed, and a complete decoking procedure will be described. This is all good practice for any engine that has been neglected for any considerable length of time.

The inspection and recommissioning of ancillaries such as the fuel pump and carburettor will also be discussed.

After some fettling with the ignition, the demo 109's engine was capable of starting and running, proving it was not seized.

Complete engine restoration is a very technical subject, beyond the scope of many home restorers, and for the purposes of this vehicle's rebuild, the pistons and the crankshaft will remain in the block. Instead, most of the outer components of the engine will be stripped, with a view to the following:

- Assessing the ancillaries, and restoring or replacing as necessary
- Inspecting the valve gear (inlet and outlet)
- Inspecting the cooling system

This 109 engine was rebuilt by Litchfield Motor Engineers Ltd in Adelaide in April 1969.

> ### *ADVICE FROM LAND ROVER ENGINE SPECIALIST COX AND TURNER*
>
> Ian Cox, of Land Rover engine specialist Cox and Turner, has this advice:
>
> The cylinders of all three of the engines (1.6, early and late 2.0-litre) can be bored by .060in and all the crankshafts can be ground by .060 on both mains and big ends. The crucial thing is that the appropriate parts are obtained *before* the block or crank are machined. This is particularly important with the early crankshafts where the centre journal has integral thrusts on the bearings.
>
> Pistons from different manufacturers also require different clearances, so it's important that the machine shop has the pistons before finishing the cylinder bores. Liners can be fitted to all the blocks to reclaim worn or damaged bores, however great care should be taken with early 2.0-litre engines because of the small distance between the pairs of cylinders. All engines should have liners fitted the full length, as original, to preserve the combustion chamber volume, otherwise poor starting and low power will result. Liners can be bored for oversize pistons up to +.030 for the 1.6-litre engines and +.040 for late 2.0-litre engines, but the 'Siamese bore' 2.0-litre engines should ideally be standard bore (3.063in) after liners are fitted, irrespective of the amount of material removed.

- Checking for internal wear in combustion chambers and bottom end
- Decoking the engine
- Replacing all seals and gaskets
- Setting the valve clearances and timing
- Refreshing the paint and improving the cosmetics

Before you start, look out for any badge (usually pinned to the block) describing a previous rebuild. Our engine has a badge beside the dipstick tube, telling us it was rebuilt in 1969 using .010in main bearings, .010in big-end bearings, and the combustion chambers were rebored by .020in. These figures will determine whether there is any scope for the engine to be machined further, if required. However, the plate tells us nothing about the thickness of the liners and the size of the pistons, so it would be premature to order parts based on this information. These figures for our engine are mild, so further machining would be possible.

DIFFERENCES BETWEEN ENGINES

Three engines were originally installed in Series Is. The petrol engines are all related to one another, each being an evolution of its predecessor:

1.6-litre petrol (1947–1953)
2.0-litre petrol 'Siamese bore' (1953–54) and 'spread bore' (1955–58)
2.0-litre diesel (1957–58)

In all Series I petrol engines, the inlet valves are located in the head, while the exhaust valves are in the block – hence the term 'inlet over exhaust' (IOE). Each set of valves has its own rocker shaft. The exhaust rocker takes its drive from the camshaft, and pushrods transmit the motion from the camshaft up to the inlet rockers, which have their own shaft mounted in the head. (The very early 1.6-litres are known as 'side-plate' engines, as they have two plates on the side of the block, covering the water jacket. These were replaced with core plugs during 1949.)

The diesel was a new engine altogether, with overhead valves, and unrelated to the side-valve petrol engines. Despite being advanced for their time, they are noisy and laborious to drive compared to the petrols. Few Series Is were ordered with a diesel engine when new, and they are rare today.

Over the years, many non-standard engines have been fitted to Series Is. Popular fitments included 2.25-litre engines from later Series Land Rovers, and Rover V8s, which were particularly popular among triallers. Overseas, conversions include Holden 6-cylinder engines and Chevrolet V8s.

Restoration implies (but does not necessarily require) retention of a genuine Series I engine, ideally the same engine that was fitted when the vehicle was new. If an engine swap is required and a decent Land Rover engine can't be found, one common option has been to use a variant of the same engine, as found in Rover saloons of the era. The 1.6-litre engine was used in the Rover Sixty (P3) in the late 1940s, and a spread-bore version of the 2.0-litre engine was used in the Rover 60 model of the P4 in the 1950s. There were very few differences between the Rover car and Land Rover versions, but the 2.0-litre Rover engine uses a 1¼in SU carburettor, while the Land Rover engine uses a Solex 34IB. The inlet manifold is removable from the cast-iron head, whereas the Rover's inlet manifold is integral to the cast-aluminium head, and gives higher compression.

(Incidentally, the later 2286cc OHV engines and the 2638cc IOE straight-six engines were also used in both Series Land Rovers and Rover saloons.)

It is almost impossible to know how much time and expenditure an engine may require until some of its major components are disassembled. Even if the vehicle seems to run and drive without problems, you'll often find once you start investigating that it requires serious intervention to preserve the vehicle's longevity. Some of the hidden costs that we encountered with the demo 109's engine strip included a scored flywheel, but we were quite lucky overall. Less fortunate is to discover major wear in the cylinders or bottom end bearings, requiring the engine to be sent away for a full rebuild, including honing of the bores and bottom end. This kind of work requires specialist machinery.

Note: Sometimes we refer to the left- and right-hand side of the engine – this is as if the engine is mounted in the vehicle, and viewed from the perspective of anyone sitting in the car. So in the UK, left means nearside (passenger's side), and right means offside (driver's side).

ENGINE STRIP PART 1: MANIFOLDS AND FLYWHEEL

An engine stand makes it much easier to inspect and work on an engine, so it's worth spending a little time fabricating one. The vertical posts of a stand should be the same distance apart as the engine mounts on the chassis, and a block on the base of the stand supports the rear. Don't under-

The engine is thoroughly steam-cleaned before disassembly, and its coolant passages are flushed.

estimate the weight of the engine, and ensure the verticals are well braced so they don't collapse under lateral load from the engine rocking while you're working on it.

Once the engine is in a clear working environment, the top rocker cover is unbolted, and then a start can be made on removing all the ancillaries. The ignition components are a good place to start, so the HT leads are pulled off the plugs first. In most cases it is good practice to label each lead with the number of the cylinder it relates to, to aid reassembly, but if their age or condition is unknown then they will be discarded and replaced anyway.

The engine, ready for disassembly, after a basic clean.

Number 4 sparkplug being removed.

HT lead to plug number 4, headed for the bin.

The distributor being unbolted from the block.

Removing the distributor requires the single bolt to be undone at its base. On 1.6-litre engines there is also a horizontal bolt that will need to be removed.

Once unbolted, the distributor will pull out, complete with its retaining clamp. This is a Lucas 25D distributor, which is the correct spec for this engine. Distributors are reasonably reliable, but some of the internal parts are service items. We will shortly be replacing the points, rotor arm, leads and cap. In the meantime, a clean rag needs to be stuffed into the aperture the distributor has come out of.

The spark plugs can come out next. Again, it's good practice to stuff the holes with clean rags to prevent dirt falling into the threads and the bores.

Moving round to the back of the engine, we remove the clutch cover next. It's held on with locknuts that must be replaced with new ones when you come to rebuild. Note the lozenge-shaped plate on the housing, which can be removed to reveal the timing marks on the flywheel. We'll come to this later when we calibrate the engine's static timing.

Removing the clutch cover reveals an asbestos friction plate (the removable disc) and the face of the flywheel that it is pushed against. The friction plate is a service item that generally lasts about 50,000–60,000 miles (80,000–96,000km) before having to be replaced – although this figure is very dependent on usage. The demo 109's is an asbestos friction plate, so it is at least as old as the 1970s and probably dates from when the engine was rebuilt in 1989. Friction plates are not very expensive, so replacement is a good idea whenever the engine and gearbox are parted.

Pulling off the friction plate reveals the surface of the flywheel, and a problem: it's scored and slightly rusty, and therefore needs to be refaced. When a flywheel surface becomes rough, it

Unbolting the clutch cover.

Flywheel being revealed behind the clutch cover.

causes uneven wear on the friction plate, as well as clutch judder when taking up drive. The problem is more noticeable with a riveted friction plate (as on Series Land Rovers) rather than a later bonded type.

Refacing the flywheel is a specialist job requiring a lathe, so the 109's is sent it to a specialist who can machine the surface smooth. Rover recommended that the maximum amount of metal that can be removed was only .030in (0.75mm), so if there is scoring that seems deeper than this, a new flywheel may be required. The flywheel is removed by bending back the locking plates round the six nuts round the centre, and unbolting it. Discard the plates, as new ones are available.

Out comes the distributor.

Worn friction plate, held in position against the flywheel.

Unbolting the rocker cover for the exhaust valves.

This flywheel is scored and needs refacing.

simply be cleaned, repainted and refitted.

These exhaust manifolds can develop cracks, which may be repairable by welding – but welding cast steel presents a different set of complications to welding the plate steel used for chassis and bulkheads, and we would recommend having this work carried out by a professional.

Currently there are no reproduction exhaust manifolds being made. The symmetrical version fitted to 80s is usually easier to find second-hand than the later offset type, whose

The exhaust manifold is held in place with lozenge-shaped clamps, and bolts underneath.

Once the flywheel is removed, the phosphor-bronze spigot bush is knocked out with a drift. It's good practice to replace this with a new item. When worn they make a loud crunching noise when the clutch is disengaged.

Now we move to the exhaust valve gear on the left side of the engine. Because this is a side-valve engine, the exhaust valves are mounted in the block rather than in the head (where the inlet valves are). The exhaust valves have their own rocker cover (beneath the exhaust manifold), which is removed by undoing the three bolts along its top.

Any corrosion that has developed on the valve gear could be problematic, as rust particles mixing with oil will increase engine wear, so this must be addressed. All these components will be removed later, scrubbed with a wire wheel and chemically treated to remove the corrosion.

After undoing the two bolts either end of the exhaust manifold, the three clamps that also hold it in place are slackened off. Unless the engine is being completely stripped, there is no need to remove the clamps – just slacken them enough for them to let go of the manifold. The 109's manifold is in quite good condition, so it will

The valve gear can become rusty if the vehicle has been sitting in a damp environment.

The starter motor (not the original type) being unbolted from the flywheel housing.

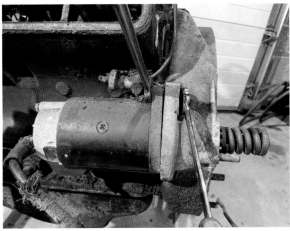

threads in the outlet flange are more prone to damage.

Removing the aftermarket starter motor is simply a case of undoing any wiring that may still be attached, and undoing the two bolts securing it to the flywheel housing. Note that there is no gasket here, and there does not need to be. This type of starter motor is from a later Series Land Rover (although it does work perfectly) – we will be replacing it with an original Series I type.

Next to the starter, the banjo securing the small pipe that delivers oil up into the head from the oil gallery in the block also needs to be detached. This pipe is easily forgotten, and can easily be damaged if you attempt to remove the head with the pipe still attached. The two copper washers on either side of the banjo will need to be renewed.

Where the feed enters the block, you will find another banjo union together with an oil-pressure switch. This switch can't easily be tested in isolation, and at this stage it is safest to assume it doesn't work unless you have reason to believe otherwise, and to replace it. This ensures that, if there is inadequate oil pressure when your engine is fired up, you should be notified via the warning light on the dash. It can be difficult to find a suitable modern

Unscrewing the throttle linkage from the carburettor.

Unbolting the carb from the inlet manifold.

Inlet manifold, minus carb, ready for removal.

Unbolting the oil-pressure switch from the block.

Easily forgotten oil banjo union that supplies oil to the inlet rocker shaft.

Inlet manifold showing the amount of dirt inside. The central branch is for coolant.

Right-hand side of the engine, with the inlet manifold removed.

It's time to remove the oil filter, but first a suitable receptacle needs to be slid underneath to catch the oil. The bolt at the bottom of the housing is then undone, and the housing is pulled away. The oil will flow from the rim as soon as it begins to let go.

The oil-filler mount will also be unbolted from the block in order to clean it and renew its gasket. The other reason to do this is to give access to the middle core plug behind it.

There are four studs holding the oil-filter housing to the block. As you can see, three of those studs came away, and one remained in the block, where it can stay. Note the orange gasket compound, which is completely unnecessary as the passageway between the block and the filler mount is lower down.

The dipstick is the wrong length so it needs replacing with the correct part. The dipstick tube is also removed by undoing the nut at its base.

There is now good, clear access to the core plugs (three on the side, plus one on the back). They block up the holes left by the casting process, and also act as a pressure-release mechanism in the unlikely event of coolant

Oil draining from the oil-filter housing as it's removed.

Oil pan with the old oil filter and its housing.

balljoint for the throttle linkage that needs unscrewing next, followed by the two bolts that hold it to the inlet manifold.

The carburettor is relatively fragile and at risk of contamination from dirt, so keep it in a sealed container or bag.

The throttle linkage can remain attached to the inlet manifold for now, and the manifold is removed from the head simply by unscrewing the nuts. There might be some coolant remaining inside it, so have a rag ready to catch it. In our case however, the engine is clearly dry.

Pulling the inlet manifold away reveals plenty of dirt that needs cleaning away. The stubborn remnants of the inlet manifold gaskets will also need removing from the manifolds and block to provide clean surfaces for the new ones to mate up against. A gasket scraper or razor blade is useful for this.

The oil-filter housing, showing the nut that passes into the block.

oil-pressure switch that works reliably with positive earth.

Moving round to the right-hand side of the engine, the next task is to remove the carburettor, before separating the inlet manifold from the head. Keep some rags ready to catch any fuel that escapes, then detach and retain the fuel pipe. Then undo the small copper pipe, which is the vacuum advance pipe between the carburettor and the distributor. There is a small

The filter housing removed, and the dipstick tube being unscrewed from the block.

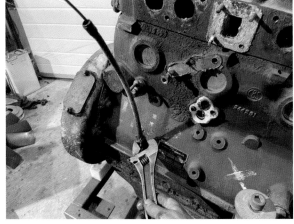

freezing and expanding inside the block. Core plugs are normally steel and they corrode internally over time, leading to sudden coolant leaks when the rust finally breaks through. Replacing them is a standard part of recommissioning – however, the 109 engine has an extremely rare set of brass core plugs that are clearly in perfect condition. Brass is far better than steel at resisting corrosion (it does not contain iron), so the core plugs will be left in place.

To remove the core plugs, carefully puncture them with a small chisel, and use this hole to then lever them out with a pry bar. Once they're out, use this access hole to help flush the muck and coolant residue out of the block, and scrub away any corrosion from the apertures with wire wheel on a drill. The new plugs can then be driven home using a mallet and a block of wood, ensuring the wood is wider than the aperture so the rim of the core plug ends up sitting flush with the wall of the block.

ENGINE STRIP PART 2: COOLANT PARTS AND TIMING GEAR

The next task is to go to the front of the engine to remove the fan, coolant pump and timing chest, and inspect the timing gear.

Note that the front pulley on this 109 has a spare V channel, meaning it is designed for an engine with a governor. (An engine governor is a device that automatically applies small amounts of throttle to compensate for any dip in engine revs caused

A different engine, showing the governor mounting bolts that the 109 engine lacks.

by a variable load from the optional power take-off.) Engines fitted with a governor had special mounting bolts protruding from the front of the thermostat housing, which the governor would bolt to. These are absent on the project 109's engine, so it can be assumed that this front pulley is not original. It will be replaced with a standard item.

The housing sits at the front of the head, and water passes up through it from the coolant pump beneath it. A rubber O-ring seals the join between the coolant pump and the thermostat housing.

First, the water pump pulley is unbolted, along with the fan. Next come the four horizontal bolts that hold the thermostat housing to the head.

These bolts often seize into the

thermostat housing and are difficult to extract, though less so in Australian examples. Series Is built for the UK market had an aluminium thermostat housing, whereas some export models used cast steel (bolts in a steel housing don't corrode as badly as they do in an aluminium housing). Because the shanks of these bolts are long, they can twist easily, creating the illusion that the thread is turning, when in fact you're on your way to shearing the bolt. This needs to be done gently and slowly, using penetrating fluid, and winding the bolt back in and out a few times to help ease it out. This coolant pump has a steel housing so the bolts come out relatively easily.

The radiator fan is the first to be unbolted.

The top pulley being removed.

The front of the 109 engine. Note the front pulley, specified for engines fitted with a governor.

If your thermostat housing is aluminium, these bolts are more likely to be seized.

Removing thermostat reveals sediment in the coolant passages in the head.

The impeller on this water pump is exceptionally rotten.

There is a cork gasket between the thermostat housing and the head. This obviously needs to be replaced, along with every other gasket we come across.

You will often find a severe amount of sediment when you pull off the thermostat housing. A lot of rust in here would suggest that the engine has been run with too much water and not enough proper coolant. (Coolant acts as a corrosion inhibitor, in addition to raising the boiling point of the water.) All the dirt will need flushing out as thoroughly as possible.

The metal pipe can now be unbolted from the coolant pump. Its lower portion is secured to the timing chest, so this bolt also needs to be removed. This pipe often corrodes from the

The replacement pump shows what the impeller should look like.

The nut securing the crankshaft's large pulley in place.

inside out, and the Series One Club has recently commissioned new ones to be made.

This leaves the coolant pump ready to be detached. Reproduction pumps are cast steel, but original pumps for UK-market Series Is are aluminium (like the thermostat housing) and the bolts therefore seize easily. There are eight of them, so it's common to find at least one of them seized, but if the bolts are in good condition they can be reused.

The bolts being removed from the timing chest.

The bottom pipe coming off the water pump. A rubber hose connects this pipe with the radiator.

These bolts securing the water pump can easily seize.

The timing gear, revealed after removing the chest. All looks good.

Old (left) versus new (right) camshaft sprockets. Note the blunt and damaged teeth.

Old tensioner sprocket. The top of the teeth have been worn on either side.

These tensioner sprocket teeth are worn on one side into a shark-fin shape.

The impeller of this pump had totally rotted away, so the coolant had no means of circulating round the engine – suggesting this engine had not been run up to temperature for a long time. Impellers can sheer off, but it's very unusual to find them as rusted as this. This issue was not noticeable without removing the pump because there were no outward signs of failure, so this reinforces how important it is to strip the ancillaries of an unknown engine before relying on them. This pump will be replaced with a new one.

To access the timing gear, we first need to pull back the lock tab and undo the large bolt in front of the crank pulley. This slots on to a woodruff key on the front of the crankshaft.

The bolts surrounding the timing chest can then be undone. These are not all the same length, so try to keep them in order so as to aid with reassembly later. These bolts are aluminium, so take care not to sheer them off. There are also two studs at the bottom joining the timing chest to the engine sump.

The timing chest can then be pulled away to reveal the timing gear. The large upper sprocket turns the camshaft (just beneath the exhaust rocker shaft). The middle sprocket tensions the chain, and receives its pressure from a piston filled with engine oil; there is also a ratchet mechanism to stop the tensioner from becoming slack.

It is possible to assess the level of wear in the timing chain by pulling the long length forwards and feeling for play. This is not an exact science, but you should detect very little movement. Once the timing chain is removed, another technique is to hold the chain horizontally and see how much downward deflection there is. Again, there should be very little.

The sprockets also need assessing for wear. Their teeth should be symmetrical and not smoothed over. The example photos show some typical wear patterns on the timing gear of a later 2.25-litre Series Land Rover engine. Although these components are not identical to those in a Series I, they are very similar, and wear presents itself in the same way. Notice how some teeth have lost their sharpness, and some (on the larger sprocket for the camshaft) have broken off or become asymmetrically shaped. This timing gear was renewed immediately.

The timing chain and sprockets in the demo Series I are in perfectly reasonable condition, so we felt confident in retaining them and leaving the sprockets attached to the block. If the timing chain were being replaced, it would be good practice to replace the hydraulic tensioner at the same time.

ENGINE STRIP PART 3: THE HEAD

Series I cylinder heads have hardened valve seats from new, so they do not require hardening for unleaded fuel. Removing the cylinder head might therefore seem unnecessary if your engine is capable of running, but there are advantages to doing it. With the head off any carbon can be cleaned away (known as decoking), the condition of the bores can be assessed, and you can look for a stamp on the piston crowns that will tell you if the engine has previously been rebored. These indicators may help you decide when a larger rebuild might be necessary. The rebuild phase is also a good time to reset the timing and valve clearances, which helps to ensure efficient combustion.

We are working on the engine after it has been removed from the vehicle, but this work can be done with the engine in situ – for example, if the head gasket had blown or if a valve had burned out.

For the purposes of this inspection, the outlet rocker shaft will remain in position, but the inlet rocker shaft needs to be removed so that the head can be separated from the block. This shaft is always under tension from one valve spring at a time.

The top rocker cover is unbolted to reveal the rocker shaft. Then there are six $^5/_{16}$in bolts securing the inlet rocker shaft, two of which use long bolts

One of the head bolts that secure the rocker-shaft pedestals.

Keep a record of which head bolts came from which holes. The most usual way of doing this is to punch twelve holes into a sheet of cardboard in a pattern that corresponds to the head-bolt arrangement, and to push each bolt into the corresponding hole.

With the head bolts removed, the head can be lifted away. It's heavy, so be careful to avoid injury while doing this, and wear protective gloves.

Removing the head of the demo 109 has revealed a lot of coke deposits around the combustion chambers, especially on cylinder 4. It's bad, but this is not unusual for these engines. The coke means a less efficient combustion, although it partially compensates for itself by increasing the compression ratio. Problems arise when the coke prevents the valves from sealing completely, and it can also cause overrun because the hot coke can ignite the fuel-air mixture too soon. All this will be cleaned off.

The head gasket must always be renewed, even if it seems in good condition. Ours is an original tin gasket, rather than the alternative copper version. Tin gaskets give slightly higher compression than copper because they are thinner, bringing the head slightly closer to the top of the piston, effectively making the compression chamber smaller.

Once the gasket is removed a careful check can be made for any cracks in the block around the cylinders. If any are found, an engine specialist will be able to determine whether or not a repair can be made.

The water jacket of the demo vehicle's engine is clearly very rusty and dry, and there are some severe carbon deposits around the valves, but other-

Removing the end pedestal nut.

The rocker shaft being removed.

that pass straight through the head and into the block. These all need to be undone, then the shaft can be removed complete.

Next come the four pushrods, which are simply lifted out. These actuate the inlet rockers, and they are pushed upwards in the correct sequence by the

camshaft in the block. Each one needs to be inspected for perfect straightness by rolling it along a flat surface and checking for any oscillations.

Now the head bolts can be undone, and the head can be lifted away from the block. There are twelve bolts of three different lengths. These are not 'stretch' bolts, so they can be reused (they are not under very much tension compared with modern engines).

Removing one of the four pushrods.

Undoing the shortest of the twelve head bolts.

The lower face of the head, showing plenty of coke stuck to it.

The block has a badly rusted water jacket, but is otherwise all right.

The exhaust valves in the block have particularly bad carbon deposits, but there was no scoring on the bores.

The sump is severely damaged, so we sourced a replacement.

wise there are no structural problems with the block. It's important to check very closely for any cracks around the top face of the block; however, these are unlikely if the engine is known to be running normally.

The other check to make is for any wear in the bores, which would mean the engine needs to be rebored. This is more difficult to spot, but under bright light you should be able to see a fine cross-hatch pattern on the surfaces of the bores, caused by the honing process. The pattern gradually wears away over time on the thrust side of the bore (sometimes known as 'glazing', as the surface goes shiny). If this is the case, the bore will need to be measured using a bore gauge, and if any ovality is detected then the engine is due for a rebore. Using the bore gauge requires the pistons to be extracted from the block, something which is beyond the scope of this book.

More obvious problems include scoring or corrosion within the combustion chamber, so run a clean finger round the inside of each bore to make

The bottom of the engine with the sump removed. The dirty round disc is the oil strainer.

sure they feel smooth. If a piston ring has seized due to the engine being left standing, bore corrosion is often the result.

ENGINE STRIP PART 4:
THE BOTTOM END

The aim here is to check for wear in the crankshaft bearings, which can be done without removing the crankshaft from the block. The first stage is to drain all the oil from the sump, if

this hasn't been done already. The rest of this procedure is much easier with the engine on its side, but obviously its weight means that extreme care needs to be taken when rolling it over.

If the vehicle has been abused off-road, as has this 109, you might find the sump has been bashed in. If it's not too severe you can knock it back into shape, but this 109's was buckled too far so we had to source a second-hand replacement. Not all Series I engine sumps are the same; they differ in overall shape and in the design of the baffles inside, so be sure to buy one that is correct for your engine type.

Once the oil is drained, the bolts surrounding the sump are undone, and the sump is pulled away. If it is severely buckled – as the demo 109's – it may be in contact with the strainer at the base of the oil pick-up, potentially interfering with oil flow by submerging the mesh in sediment. This was probably happening with the demo's engine, as can be seen from the state of the mesh. There's a lot of dirty slime here, which is terrible for an engine's longevity but not uncommon. All this needs to be thoroughly cleaned before reassembly, and it will probably involve digging the sediment from the sump with a chisel or trowel.

The oil pick-up has a dish-shaped strainer that is in two halves. Undoing the nut and split pin at its base enables the base to be removed, so the two sections can be pulled apart for proper cleaning. The strainer obviously needs to be free of sediment for the oil to be pumped round the engine. A parts washer filled with degreaser is the best way to get it clean, but some time spent with petrol and a small brush will do the job. Make sure it is dry before reassembly.

The next task is to remove and inspect the conrods' big-end bearings. These are half-moon strips, or 'shells' – consumable strips of metal that are clamped round the crankshaft by the conrods at the top, and the conrods' caps at the bottom. There are eight altogether, two for each conrod.

Conrod is short for 'connecting rod', as they connect the piston with the crankshaft. As the crankshaft turns, it must rotate within the big end of the

Pulling out the split pins for the nuts that hold the conrod shells in place.

conrod. This friction wears down the bearing shells over time.

These engines will actually run reasonably well with worn bearings, but aggressive rumbling noises will eventually emerge from the lower part of the engine when under load, at which point a rebuild is urgent. As the demo engine has never properly been driven, the amount of wear at this stage is completely unknown to us.

The bottom caps of the conrods are secured in place with castle nuts. Undoing them requires the split pins to be removed first, which should be replaced with new pins when you reassemble.

As we suspected, our bearings are in healthy condition. We can tell this because the metal is a uniform colour across its surface and not excessively scored. By contrast, a worn bearing will show different shades of colour, as the grey top layer will have worn down to reveal the copper layer below.

New shells must not be added to worn bottom ends, or they will be destroyed quite rapidly. The main bearings and big-end bearings must be machined to match the new shells.

A used but healthy conrod shell.

The crankshaft rotates through three main bearings, not to be confused with the conrod bearings. These have to endure extreme levels of thrust, and tend to wear faster than the conrod journals (which is partly why, during Series III production, Land Rover would upgrade to five main bearings instead of three, to spread the load). The main bearing caps have two shells alongside each other, and their condition can be

The oil pick-up strainer assembly comes apart after undoing its bottom nut.

A worn conrod bearing, taken from a different Series I engine. Note the copper layer showing through – a sure sign of wear.

These main bearing shells are in good condition.

assessed in just the same way as for the conrod bearings. These are in good condition.

Not all bearing sizes are available, so in some cases the conrod may need to be machined to match whatever size of bearings are available to you. If the crankshaft journals are not being machined, the bearing shells must be reinstated – otherwise the contour of the partially worn journal will not fit perfectly against the new shell, and the shell will wear very rapidly.

It is also important to ensure that the piston rings are not seized. Seized rings cause poor compression, because they remain stuck in their grooves round the piston rather than pushing out against the walls of the cylinder. This can happen in an engine that has been left standing – a typical symptom is a pressurized crankcase, as pressure from the combustion chamber is forced down past the pistons and into the sump. A typical indication of this happening is visible oil vapour being emitted from the crankcase breather on the top of the rocker cover while the engine is running – but even if this has not been detectable, it is worth checking the rings anyway at this stage.

This inspection can only be made when the conrods are disconnected from the crankshaft, and when the head is off, as each piston needs to be pushed up from below until the rings just begin to emerge from the block. If the piston comes all the way out then you will need a piston ring compressor to squeeze them back into the bore, but it should not be necessary to withdraw the pistons this far. (On both 1.6- and 2.0-litre petrols, the conrod's big end is too big to pass all the way out through the cylinder.)

You should see them pop out as the piston emerges, and not remain flush with the piston, which would mean they're seized. A flat screwdriver or thin pliers may help in manipulating the ring to free it off. If any ring is found to be rusty or cracked, it will need replacing. If the position of the rings is adjusted, or new ones fitted, it is important that the gaps around the rings must not all line up.

None of the piston rings showed any signs of sticking, so they were left in place.

We can now reassemble the conrods' bottom caps, bearing shells, and the crankshaft main bearings, with a smear of engine oil around all the mating surfaces. The torque on these nuts is particularly important; on this vehicle the conrod nuts must be tightened to 40lb/ft, but Land Rover specified 30lb/ft for engines built up the 1953.

We also reattach the sump with a new gasket.

DECOKING THE ENGINE

Note: The photos in this part of the chapter show a 1954 petrol engine from an 86in Series I being decoked. Although this is an earlier Siamese-bore 2.0-litre engine rather than the spread-bore version in the demo 109, the procedure is identical.

'Coke' is the build-up of carbon deposits caused by unburned fuel and oil in the combustion chambers. Removing these deposits used to be a more common job when fuel was of poorer quality than it is today, but Series Land Rover engines still do need decoking from time to time. Otherwise, two problems can occur. First, the engine can suffer pre-ignition symptoms when hot, because the coke retains its heat and ignites the fuel/air mixture too early in the combustion cycle. Second, the engine will lose efficiency as coke build-up around the edges of the valves prevents them from closing fully. This is where valve lapping comes in.

A small number of dedicated tools is required, but none is particularly expensive.

The top of the block is thoroughly cleaned to remove any residues of the old gasket. This is done now to prevent dirt being knocked into the bores after the pistons have been decoked. We need to avoid introducing any unevenness into the surface of the block while doing this, so here 40grit on a wooden block is used. As always when prepar-

A valve spring compressor will be required.

The piston rings should pop out lightly, like this.

Care must be taken to prevent creating irregularities in the flatness of the top of the block.

ABOVE: *A wire wheel cleans the coke deposits from the underside of the head.*

LEFT: *Each piston crown is scrubbed at TDC.*

ing mating faces for gaskets, it pays to take your time and be thorough.

Coke on the piston crowns is also scrubbed away, using a brush on a wire wheel. It is extremely important that each piston is at TDC before doing this, otherwise the wheel would scratch the lining of the bore. The combustion chambers around the exhaust valves are scrubbed with each valve in the closed position.

Brake cleaner is used to wash the loosened deposits from the surfaces of the head and piston crowns. This also removes any old residue of engine oil, which is needed for lubricating the bore lining when the engine is fired up again, and for preventing corrosion, so the wash ends with a generous squirt of engine oil mixed with WD40.

The inlet and exhaust manifolds have their insides cleaned using a small wire wheel and a flush of degreaser.

Now we need to remove the valves from the block and the head, to access any deposits around the valve seats. This process is similar for both sets of valves, and each valve must be in the closed position before it is removed. First, one side of the spring compressor is placed over the flat face of the valve. The compressor is then adjusted so that the other end is able to slightly compress the valve cap when the handles are squeezed inwards and locked together.

Once the valve spring is slightly compressed, the collets can be extracted using a fine screwdriver, then the compressor is released and the valve cap should drop off, together with the spring. The valve is then free to be removed. Keep the valve together with its collets, spring and cap, as these are small parts and easily lost.

The rear faces of the valves are scrubbed using a wire wheel (a bench-mounted version is useful for this).

The exhaust manifold, held in a vice, being scrubbed from the inside. The inlet manifold receives the same treatment.

Valve spring compressor removing inlet valves from the head.

An example of pitting on a different Series I head, requiring new valve seats to be cut.

LEFT: *The same process for the outlet valves in the block.*

Care must be taken not to erode the metal, but the valves are made of very hard steel so they can withstand quite thorough scrubbing.

Afterwards, inspect each one carefully for any pitting, which will prevent the seal from making a perfect seal. Even a small amount of pitting means that the valve needs to be replaced.

The inlet ports in the head are also cleaned using a drill with a small wire brush attachment. Again, you will need to inspect closely for pitting round the valve seat. If any is found, the head will need to be sent to an engineering firm with the equipment necessary to cut

Lapping valves by swizzling them against their seat.

new seats; however, this is not very common.

Valve lapping is the final step. This ensures that each valve mates perfectly with its seat, and requires a lapping kit consisting of a suction cup on a stick, and a pot of abrasive paste. Smear some of the paste round the valve seat, then stick the suction cup on to the face of the valve and drop the valve into position. The stick is then rubbed between the palms while pressing down firmly, spinning the valve against the seat. This is repeated for a couple of minutes on each valve, until a bright polished ring has been created around the seat. The process is then repeated for all the remaining valves, followed by thorough cleaning to remove any deposits of the grinding paste.

Both sets of valve gear are ready for reinstallation, but there is some cosmetic work to do first.

All these deposits must be scrubbed off, while checking for pitting.

A bench-mounted wire wheel is ideal for cleaning individual parts such as this.

PAINTING AND SURFACE PREPARATION

Cleaning the engine, preparing the surfaces and applying paint is a time-consuming process, and different methods are required depending on the surface in question. For soft metals such as aluminium – as used in the timing chest, top rocker cover and flywheel housing – vapour blasting is recommended, and this work is outsourced to a specialist. The process is effective at removing ingrained dirt, and is less abrasive than grit blasting. It also avoids warping caused by heat that results from the friction of the grit-blasting process. (For structural steel components such as the chassis and bulkhead, grit blasting is more efficient.)

The steel parts are all painted before reassembly. In each case the process

Sanding the old paint from the air-filter housing of an 80.

New coolant pump, painted with synthetic paint that does not require primer.

Note the correct area of missing paint around the engine number on this restored 1948 engine.

The radiator fan, front coolant pipe, engine mounts and alternator bracket are all etch primed and painted black.

GASKETS

Gasket technology has advanced over the decades, but not all modern gaskets for old engines such as these Rover units are made to a very high standard. If you buy cheaply you can end up with gaskets failing prematurely. This is especially true of modern exhaust manifold gaskets, which are often inferior to new-old stock versions. All the gaskets used in the rebuild of the project 109's engine came together as part of a new-old stock engine gasket kit. There aren't many left but they are worth looking out for, as the quality is good, and it saves a lot of time.

begins with a thorough cleaning with degreaser – brake cleaner is ideal – and then scrubbing using a wire wheel on a drill. For certain flatter surfaces, a sander with 80-grit paper can be used.

Never shotblast an engine, because any grit in an oil gallery or bore will cause a lot of damage. One old Land Rover engine is known to have lasted only 30 miles (50km) after being shotblasted, as grit had worked its way into the oil and caused terminal damage.

A coat of etch primer should precede any application of paint, to ensure a thorough bond.

After thorough cleaning, the engine block is brush painted with grey, heat-resistant, gloss coach-enamel paint, which does not require priming. The same paint is used for the coolant pump and the head.

When it comes to deciding which colour to paint your engine block and head, as a rule the 1.6-litre engines were dark blue and 2.0-litre engines (from 1954 onwards) were grey. The demo vehicle's had previously been changed from grey to blue, so a little authenticity was restored to the engine by returning it to the original grey.

Originally the engine block and head would have been painted very early on in the build process, before they were machined, so none of the machined surfaces on the finished engine would have left the factory with paint on them.

Always apply these coats in a well ventilated area.

When spray painting, use scrap cardboard to catch any overspray. Another method is to hang the parts from a wire while painting, which gives better access all round the component. One downside is that this creates excess vapours in the air (overspray) so you will need to wear a respirator mask.

The exhaust manifold is given a coat of black using heatproof paint that is designed to withstand extremely high temperatures and gives a wrinkle finish. Although black has been commonly used, early 80in Series Is originally left Solihull with cream-coloured exhaust manifolds.

Once the paint is dry, and all the mating surfaces have been scrubbed clean and perfectly flat, we're ready to start reassembling the engine.

The heatproof paint used for the demo exhaust manifold.

The original exhaust manifold after painting.

REPLACING THE HEAD

With the cleaned head still on the bench, the inlet valves are returned to their original places, using any new parts that may be required. (In the case of the project 109, all the original parts could be reused.) When building each valve assembly, the valve, spring and cap are held with the compressor, which puts enough pressure on the spring for the two collets to be inserted in the groove in the gap. A small smear of grease will hold the collets in place while the compressor is released.

Before replacing the head, smear a little gasket compound round the combustion chambers to help the new head gasket seal efficiently. Only use compound that is designed for this high-heat application (Hylomar Blue was used for the project 109), and be careful to avoid the risk of any extrusion into the combustion chamber or the coolant passages.

(For the project vehicle a new-old stock tin gasket is used, although reproduction copper equivalents are more readily available.)

Once the gasket is in position on the block, the head is lowered into place, and its bolts are dropped in but only gently tightened. The head

Pushrods being inserted into the newly replaced head, before the head bolts are tightened.

The rocker shaft being refitted, before the head bolts are torqued down.

must not be torqued down until the inlet rocker-shaft assembly is in place, because two of the shaft's pedestal bolts go down into the block, so these need to be part of the head-bolt tightening sequence.

A thin smear of compound is applied round the combustion chamber apertures, on both sides of the gasket.

The three lengths of head bolt, accounting for the tapering height of the head.

This is the sequence for tightening the head bolts, as stipulated by Rover. (The front of the engine is at the top of the image.)

Ideally you will have kept a record of which head bolts came from which holes. There are twelve bolts, in three different lengths, with four of each length. The long ones go in the taller side of the head. Once the head is in place, the four pushrods (which are all the same length) can be dropped into position. The head is then ready to receive the inlet rocker shaft.

With the rocker shaft bolted to the head, the head can be torqued down into the block. The $^{7}/_{16}$in bolts require 50lb/ft and the $^{3}/_{18}$in bolts require 30lb/ft. It's essential that this is done accurately, and that the bolts are tightened in the correct sequence, specified by Solihull. This sequence starts in the middle and works outwards, to ensure the compression forces are applied as evenly as possible. When all the bolts have been tightened, go round them all again to check. You will need to torque them down again after 100 miles (160km) (*see* Chapter 18).

VALVE CLEARANCES

The clearance between each rocker arm and its corresponding valve stem needs to be carefully adjusted to the factory specification, when each valve is closed. This ensures that the valves open and shut fully, and at precisely the right moment. Calibration is required for both inlet and exhaust valves (with different clearances for each, as described below), and the exhaust valves come first.

Beginning with the exhaust valve of cylinder no.1 at the front of the engine, the crankshaft is turned until the corresponding lobe on the camshaft is off-peak. At this point, the rocker arm should not be exerting any pressure on the valve stem, and a feeler gauge can be inserted between the two. The target clearance for the exhaust valves is

The reconditioned head being tightened into the block.

The feeler gauge setting the clearance for one of the inlet valves.

.010in. To adjust the clearance, slacken the nut on the rocker arm and adjust the screw until the feeler gauge is held gently (not pinched tight), then lock the screw in place by tightening the nut. The precise order in which the remaining exhaust valves are adjusted is unimportant; simply adjust whichever valve is off-cam, rotating the crankshaft until the rocker arm lifts fully away from the valve.

The process is then repeated for the

inlet valves, but with a different target clearance of .012in.

Once the inlet valve clearances are set, they are brush painted with a coating of clean engine oil to prevent wear when the engine is fired up.

FLYWHEEL AND CLUTCH

The 109's flywheel has returned from the engineering firm, who refaced it at a cost of about £40. It can now be

The feeler gauge setting the clearance on exhaust valve no. 1.

Eight bolts attach the cleaned flywheel housing to the newly painted block.

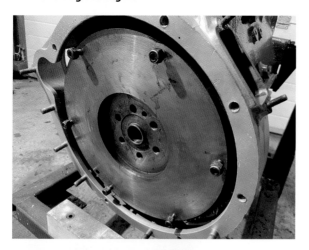

The refaced flywheel is in place, but the spigot bush hasn't been added.

The new clutch plate is located against the flywheel using the DIY clutch alignment tool.

The spigot bush is driven in using a drift.

Clutch cover/pressure plate bolted in place, prior to removal of the alignment tool.

requires a clutch alignment tool. This ensures that the friction plate is centralized to the flywheel, allowing for ease of mating the gearbox first motion shaft to the splines in the clutch plate and the spigot bush.

Generic clutch alignment tools can be bought, but a DIY tool made from a cut-down first motion shaft is easier to use and gives the best result. To use it, push the splines into the centre of the friction plate, and locate the smooth end of the shaft into the spigot bush. This is left in place while doing up the pressure plate.

The pressure plate on the demo 109 is renewed in addition to the friction plate. With the friction plate held in place, the pressure plate is pushed on to the six studs round the edge of the

flywheel, and held in place with new locknuts. The nuts need to be tightened in a star pattern to spread the forces evenly: top, bottom, top right, bottom left, bottom right, top left.

If you are trying to understand for the first time how the friction and pressure plates move in relation to each other, it is helpful to think of the friction plate as being part of the gearbox rather than the engine, because it spins with the first motion shaft. The pressure plate, however, is coupled to the engine, as it is bolted to the flywheel and therefore spins at the same speed as the crankshaft.

VALVE TIMING

The valve timing needs to be calibrated after the valve clearances have been set and the flywheel and its housing have been added, but before the addition of the timing chain. The timing ensures that the camshaft and crankshaft are correctly co-ordinated with each other, so the valves open and close at the correct point in the combustion cycle. Doing this accurately requires a dial gauge to determine the exact position of the valves. (This process should not be confused with ignition timing, which is adjusted later.)

The spigot bush should be flush with the hole in the flywheel, as shown here.

returned to the engine with the flywheel housing and clutch assembly. The first stage in the reassembly process is to attach the flywheel housing, which has also returned to the workshop after being vapour blasted.

The flywheel is bolted to the end of the crankshaft with six new bolts, not forgetting the three brackets whose corners need to be bent forwards to prevent the bolts from undoing.

Next comes the spigot bush, which is tapped home with a drift. The spigot bush is what supports the smooth (non-splined) end of the first motion shaft, which comes forwards from the gearbox. It's important that the bush isn't driven in too far – stop when it is flush with the hole.

Attaching the clutch to the flywheel

The end of a first motion shaft makes the best clutch alignment tool.

The new pressure plate (left) and friction plate (right) ready for fitting.

To set the timing, the letters EP on the flywheel need to be aligned with the marker.

The timing chain in position on its sprocket, with the tensioner added.

It is easier to have the crankshaft damper already attached before doing this, as it can be used to rotate the crankshaft, but you will need to remove the damper again in order to add the timing chain.

The first step is to rotate the crankshaft until the letters EP on the flywheel align with the marker in the timing window. EP stands for 'exhaust peak', denoting the point at which the exhaust valve on cylinder 1 (nearest the front of the engine) needs to be in the fully open position.

With the crankshaft left in this position, the camshaft sprocket is turned until the exhaust valve on cylinder 1 is fully open: a dial gauge is used to determine this point exactly. The gauge's magnetic base is attached to the crankcase, and its pin is rested against the end of the screw adjuster on the rocker for cylinder 1. You will need to rock the camshaft back and forth while watching the gauge needle to home in on the exact point at which the rocker arm ceases to compress the valve spring.

This position is then locked in place by adding the timing chain and its tensioner to their sprockets. As the timing chain is fitted, it needs to be kept tight on the drive side; this may require you to remove and reposition the camshaft sprocket, which has three irregularly spaced 'keyways' to make this easier.

FRONT REASSEMBLY

Our timing chest needs to receive a new crankshaft seal before being refitted. The old one is removed with a seal pick, taking care not to scratch the surrounding metal, and the new seal is gently tapped in with a wooden mallet.

Both the timing chest and the mating face on the block receive a smear of gasket compound, in addition to the new paper gasket. The gasket compound is used primarily to hold the gasket in place, helping to align it over the bolt holes. The chest is then offered up to the block, and bolted in place.

The new paper gasket stuck in position with Hylomar.

The old crank seal being removed from the timing chest.

The new cork gasket and O-ring, ready to receive the thermostat.

The dial gauge in position against exhaust valve 1, with the timing chain added.

The thermostat housing in place, prior to the addition of the thermostat.

The new thermostat going in, with its two fibre washers.

The coolant pump assembly is the next to be fitted. Note that the timing chest and pump need to be fitted in this order, because the pump slightly covers the chest.

The lower pipe connecting to the coolant pump at the bottom of the radiator is then added, followed by the thermostat housing, which is added to both the head and the coolant pump. Don't forget the fat little O-ring that sits on top of the pump (part number 01970; the copper tube that sits inside it is 01917). This is not included with the new water pump so it's easy to overlook, but it comes with the engine gasket set, together with the cork gasket that sits between the thermostat housing and the head.

The thermostat housing can now be added. (The demo 109's is a cast steel version, whereas those built for the UK market are usually aluminium.) The brass bung is where the pipework would be connected for a heater – an optional extra not fitted to this vehicle. Another option is that the black blanking plug in front would take the capillary for a water-temperature gauge.

The new thermostat is then fitted into the housing. We've used an 88°C wax-based thermostat, the modern equivalent of the original but obsolete 'bellows' type (which was also set to activate at 88°C). The thermostat requires two fibre washers; one goes beneath it, and one sits on top.

New-old stock bellows thermostats can sometimes be found, but they are rare and more expensive.

It is possible to check that your thermostat is specified to open at the right temperature, using a kettle, a jug and a thermometer. Place the thermostat and thermometer in the jug with a little warm water, and gradually bring up the temperature using boiling water from the kettle. When the temperature reaches 88°C, the thermostat should visibly open.

Before proceeding to fit the manifolds, we need to fit the dynamo's two little mounting plinths to the block, because there isn't enough clearance to reach one of the bolts with the inlet manifold in place. These same parts are used whether it is a dynamo or a dynamator being fitted. We have

cleaned and spray painted them black before reassembly.

MANIFOLDS, ROCKER COVERS AND OIL PARTS

The exhaust manifold is bolted to the block using a new two-piece gasket and all the original fixings, which have been thoroughly cleaned and derusted. (The gasket is RTC3326, a three-part gasket for a later 2.6-litre 6-cylinder Rover engine, but the middle section is simply discarded.)

The exhaust rocker cover is also fitted, with a new gasket aided by compound to hold it in position. The oil feed pipe running to the head from the oil pressure switch on the block

The exhaust manifold bolted in place with the original studs and brackets.

The exhaust rocker cover being placed over the new gasket, adhered with Hylomar.

The dynamo's mounting points must be added before the inlet manifold.

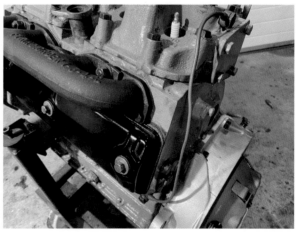

The oil feed pipe is added.

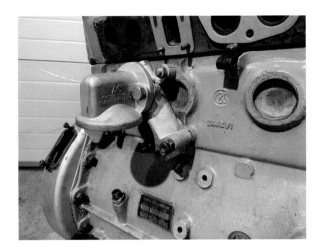

The oil filter bracket is attached to the block with the new gasket.

The dipstick tube and reconditioned oil filter housing in place.

The new inlet manifold gaskets in situ, with the oil filter housing and dynamo plinth attached. Note that the mating face of the block has not been painted, to ensure better sealing.

New plugs being added to the head.

is then reattached. The banjos use four copper washers, which should all be renewed. Testing the oil pressure switch is not easily achievable, but these are readily available to buy if yours is non-functional.

On the opposite side of the engine, the oil filter bracket is bolted to the block using the new gasket round its lower section, and the inlet manifold is fixed back in place. The manifold requires three gaskets, and the mating faces of both the block and manifold are given a smear of gasket compound to aid adhesion. The four inner studs (¼in UNF) round the water jacket are tightened first, followed by the outer studs ($^5/_{16}$in UNF) round the inlet ports.

The dipstick tube is bolted back in place, and a new paper oil filter is added in the freshly painted housing that screws into the bracket. The part number for the Series I oil filter was discontinued, so a filter for a 6-cylinder engine, RTC3182, will need to be used.

At the top of the engine, a set of new NGK BP6ES spark plugs is added. Many early Rover engines use NGK B5ES spark plugs whose electrode does not protrude, and are now discontinued. The protruding electrode design of the BP6ES plugs helps older Rover engines run more efficiently with modern fuels.

The vapour-blasted inlet rocker cover is then added, using new nuts and fibre washers, and a new cork gasket. The top of the thermostat housing is bolted in place. The inlet manifold's coolant passage is connected to the thermostat, using an elbow that was missing from our engine and had to be sourced second-hand (costing around £25). A new rubber bypass hose with jubilee clips connects the elbow to the manifold; the hose and clips used for the demo vehicle are not period correct, but they are more reliable and easier to use than the original wire hose clips.

The freshly painted exhaust rocker cover is also added, with an even smear of Hylomar keeping the new gasket in place while the cover is offered up to it.

A replacement starter motor is

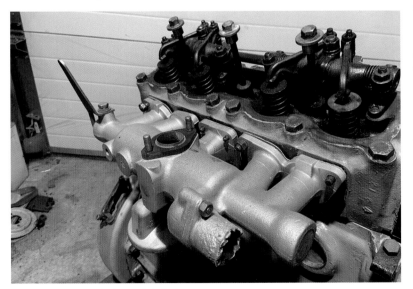

The cleaned inlet manifold, partially bolted on.

Inlet rocker cover gasket bolted in position, plus thermostat top.

Coolant elbow joint added with a new gasket.

Bypass hose and jubilee clips are not period correct, but serviceable.

New starter motor being added.

bolted to the flywheel housing. This model is the type used on later Series Land Rovers, but is outwardly similar to the original, does the job perfectly, and is much more affordable. Note that no gasket is required between the starter and the flywheel housing.

FUEL PUMP REBUILD

In the case of the demo 109, more than 80 per cent of the cost of replacing the fuel pump was saved by refurbishing it with new parts supplied as a kit by Burlen Fuels. This is vital for reliability and performance (especially with a particularly dirty engine), and ensures that the internal components are compatible with modern fuels, high in ethanol.

The kit comes with its own set of instructions. Cleanliness matters, and you will want to have spare rags and a container ready to catch any spilled

fuel. The process should take an hour or two, even if you have never done this before.

Various specifications of SU fuel pump are available. When choosing a new pump, or ordering a refurb kit for an old one, you need to know which model number suits the vehicle. The correct version is AUA25, pumping 8gal per hour, but you can also opt for an AUA66 (also fitted to Morris Minor 1000s) if you swap over the outlet union from your original AUA25 pump. It is easy to get caught out and buy a pump that looks right, but which isn't matched to your fuel system's layout (the bulkhead-mounted AUA25 is

Our SU pump, prior to disassembly. Black cap comes off first.

designed to suck a long way and push a short way, rather than vice versa). To be sure, you can measure how high the fuel pump will be from the base of the fuel pick-up in the tank, and check this figure against the pump manufacturer's specifications.

The refurb kit (part number EPK700) consists of a new set of points, a diaphragm and its return spring, gaskets, non-return valve, gauze filter and various washers. The components that typically wear out first are the diaphragm and the non-return valve. Throughout this process it's important to clean any dirt, rust and debris from all the components that are being reused, and to keep track of the many small parts. As always, photographing parts as they are removed will help remind you how it goes back together.

The pump contains a diaphragm, attached to a rod that passes through the middle of the pump. The oppo-

Rebuild kit from Burlen Fuels, part number EPK700.

Holding the points arm, after it has been unscrewed from the body.

Bakelite mounting plinth, turned upside down to reveal the points.

Removing the bolts that hold down the plinth. The nut has been undone from the threaded post.

New points (with attached wire) secured to the plinth with a new pin.

Screwing the new points arm on to the Bakelite plinth.

site end of the rod is secured to the pivoting mechanism that pushes it up and down, activated by an electro-magnet.

First we take the end cap off the pump, and unscrew the points arm. The threaded post receives the live feed (positive or negative, depending on whether your vehicle is positive earth or negative). The little wire that comes off the post magnetizes the electromagnet; the nut holding this wire in place is undone next.

The other small (unsheathed) cop-

per wire comes up from the points and is earthed by the screw. This screw is now undone, along with the similar screw opposite it. Before the Bakelite plinth can be lifted away from the pump, it needs to be unscrewed from the rod that passes up through the pump from the diaphragm. This means undoing the six fixings round the out-side of the casing to detach the main sections of the pump and reveal the diaphragm, together with the white plastic spacer that restricts the move-ment of the diaphragm and the throw of the spring.

The diaphragm is then unscrewed, and the points are removed by extract-ing the pin they pivot round. They are replaced with the new points from the kit, along with a new pivot pin.

The main body of the pump is given a coat of paint; when dry, it's ready for reassembly. The Bakelite plinth assem-

This bracket is retained, rather than fitting the washers contained in the kit.

bly is reattached, and the new dia-phragm is screwed up into the points mechanism. The two large screws are added to fix the plinth in place – not forgetting to attach the little wires – and a new points arm is added.

The white plastic bracket can then be slotted back into position against the diaphragm.

Pulling out the pin that the points pivot round.

Removing the old outlet valve, a common failure point.

The old outlet union is added to the new valve and washer.

The little filter for renewal, unscrewed from the base of the housing.

Removing the spring clip, which must not be lost.

The pump (with diaphragm) is placed over the diaphragm housing, with its new gasket.

Next, the main body of the pump (left) can be unscrewed from the diaphragm housing, and the inlet and outlet unions can be removed from the body. Behind the outlet there is a non-return valve that needs to be disassembled and replaced, using the contents of the kit.

Disassembly of the outlet valve involves removing the little spring retainer with pliers. Be careful not to lose it because a new one is not supplied in the refurb kit. You do, however, get a new valve body and 'penny',

which sits inside it. Before installing the new valves, the housing is given a thorough scrub and a wash, as it's important not to introduce any dirt to the inner workings of the pump.

The outlet valve can now be reassembled, with the old spring clip holding the penny down in the valve, which can then be positioned down into the main housing. A new fibre washer is now fitted, and the old union can be screwed back into place.

The inlet union is unscrewed and replaced, using another fresh washer

from the kit, and taking care to remove any dirt from the inlet area. The pump body also has a gauze filter that needs to be unscrewed from the base and replaced with the new filter in the kit, together with its new fibre washer. These are usually clean anyway, because the fuel has already passed through the sedimenter by the time it reaches this point.

The diaphragm housing is then cleaned and reattached to the base of the pump, using a new gasket. The assembly is reattached to the main

Placing the new penny into the new valve before reassembly.

Screwing the main sections of the pump together.

The finished item – an original pump with new innards.

Dirty sedimenter, ready for refurbishment.

body of the pump using another new gasket, and the six outer screws are added to hold it all together – not forgetting the little earth terminal that is attached to one of the screws.

The plastic cap is placed on top, with some discreet black tape to prevent any water ingress, and the pump is complete. Applying tape may seem odd, but new SU pumps also use external tape here (with SU branding) for the same purpose.

The fuel pump will be added to the bulkhead later.

THE FUEL SEDIMENTER

The fuel sedimenter (similar to that on later Series Land Rover engines) was missing from the project vehicle, so a second-hand replacement was sourced. It's a simple device that mounts to the bulkhead, and is cheap and easy to service.

Undoing the large nut at the bottom enables the clamp to be swung clear so the glass bowl can be removed. As you can see, there was plenty of dirt and old, crystallized fuel that was cleaned out using WD40 and wire wool.

The brass gauze is sometimes found to be rotten and replacements are available, but if it is in good condition it will simply need cleaning (as the demo 109's). In some cases this gauze may be blocked with a gungy mat of small fibres. This happens when an old, braided fuel hose comes in contact with modern petrol. The rubber degrades and the fibres come loose, then flow into the sedimenter and get sucked up against the mesh. This is an easily overlooked cause of poor running.

Undoing this bottom screw releases the clamp and the bowl.

There is a great deal of dirt on each side of the gauze.

Without fuel filtration, here's what happens: this Solex carburettor came from another Australian Series I project and it is severely clogged with sand, mud and bugs in the float chamber.

The cleaned gauze, with the new rubber seal ready for installation.

A vice is useful for removing the top nut.

Small tap mechanism, with a rubber seal.

Replacing the cleaned outlet union.

The refurbished sedimenter, ready for installation.

The brass unions were also removed from the housing and cleaned. The outlet adaptor has two threads: one side is coarse threaded, the other is fine, and the fine side is tapered so it tightens up against the body of the fuel sedimenter. Adjacent to this on the housing is a screw tap that enables the flow rate to be adjusted; the tap needs to be unscrewed and cleaned, and the condition of the rubber seal needs to be assessed, but it is rare for this to be perished. Count the number of turns as the tap is undone, as it must be reinstalled by the same amount.

In practice, the regulator tap is of limited utility. It is unlikely that you will leave it too far open, because when the float chamber in the carburettor is full, the back pressure will automatically turn off the electric pump. However, the tap can be wound too far in, reducing fuel flow and causing the sedimenter bowl to empty before fresh fuel can replenish it, resulting in fuel starvation. If you are not sure how far to wind the tap, half way in is a good option.

The mounting bracket and the clamp for the bowl received a coat of black paint, then the unions were returned to the housing. The bowl was reattached with its mesh filter, using a new rubber seal that received a small smear of grease on each side to prevent it pinching when compressed, and to ensure a good seal. The clamp's bottom nut should tightened by hand, enough to create a good seal.

Once dry and reassembled, the sedimenter is set aside ready for when the bulkhead has been added to the chassis.

CARBURETTOR

All Series Is were originally fitted with a Solex 32PBI carburettor. Those fitted to the 2.0-litre engine have a slightly larger jet compared to the 1.6-litre version. The 32PBI has three common problems:

Problem 1: Wear in the housing where the throttle spindle passes through it. This is the most common issue, and results in air leaks down the side of the butterfly, causing a lumpy idle and poor acceleration. A carburettor

specialist should be able to machine a new hole and replace the spindle with a slightly thicker one to compensate.

Problem 2: The accelerator pump can seize. Patience and plenty of penetrating fluid may or may not be able to get it moving again.

Problem 3: When unscrewing the main jet of 2.0-litre type, the housing into which it screws can crack – as happened with our vehicle's carburettor. There is nothing that can be done about this, so take great care to avoid putting too much pressure on the jet when unscrewing it.

Wear in this spindle is a common problem.

Indicating the accelerator pump, which can seize.

The central housing can sheer around this point.

Our replacement carb is new, but a more 'perfect' restoration would use a genuine Solex.

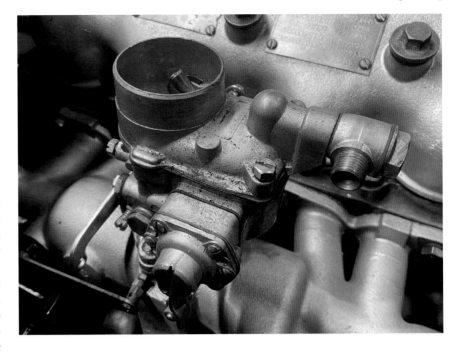

The demo 109's carburettor was beyond repair, not only because there was a large amount of wear in the throttle spindle, but also because the thread broke round the jet when we attempted to unscrew it. As a cheaper option it is possible to install an aftermarket remake of the original Solex 32PBI. However, if the carburettor is not too deteriorated, we would recommend having it rebuilt by a reputable specialist such as Carburettor Exchange. A good rebuild of an original Solex will usually be of significantly better quality than a new aftermarket version.

Rebuild kits are available, enabling you to replace the gaskets, diaphragm, washers and float needle valve assembly. Note that good seals are vital when working on a carburettor, to prevent the mixture being altered and to prevent seepage of petrol. When removing gaskets they should always be replaced with new items, and care should be taken to make sure that all mating surfaces are clean. A clean working environment will help.

The carburettor's linkage inside the engine bay incorporates two arms that rotate round phosphor-bronze bushes on a pivot, which is screwed into the side of the inlet manifold. These bushes need checking for slackness, as they will sometimes wear and introduce play that will make it difficult to calibrate the many linkages accurately.

The project 109's were in good condition, but dismantling them, painting the arms and lubricating the bearings with grease was still a worthwhile procedure. The order of events for dismantling is fairly self-explanatory, but it is advisable to take photos as you do so, to act as a reference for how it fits together again.

The mechanism can then be bolted to the inlet manifold, ready for the carburettor to be added later.

Throttle linkage prior to disassembly. The arm with the wire attached is the hand throttle linkage.

The reverse of the same mechanism, showing the small slip pin that needs to be removed to access the bushes.

Sections coming apart, revealing the bush (top left) and the perishable ball joint (bottom left).

The central pivot that screws into the manifold.

A POPULAR PERIOD MODIFICATION

A popular period modification was to swap the cylinder head with one from a Rover 60 (P4). These use a side-draft HS4 carburettor made by SU, which was easier to tune and offered easier access.

Check for lubrication and signs of excess wear.

DYNAMO

The finished engine with the refurbished carb linkage attached.

The dynamo (known as a generator outside the UK) was the forerunner to the modern alternator, and all Series I engines were originally fitted with a Lucas C39 or C40 model. In the demo 109 the dynamo was seized solid, so it will be replaced with a modern remake. This is more cost effective than having the original rebuilt, which is usually twice as expensive as sourcing a new dynamo.

These new models are very similar to the originals, although not quite identical. A different arrangement of the brushes inside means that the modern version does not have an inspection plate on the main casing, as the original does. Also, the terminals on the rear of the new model are spade connectors, rather than the original pegs, so we will need to modify our new wiring loom accordingly (*see* Chapter 17).

A small modification is also required to the spacer washer that sits between the pulley and the dynamo. The spacer that comes with the new dynamo is too thick, meaning that the belt will sit slightly further forwards than the fan pulley and crank pulley. The washer is given to an engineering firm, who shrinks it in a lathe.

The original pulley would have been painted black at the factory, but the demo 109's came unpainted, so it is painted matt black before installation. The bolts securing the dynamo in place are left slack while the fan and its pulley are bolted to the front of the coolant pump. The slider bracket is also added to the timing chest and loosely bolted to the bottom of the dynamo. A new belt is run round all three pulleys, then the dynamo is pulled upwards, tightening the belt. (Too slack and it will skip when resistance is by the dynamo, causing it to squeal – too tight and it will overload the water-pump bearing.) Its position is locked by tightening the slider and then the two mounting nuts.

The new dynamo. The pulley will be painted, and its spacer washer is too thick.

Old, seized dynamo. Note the clamp on the left-hand side, giving access to the brushes – absent on the modern version.

The new dynamo in position, with the fan pulley. The slider bracket needs adding next.

The new belt tightened into position, and the front end of the engine is complete.

The old internals, after removal of the cap.

There are alternatives to fitting a dynamo. The originals generate up to 25amps – not much by the standards of most modern alternators. Alternators also create a steadier supply of current and tend to be more reliable. They do require converting the vehicle to negative earth, but they are a sensible upgrade if you plan to use the vehicle regularly, or to place extra demands on the electrical system by adding lights or other accessories.

(SU's AUA25 fuel pump can be fitted to both positive- and negative-earthed vehicles.)

The aesthetic element is worth considering, as alternators do look out of place in a Series I engine bay. The solution is a 'dynamator', which is an alternator built to resemble a dynamo, combining period looks with modern functionality. A dynamator will usually come supplied with instructions showing how to make

the necessary changes to your wiring harness.

DISTRIBUTOR

All Series Is from 1954 onwards have a Lucas 25D side-exit distributor, like this one. To guarantee a reliable spark, it's important to replace the condenser, points and HT leads. In this case the vacuum advance/retard module will also be replaced, as the project 109's

The new advance/retard module. The original one had sheared.

New advance/retard module in situ.

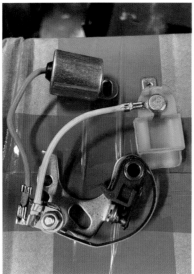

New points, condenser and feed wire ready for installation.

The body of the distributor is added to the block using the original mounting post and plate, with a new O-ring.

had seized to the extent that it broke off as we attempted to remove it – which is quite common.

For ease of access, the 109's distributor is placed in a vice, although this work can be done with the distributor already attached to the block.

Inside the distributor housing, a set of weights and springs controls the degree of timing advance, governed by the engine's rpm. This doesn't take into account engine load, which is why an advance system is required, and takes advantage of the variations in air pressure inside the carburettor. The advance module incorporates a knurled nut on the outside of the distributor body for fine-tuning the timing. Original items have a nut on the opposite end of the vacuum advance module, with a male thread for receiving a union for a copper pipe; our modern replacement is more typical of later types, with only a push-on nozzle to receive a plastic pipe.

The new vacuum module is slotted into the housing, the knurled nut is placed over the end of the adjuster rod, and the little hoop on the spring arm is hooked over the vertical peg next to the points.

The old condenser, points and feed wire are then unscrewed from the distributor. When fitting the replacement parts, it may be helpful to attach them together before installing them. In our case we ordered a kit so they arrived preassembed.

With the points only loosely screwed down, rotate the cam so the points

Locking the points gap, with the feeler gauge in position.

Unscrewing the flat screw down the centre of each post inside the distributor cap.

The rebuilt distributor, in position. Note the arrangement and sequence of the HT leads. The central lead comes from the coil.

The earlier type of Lucas DVX4A distributor.

An original-type copper vacuum tube is added to an earlier-type distributor.

arm is touching one of the four peaks on the cam. Then insert a .015in (0.38mm) feeler gauge into the points gap, and slide the points on their screw slot until the feeler gauge is fitting snugly. Then tighten the screw, remove the feeler gauge, turn the engine through one complete rotation, and recheck the gap to make sure it hasn't altered.

The body of the distributor is added to the block using a new gasket and the original clamping mechanism. When installing the earlier type, you will also need to reinstate the mounting post and plate, with the thick cork gasket that sits in the top of the post.

This type of distributor cap requires the HT leads to be screwed into place, unlike the simpler pull-on/pull-off leads found on later vehicles. In the centre of each post in the cap is a flat-head screw that pierces through the insulation of the HT lead, creating the electrical contact and holding the lead in place. The demo 109's old distributor cap was unserviceable due to corrosion in the screws, so a new replacement had to be sourced.

To replicate original spec, HT leads with the older-style copper core will need to be used, but better performance is possible with a more modern carbon core.

The revitalized engine, ready for reinstallation.

It is vital to add the leads to the correct plugs, remembering that the rotor arm rotates in the direction of the arrow on the distributor body (anticlockwise for the project vehicle). As the arm rotates, it needs to pass the brush points for the leads in the following firing sequence: 1-3-4-2.

Once the distributor is in place, the vacuum advance pipe is attached, connecting it to the carburettor.

The new vacuum advance module meant that a later-type plastic pipe had to be used, rather than original-type copper tube. The plastic pipe is an inferior alternative, as it is liable to melt if it comes loose and rests against the exhaust manifold, so make sure it is firmly attached.

For reference, the images show the earlier-type DVX4A Lucas distributor with side-exit cap (whose parts are very expensive), fitted to a 1.6-litre 1948 engine. The earlier model is sig- nificantly larger, but the principle of operation is the same. The only differences are the method of mounting it to the block, the terminal where the wire from the coil joins the body of the distributor, and the type of HT leads used.

COMPLETE

Finally the project 109's engine was assembled and ready to be lowered into the chassis.

10

Bodywork Restoration

In this chapter some of the techniques and principles for refurbishing the bodywork of the project Series I will be outlined, and some of the repairs that the vehicle required will be described. (The bodywork will be reassembled in Chapter 15.)

When repairing original bodywork, a 'concours' finish is often impossible. Small creases are likely to remain, and perhaps some uneven edges caused by corrosion. There may also be areas where damaged sections have to be reinforced with strengthening pieces, together with adhesive or new rivets. A non-factory finish such as this is traditionally not considered a 'concours' restoration (although there are exceptions – mentioned below).

Typically, the bodywork of a concours winner will have had much of its bodywork replaced with new-old stock panels, or unmarked panels from another vehicle. In other words, it's sometimes arguable whether the bodywork has been 'restored' at all.

Great care is being taken with this restoration to preserve and restore all the original bodywork. The intention is to explore what is possible, and to illustrate some achievable ways that any home-based restorer can use to breathe new life into battered bodywork – even if a perfect final result is going to be impossible.

DIFFERENT APPROACHES

For many high-end prestige classics, the aim is usually to make the car as immaculate as possible. But old Land Rovers are expected to acquire battle scars over time, and there has been a growing trend in recent years for 'patina restorations', which retain this kind of light damage and weathering as authentic signs of a life well spent. These restorations preserve and celebrate those elements that make each vehicle unique, and set it apart from the more uniform 'trailer queens'. Therefore retaining old bodywork should not be looked down upon if the repair is strong and safe.

Less conspicuous details are also worth retaining – for example, holes showing where accessories were fitted, or subtle traces of previous accident damage or repair. Depending on the story that comes with them, unique details such as these can make each restoration unique and interesting.

One high-profile 'patina restoration' is that by Julian Schoolheifer of JUE 477, the first production Land Rover, chassis 860001, which won the award for 'Best 1940s Car' at the Hampton Court Concours d'Élégance in 2020. JUE (or 'Juey') was restored at great length to ensure that every possible salvageable component was retained, and new components were given considerable thought. Author Martin Port's book dedicated to the restoration (Porter Press, 2020) describes how, for example, a unique replica of the original bronze badge was made by hand, and the replacement wheels were painted to blend in with the patina of the original bodywork.

A similar but different approach was taken by Ben Stowe with the restoration of Oxford, the First Overland expedition Series I. This car was reassembled with the original patina bodywork, but due to heavy corrosion of the bulkhead and chassis, and the intrepid plans for the vehicle, new replacements were required. It was important for this restoration that the original parts were clearly distinguishable from the new, so the bulkhead, chassis and repaired rear quarter were treated to fresh paint, while the original components retained their original patina. Since then it has driven from Singapore to the UK, and is now travelling the world in the custody of various Land Rover clubs and enthusiasts.

The Series I Oxford, being rebuilt on to a new chassis.

Oxford's *new bulkhead, painted without artificial patina.*

Painting the new rear quarter of Oxford *helped showcase the originality of the surrounding panels.*

Sometimes a vehicle's unique history may be secondary to its overall functionality and aesthetic appeal. This could be said of the 1949 Series I that Ben built for his own use a few years ago. This car was never intended to be period correct, although the mechanical alterations are in keeping with the era. The vehicle uses a Rover 60 engine that has a high-compression head and an SU carburettor, with higher ratio differentials for easier cruising, and some modern electrics, among other alterations – but much of the original character has been retained thanks to the use of original bodywork. It has been a reliable long-distance vehicle for many

trips into Europe and around the UK, sometimes with a similar 80in that Ben was also commissioned to build.

Usability need not require loss of originality, as can be seen with Ben's 107in Station Wagon (*see* overleaf). Although this vehicle has some

upgrades under the skin (including servo-assisted brakes), considerable time was spent salvaging the original bodywork, which had been badly damaged by a falling tree. Some panels had to be replaced, but much of it was salvageable – even the top skin for the

The Series I Oxford, *with original bodywork but new bulkhead and chassis.*

Both these 80in Series Is (pictured in the Alps) were restored for long-distance travel, using some later spec mechanical components but retaining the heavily patinated bodywork.

tropical roof. Making a 'perfect' repair is sometimes impossible, so under the right light there are places where you can see signs of the old damage, but this only adds to the vehicle's indi-

Many of the panels on this 107in Station Wagon have been straightened back into shape.

viduality and is arguably for the better. What matters more is the car's safeness and integrity, and the result was a good level of continuity and authenticity, with some financial savings. All the

Australian Series I, painted with details of an original owner.

fresh paint was applied with the cappings still in place.

In the case of Australian Series Is, often the name and region of an original owner will be found hand-painted on to the front wings. In some cases it would be a shame to paint over this and lose the sense of history. One of the project 109's front wings had the remains of some hand-painted lettering, but not in any particularly attractive way, so we had no qualms about painting over it.

At the opposite end of the spectrum is Ben's restoration of a 1948 Series I, which won the award for Best Restoration at the 2018 Series One Club National. Only the driver's side outer wing skin and rear tub outer side skins were replaced. All the other panels were chemically stripped, refinished and repainted to the best possible standard, and great care was taken to use period-correct fixtures and fittings.

So will you aim for factory-fresh perfection, or a patina restoration with as much original character as possible, or somewhere in between?

NEW METAL

The higher prestige given to 80in Series Is, and the larger budgets of those who restore them, has meant that the availability of new panels is much better for these earlier cars, compared to 1954-onwards Series Is. With a later car such as the project 109, it is much more likely that the restorer will have to 'make do and mend' when it comes to the bodywork – although some genuine new-old stock panels can occasionally be sourced.

When ordering new bodywork sections, it is sometimes easy to order the wrong part thanks to the frequent evolution of the Series I during production. For example, there were three types of lower tailgate designed just for 80in Series Is. A fourth type was fitted to both 86/88in, and another taller type was used for 107/109in vehicles. For a 107in Station Wagon, the lower tailgate is identical to the front-right door bottom, so the two are interchangeable. (On an 86in Station Wagon the hinge bracket is lower and the hinge itself is mounted upside-down.) The lower tailgate from a Series II or III can also be made to fit a 107in, as the aperture is the same.

Not all retailers are very clear about which item is which, so it helps to know the part number of what is needed.

Bear in mind that the availability of certain bodywork parts fluctuates, often due to small-scale manufacturers retiring. At the time of writing, there is a hiatus in the production of new 80in door tops, as the one current provider has recently stopped making them.

Extremely early Series I, battered and broken, as found in a barn after thirty years.

The same car, restored by co-author Ben to factory-correct 1948 specification, with a prize-winning finish.

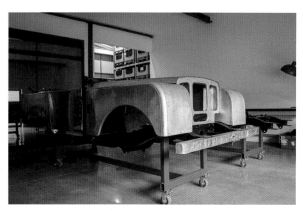

A full, new set of early 80in bodywork, made by CKD Shop.

LEFT: *The last set of new 80in door tops, pictured at CDK Shop.*

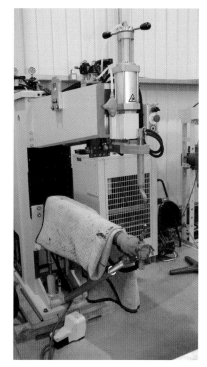

RIGHT: *Spotwelding machine used by CKD Shop to produce Series I bodywork.*

BIRMABRIGHT

The body panels of all Series I Land Rovers were made from Birmabright. This was an alloy of aluminium and magnesium, produced by Midlands-based firm Birmetals Ltd until the late 1970s. Birmabright alloys ranged from 1 to 7 per cent magnesium, and the grade supplied for Land Rovers was 2 per cent (known as BB2). This meets the Old British Standard 'N4'.

Birmabright was in widespread use during World War II, due to its combination of strength and lightness. According to legend, surplus stocks of cheap Birmabright in the aftermath of the war made the choice of material an obvious one for Rover – although this has been disputed by Arthur Goddard (the vehicle's original lead engineer from 1947), stating that it was chosen simply because it was the right material for the job.

Suppliers such as CDK Shop have greatly improved the availability of parts for 80in Series Is in particular, including numerous body parts in their catalogue of 650 parts (and counting). Although Birmabright is no longer made, alloys of an equivalent grade are available.

Alexander Massey, co-director of CKD Shop tells us that from 1949 onwards, the main panels all round the vehicle were standardized at 1.2mm, but thicker grades were used for various strengthening pieces, including parts of the seat box, and the tailgate was 1.5mm. Before 1949, panel thickness was much more variable from one vehicle to the next. 'We use 5000 Series aluminium that we've chemically matched to Birmabright, so it's as close as you can possibly get to the original with what's available today. If you tap the panels they'll sound how they should.'

Accurate reproduction of complete bodywork sections is a highly technical procedure, outside the scope of most restorers. One of the main difficulties is the requirement for spotwelding the metal, which requires specialist machinery.

A restoration to show-winning 'concours' standard will usually involve sending away the galvanized areas of the vehicle for hot-dip regalvanizing – primarily the cappings, door frames, front bumper and windscreen surround. However, this isn't always essential, and we are choosing not to do so for our 109's restoration. Regalvanizing results in a bright, gleaming finish that looks smart if 'showroom' freshness is your goal. But if you prefer to retain a sense of the vehicle's history and character, as is being done here, the mellower look of the original galvanizing may be preferable. The exception is when the galvanized coating has deteriorated to the point that

rust is showing through, but this is not particularly common.

Cappings that still retain a strong galvanized coating can withstand gentle scrubbing with a wire wheel to restore some of their original lustre, which is what is done with all the exposed galvanized areas of this 109. It is important not to be too aggressive while doing this, or the galvanizing may be worn down and the steel exposed beneath.

If the cappings are to be regalvanized, the rivets holding them in place will need to be drilled out, and then sent off as a job lot to a galvanizing specialist. Select the specialist carefully, as not all galvanizers create a high-quality finish.

RIVETS

Using the 'correct' type of rivets is a common topic of debate. Around the bodywork there will be a combination of dome-headed solid rivets and a type of pop rivet with a nickel-copper alloy body – similar to a so-called 'aero' rivet – with a slightly larger hole than regular pop rivets. The alloy body of this latter type reduces the likelihood of galvanic corrosion occurring as a result of the juxtaposition of the steel mandrel with the aluminium metal around it. Although ordinary aluminium pop rivets are often used in place of the superior nickel-copper 'aero' type, they will look out of place to an experienced eye. (Pop rivets are also known as 'blind' rivets because they

can be installed without you being able to see or access the rear of the panel.)

Semi-tubular domed rivets with a slightly smoother contour than the solid rivets were used in applications such as the door seals.

As a rule, dome-headed solid rivets were used when access to the reverse was possible, and the nickel-copper pop rivets were used elsewhere. However, Land Rover was not always consistent about this, as can be seen from the two photos of the rear corners of two 80in Series Is. One was assem-

Left to right: *A standard aluminium pop rivet; an aero-style pop rivet; a solid rivet as found round the galvanized cappings; a semi-tubular rivet (used for door seals).*

All the galvanized cappings of this 109 were scrubbed with a wire wheel.

The same rivets arrayed in the same order, showing their opposite sides.

Note the different arrangements of rivets.

Rivet block or 'bucking bar', used when installing solid rivets.

bled at Solihull, the other in Australia – notice the different arrangement of dome-headed solid rivets and aero rivets.

This is why it is important to make a photographic record of rivets used before removing any, so the same pattern can be replicated upon reassembly. (This is primarily relevant when removing external bodywork pieces such as galvanized cappings.) Many restorations have used widely available aluminium pop rivets in place of the more correct aero-style versions, whose collars have a slightly different profile, but replicating a Land

Black split rivets, commissioned by CKD Shop.

Bifurcated rivets along the bonnet strip of a recent restoration by CKD Shop.

Rover's original rivets will add a highly visible layer of authenticity to a restoration.

Other rivets include split ('bifurcated') rivets made from brass, used, for example, along the bonnet strip. Although some restorers use bare brass rivets, originally these all had a black coating.

When disassembling, pop rivets can be drilled out using a 4.8mm (or $^3/_{16}$in) HSS drill bit. Using a 5mm bit will remove the surrounding metal, resulting in a slacker and weaker join when the rivet is replaced.

Dome-headed rivets will need to be drilled out, which takes patience to avoid the drill bit slipping on the curved surface. Once a hole has been drilled through the centre they can be knocked off with a chisel.

Pop rivets can be installed using a hand-held riveter, or with a pneumatic riveter. Avoid cheap hand-held versions with short arms, as these are hard work if there are a large number of rivets to install.

When installing solid rivets, a metal block or 'bucking bar' will be needed to hold against the back of them, for the rivet gun to push against. The steel block pictured is made for the purpose; its faces comprise various angles and lengths, which enable it to be fitted into a range of small spaces. This can be bought individually or as a kit, together with temporary panel-holding pins and a special tool to extract/

This type of hand-held riveter is unpleasant for jobs requiring a lot of riveting.

remove them. (*See* the bonnet refurbishment section later in this chapter for more about this kit.)

MAKING SIMPLE PANELS

Series I panels are mostly comprised of quite simple shapes, so it can be worth making your own where replacements are required. Any folds tend to be 90 degrees, which helps keep things simple. New panels can be made from 2mm aluminium, which is slightly thicker than the original Birmabright but has the advantage of therefore being a little stronger.

Slotted holes for fixings (on panels whose position is designed to be adjustable) can be replicated by drilling two holes and then using a file to merge them together. Care must be taken to ensure the holes are the correct distance apart, taking into account any widening of the original slot caused by wear or corrosion. To determine the distance apart that the two holes must be drilled, determine the desired length of the slot, then subtract from it the diameter of your drill bit; the result is the distance between the points where the drill tip must begin making its holes.

A right-angle can be achieved simply by folding the sheet of aluminium over the corner of a bench, but a much neater result will be achieved using a vice-mounted or bench-mounted folder. As noted earlier (*see* the front panel repair section) this may not be appropriate if the folded section needs to sit within another folded section, as the radius of the folds might not match – in other words, the external radius of one fold may be smaller than the internal radius of the fold it is meant to sit inside. If the radius of the fold is critical,

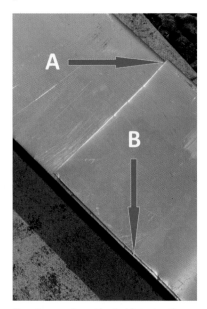

These two panels are identical, but when the internal diameter of the top panel is laid on to the outside diameter of the bottom panel (A), the bottom panel can be seen to protrude further (B). This is the margin of error that will occur if replicating the outside diameter of a curve.

a specialist firm will need to be commissioned to make the fold.

Folds introduce another complexity that may catch out a novice. When trying to replicate an existing folded section, measure the dimensions of the inside faces, and copy these on to the new sheet. It is a mistake to trace the outline of one side of the old section on to a new piece of metal and then roll the section along its folded edge before tracing the outline of the next face; if you do this, the new piece of metal will be too large. This is because you will have included the exterior radius of the original panel, where the metal was stretched when it was folded. Instead, the dimensions to replicate should come from the opposite face of the panel.

FRONT PANEL REPAIR

The remainder of this chapter is devoted to some of the specific repairs that the project 109 required.

All Series I front panels up to 1957 were Birmabright. Later Series front panels are made of steel and tend to rust conspicuously. There has been some debate over exactly when steel front panels superseded aluminium, as production of steel and aluminium

versions appears to have overlapped, but the project vehicle is quite a late 109in Series I, so its front panel is made of steel.

Aluminium front panels suffer less corrosion than steel versions, but it does happen. The more common problem is fracturing, especially in Series Is from Australia. The panels can sometimes be crudely repaired from behind using aluminium angle, and surface corrosion may be treated by skimming with filler, but in most cases it will be best to replace the panel altogether. At the time of writing, the only Series I front panels available to buy new are for 80s.

Steel front panels are easier to weld and repair. The demo 109 is a typical example, with significant corrosion around its lower areas as moisture collects in between the front section and the strengthening strip that runs behind it. Severe rust in the upper areas of the panel is less common. Restoration of rust in this area is typically fiddly and time consuming, but is the way to go if the aim is to retain as much of the original vehicle as possible, as here.

The original front panel, needing work.

The project 109's radiator was made in Australia, and is being sent off for recoring (possibly not for the first time).

Before any welding can take place, the panel needs to be stripped of its radiator and headlamp units.

It may be necessary to grind off the screws holding the radiator cowl to the radiator, but be careful not to damage the cowl itself. This late, pressed type would be expensive and difficult to source if a replacement were needed, although the earlier type made from folded sections is more available. In the demo 109, after the cowl is unscrewed from the back of the radiator, a plaque can be seen on the rear of the fins. It says that the radiator is 'a product of National Radiators, MFG PTY LTD Australia', which suggests that this unit has been recored at some stage, but it will need doing again. The radiator is then unbolted from the front panel.

The headlamps are removed by first unscrewing the retaining bezels. This is the time to inspect the chrome surface on the inside of the headlamp more closely. If it's corroded, as is the project 109's, it's no good. The headlamp can now be twisted off its adjuster screws, pulled out of the bowl (this one contained some Aussie spiders...) and unplugged from its wiring.

The bowls can then be unscrewed from the panel. There's no need to undo the three spring-loaded beam-adjuster screws in order to do this.

Note the rust inside the lamp, which means it needs replacing.

Unscrewing the bowls from the panel.

Flipped on to its front, it can be seen that the worst of the rust is along its bottom edge.

Shotblasted front panel, with perforations exposed further using a linishing wheel.

Rotten inner skin, sliced out of the front panel. This needs to be done carefully.

As can be seen, the inner skin is severely corroded, but there's just

The new repair section sitting in place.

enough of the outer (front) layer to keep. The plan is therefore to replace the inner layer with a sheet of new metal, and to keep the outer layer but repair its holes.

The first step is to slice out the inner layer, using a slitting disc on a grinder. This requires accuracy to prevent damaging the outer skin, and to result in clean lines that can be neatly replicated by the new metal.

The new piece of metal was folded for us by a local engineering firm (costing £30 at the time of writing), because the outer radius of the fold needs to

match that of the internal radius of the fold on the original outer skin. If this is not matched correctly, the new metal won't sit snugly into the original section. When asking for any work such as this to be done, make sure the engineer knows that the radius of the return is important. It's a good idea to give them the front panel so they can determine this radius for themselves.

The new section has the same width along the bottom as the original, plus a tab at each end, and it extends up to the large aperture in the panel. It is clamped into place while the three mounting holes along the lower edge are drilled out, after which it is ready to be welded into place.

Turning the panel on to its back, the front skin can now be repaired by welding small pieces of new metal into the holes, after first tidying up the rough edges with a small cutting wheel. Letting in such small and irregular sections of new metal is a messy-looking process, but it soon improves once the welds are ground smooth using a flap disc. Any remaining blemishes should be small enough to disappear after the

Adding a bottom mounting hole to the new section of metal.

The perforated lower edge with the new metal now welded in behind it.

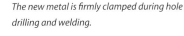

The new metal is firmly clamped during hole drilling and welding.

The outer skin, with the new metal let into the perforations, and ground down.

application of a small skim of filler or high-build primer.

FRONT WING REPAIR

Wing damage is common on Series Land Rovers of any age, especially on the passenger side. Both wings of the demo 109 were badly battered, and very close to being beyond repair. If we were aiming for a prize-winning finish, the sensible option would be to replace sections of them with new panels. But to illustrate what is possible, it was decided to rescue them and to get them looking as good as we could. This involved beating out the dents as accurately as possible, and restoring the original contours with the careful use of filler. In one section it also involved creating a concealed strengthening section to reinforce an area of torn metal. It wasn't quick, but the result has a much more authentic feel, and it saved some money.

Wings from 80s and 86s are interchangeable with each other, but they are different, as the inner wing of an 86 is made up of two pieces, whereas an 80 is one longer piece. Changes were also made to the wings of 88/109 Series

Is, which were lengthened between the bulkhead and the arch to accommodate the longer chassis. At the time of writing, new wings for 80in vehicles are around £700 each, while wings for 88/109in Series Is are unavailable, so the only alternative in this case would have been second-hand wings, which might also have needed some degree of repair.

The first job is to sand down the wing to remove all the paint. This reveals the full extent of the damage, along with any hidden imperfections caused by corrosion, and gives a stable surface for the later addition of filler and paint.

Most dents can be removed simply by tapping from behind using a ball-peen bodywork hammer. Lots of little taps will be more successful than a few big hits, but you will need to be relatively firm if the dents are deep – as they are here. Spread the hits over the complete area of the dent rather than focusing all the blows at one point. Tap as gently as possible but as firmly as necessary. In our case it was not necessary to heat the metal first, but if the Birmabright has become too brittle (or if you are concerned about how hard you are having to hit the metal) then warming the panel will intro-

The same wing, after DA sanding, showing a typical dent.

duce some malleability back into it. An electric heat gun will be gentler on the metal than a blowtorch.

The dent is repeatedly tapped from behind using a bodywork hammer.

This bodywork hammer with a small ball-peen end knocked out most of the dents for this restoration.

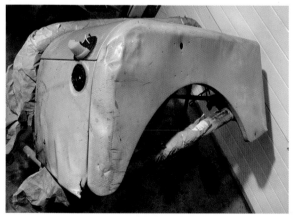

The left-hand wing, before sanding. Note the split at the bottom left corner, which needs considerable work.

The much reduced dent is now ready for filler.

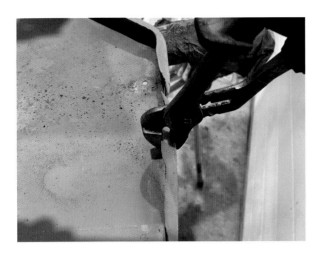

Adjustable grips are used to pull this buckled section back into shape.

Metal stretches when a dent is formed, so it will never go back exactly to its original shape. It is therefore important not to try to raise the deepest part until it is flush with the original contour, because if you do so, the metal surrounding the dent will be pushed too high – so stop before this happens. Spread the tapping round the dented area, and aim to bring it all as close as possible to the original profile. The remaining indentation can then be sculpted smooth with filler.

The 109's wing had also received some damage along the lower edge of the outer skin. The metal was carefully manipulated back into shape using a pair of adjustable grips; by pulling the metal in stages, changing the position of the grips each time, it was possible to avoid concentrating the stretch on one particular spot. The metal doesn't tear very easily, though it rarely goes back into exactly the right shape.

The front of the wing was very badly damaged – torn along its bottom, with a concealed steel plate roughly riveted to the rear face to hold it together. Ideally we would have sourced a new front panel and riveted it into the wing, but these were not available at the time. The repair involved drilling out the steel plate and knocking the metal as straight as possible with a hammer. The plate was then replaced with a length of aluminium angle, bonded along the bottom edge with Tiger Seal, and countersunk rivets were added on both sides of the tear, to strengthen the bond. The panel was clamped tightly between the angle and a metal bar while the Tiger Seal dried, which helped to straighten its profile.

Once the Tiger Seal had set, the protruding edge of the new metal was trimmed to make it flush with the bottom lip of the wing. The line was first drawn with a pen and ruler to help ensure a straight edge – always good practice – then gently filed to remove any burrs.

The finished result is strong again, and after a skim of filler, it will look perfectly tidy. This is an unconventional but workable repair that has reintroduced strength to the wing. If you are doing something similar, always make sure the repair is strong, safe and preferably discreet.

The repaired front wings then received a skim of filler, which smoothed out the remaining low spots and helped to rebuild the compound curve of the outer wing skins, especially for the left-hand side.

Some of the spotwelds had been previously replaced with rivets, where the inside edge of the front panel meets the inner wing. (Presumably the original welds had been broken.) The

Clamps and a flat wrench hold the front against the aluminium angle bonded in behind it.

Angle grinder cutting the excess off the angle to line it up with the bottom of the wing edge.

Left-hand wing before renovation. The old paint was a nice original feature which unfortunately had to be lost during painting.

Filler has been applied to the wing's low spots, and smoothed down, ready for etch primer.

The wing after application of high-build primer. Note the rivets in place of the original spotwelds.

rivets were weakened during our initial sanding, and became loose as the damaged metal was reshaped, so they were replaced before the final coat of primer was added.

After priming, the wing is finally sprayed with two coats of Dove Grey.

The left-hand wing received a similar treatment, but its damage was less severe. There was a ding in the front section that had caused a slight crack along the bottom, but nothing that couldn't be tapped out and improved with filler.

SEAT-BOX REPAIR

Whole sections of a Series I seat box rarely need to be replaced, unlike Series IIs and IIIs, which are more likely to suffer from corrosion around this area. The seat boxes of Australian Series Is are usually in better condition that those from the UK.

However, one quite common failure of Series Is of 86in onwards relates to the strengthening gusset on the

driver's side. Where the gusset mounts to the Birmabright, a combination of metal fatigue and corrosion causes the Birmabright to break away. The spotwelds along some of the seat box's seams can also fracture. The 109's seat box has both of these problems, so they need to be fixed before any painting can be done. (On the opposite side, the rigidity provided by the storage area under the seat prevents these problems, but on the driver's side the fuel tank takes the place of the storage area.)

Throughout these repairs, the seat box remains attached to the sills and the rear bulkhead, which act as a jig to hold the seat box rigid. This is useful because the seat box loses much of its rigidity when separated, and it needs to be held perfectly square while repairs are made.

Fortunately the broken piece of metal at the back of the seat box hadn't been lost, so it could be reinstated. First a small plate of aluminium is cut, which will sit underneath the broken area to

reinforce it. The fragment is bonded to the plate, and the plate is then riveted to the seat box with four original-style nickel-copper pop rivets.

The strengthening gusset on the driver's side that often breaks away.

Spotwelds have broken off on the edge of the seat box.

The seat box, still attached to the rear bulkhead.

The broken Birmabright, and the plate that will be used to repair it.

After the repair. The original fragment is bonded to the plate.

the original spec the period-correct bolts with their dished top will need to be used, and these are comparatively expensive. The domed versions are the floor screws fitted to Series IIs and IIIs, but their smoother shape makes them less likely to damage trim when removing or installing seats, so they

Unscrewing the seat box from the sills.

Where the spotwelds have broken along the vertical joins at the front corners of the seat box, strength is restored by drilling out the broken welds with a $^3/_{16}$in drill bit, and replacing them with pop rivets.

In the unlikely event that a seat box does need complete replacement sections to be added, the spotwelds that hold the damaged panel in place will need to be drilled out, the panel

replaced with a brand new section, holes added in the new panel where the old spotwelds were, and the new metal riveted in place – while leaving the seat box attached to the rear bulkhead and sills so that it can act as a jig.

Once the repairs are made, the seat box is separated from the rear bulkhead and the sills, in preparation for painting. Smaller pieces are also removed, such as the door strikers and the attached gussets that brace the rear bulkhead against the B-pillar.

Domed screws have been chosen for the seat-box lids, but to replicate

The corner of the seat box, where the original spotwelds had failed.

There is only mild corrosion beneath the seat-box hinges.

The coarse-threaded bolt that goes into a spire nut on the bulkhead, attaching the back of the seat box at the B-pillar. This is the same fixing that is used for the floor panels and the middle seat-box lid.

Removing the striker plate off the bulkhead.

New rivets being added to replace the spotwelds.

The bracing section for the rear bulkhead is unbolted prior to painting.

are arguably more suitable for this application. Their coarse Acme thread is the same for both types, and they screw into the same types of spire nut that will be found on Series IIs and IIIs.

PAINTING

Almost all the paint had bleached off much of the project vehicle in the hot Australian sun, so the bare metal was exposed in various areas, and the entirety of the vehicle required fresh paint. UK cars are more likely to have paint that is flaky and scratched, rather than bleached off altogether, and multiple layers of old paint will often be found beneath it.

If a 'concours' restoration is desired, this would typically involve detaching all the galvanized cappings and respraying each component individually. However, simply masking over them can result in a perfectly good finish if this is done carefully, so the extra work of removing the cappings is often difficult to justify. For this rebuild the decision was made to detach many of the panels (such as the seat box, and the bonnet parts have been stripped) but to leave the cappings in place.

Painting is a skill that takes practice to perfect, especially using a spray gun. If you are aiming for a perfect finish that holds up to scrutiny at close range, but you have never resprayed a vehicle before, it is advisable to send the panels to a paint shop for a professional respray. This is a perfectly valid option that is chosen by many professional restorers. However, if you follow the right procedure and get some practice first, you can achieve a perfectly good and durable finish yourself, and you will help keep your costs down – but it must be noted that two-pack is very unsafe and requires protective clothing, including an air-fed mask (government safety guidance on the usage of two-pack paints can be found at www.hse.gov.uk).

Whether you apply the final coats of paint yourself or not, you will want to prepare the surfaces as best you can. Good preparation is everything when it comes to repainting bodywork, and it should not be underestimated how long it takes to do this properly. A clean, well ventilated and dust-free environment is required, and one that is not too cold (in order for the paint to dry).

The overall process can be broken down into six stages: sanding, cleaning and de-greasing, masking, etch priming, applying high-build primer, and lastly two coats of 2k ('two-pack') paint.

Sanding

Sanding removes any loose paint, and creates a bare-metal surface for the new primer or filler to adhere to. Medium or medium-fine grit paper – around 80 or 120 grit is ideal at this stage – and a dual action (DA) or random orbital (RO) sander is best suited to this work. Slow-speed settings are for polishing, but a fast-speed setting is needed for efficient sanding.

For those intending to buy a sander, be aware that some air-powered sanders, as opposed to battery-powered models, consume a lot of air, so are best suited to large compressors, which a domestic workshop might not have.

The finished surface must be totally smooth, so you will need to run your fingers over it, and to have good light to spot any flaws. It is not always necessary to remove every last remnant of old paint, so long as what remains is firmly attached and has no defined edges.

For the 109 restoration, the wings, doors, bulkhead, seat box and all sec-

A large and robust sander will be required.

Dash panel sanded and ready for priming.

The roof being sanded.

tions of the cab were dismantled and painted separately. This included the seat box with its lids removed, and the smaller components such as the securing plate round the handbrake gaiter: everything was detached and prepared, primed and painted separately.

Cleaning and Degreasing

The surfaces then need to be clean and grease-free with no dust. A solvent-based panel degreaser, also known as panel wipe, is applied with a clean cloth to remove any remaining residue of contaminants.

Panel degreaser, important but often overlooked.

The top rear section of the cab is sanded and prepped, ready for masking.

Masking

Masking tape is applied over any galvanized capping or other areas that must not be painted. It pays to be careful with this part of the process, and to ensure that the tape goes right up to the very edge of the metal you intend to spray. For larger areas, a combination of masking tape with masking paper can be used – although in our case this wasn't required. Avoid using newspaper as the ink may contaminate the panel.

The instrument panel after priming.

The rear of the cab, sanded, with the galvanized cappings masked off.

Etch Priming

Etch primer is acidic, its purpose being to eat into the surface of the metal and so give a stronger bond for the next layer. It only needs a light coat for the next layer of primer to adhere to, and

The roof in yellow etch primer.

The front panel in etch primer, ready for high-build primer, then top coat.

there is no need to sand it down afterwards.

All external body panels are painted on the outside only. Their hidden areas, such as the wheel arches and the underside of the bonnet, were left unpainted by Solihull throughout Series Land Rover production, although there was often a little overspray inside the wheel arches, which some restorers choose to replicate for added authenticity.

Smaller, detachable items, such as dashboard accessory panels, are primed and painted separately using etch primer in an aerosol can – usually grey, rather than the yellow primer for the spray gun.

High-Build Primer

Two coats of high-build (or 'high solids') two-pack primer are sprayed over each section of bodywork, which helps create a smooth finish over any rough or dimpled areas. In between each coat of high-build primer, the surface is very gently flatted down using 400-grit paper to highlight any low spots that might need addressing – either by

The accessory panel for the period ashtray (non-standard), masked and etch primed.

tapping from behind or simply with a little more filler. (This applies primarily to already painted metal.)

Take care to ensure that the paint is fully dry before any sanding is done. Once any imperfections have been addressed, the second coat of high-build primer is added. When dry, it is gently flatted down again, this time with 800-grit wet and dry, which gives a smooth finish and a good key for the first layer of paint.

Two Coats of 2k ('Two-Pack') Paint

The gun should be held approximately 30cm (12in) away from the panel, moving steadily from left to right and back again. It is important to wait until the gun has passed beyond the edge of the panel before releasing the trigger.

The first layer, once dry, is again sanded with 400-grit paper to provide a key for the final layer.

The fully stripped bonnet, DA sanded, and about to receive primer.

The bonnet after one light coat of etch primer.

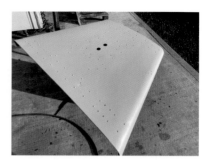

The bonnet after two coats of 2k, drying in (not too hot) sunlight.

The fresh paint will be polished later, but this will be left to the end of the restoration in case any scratches occur between now and then.

FINAL FITTINGS

After painting, any small components removed earlier will need to be reattached. The bonnet is a prime example, as it involves replacing the hinges (bolted on), the spare-wheel carrier (riveted on) and the spring-loaded latch mechanisms. When reattaching items such as this, it is useful to have a solid riveting kit, which includes a bucking bar and a set of Cleco fasteners with their associated tool. Cleco fasteners act as temporary rivets, securing the sections firmly together while the actual rivets replace them one by one. The same principle applies when reassembling any galvanized cappings

(not a task that involved the 109 restoration).

Other small fitments on our vehicle included the VIN plate on the bulkhead (which is screwed on), the two grille clips on the front panel (pop rivets can be used, but to recreate correct original spec aluminium dome rivets must be used), clips for holding the starting handle and jack handle, and the reassembly of the detached parts of the seat box.

It is also necessary to assemble the doors, complete with door locks, seals, new glazing and new window channels (for both the door and the rear of the cab). These tasks are described in Chapter 15.

As for the Land Rover badge, the demo 109 has only one, on the front grille. This was in fairly good condition, but its appearance was revived by sanding it by hand, cleaning it, and

Cleco fastener held in its tool.

PAINTING WITH A ROLLER

Although it is difficult to get a perfect finish, a roller is more forgiving than a spray gun, so a decent (rather than an immaculate) finish is easier to achieve, with spray cans being used for the corners where a roller can't fit. Many Series Is have been painted this way. There are a few important things to consider before you start:

◆ Choose your roller. There are two types of sleeve: foam or fibre. Either can be used, but a smooth foam roller is best for smooth surfaces such as bodywork. There's no need for a very large roller – a 6in or 9in sleeve is big enough.
◆ Only use a good quality sleeve: some cheap foam sleeves can disintegrate when they come in contact with automotive paint, completely ruining the finish.
◆ Prepare the viscosity: if the paint is drying too fast for a good finish to be achieved, it is acceptable to use a small amount of thinner.
◆ Always make sure your roller is totally clean and dry before use: brushing it lightly with the adhesive side of sticky tape is one way to remove dust or hairs.

Effective use of a roller involves ensuring that the sleeve has absorbed some paint all the way round, before applying the roller to the bodywork. This is done by rolling it back and forth a few times in the paint in the tray. To achieve an even finish, apply the paint in a cross-hatch motion, rolling up and down as well as left to right.

Avoid laying on the paint too thickly (the same as when spraying). Moving with slow and gentle sweeps of the roller will prevent spatter and help create a smooth finish. When replenishing the roller in the paint tray, put a little pressure on it in the tray to squeeze out the excess, before applying the roller to the bodywork again.

LEFT AND RIGHT: *Solid riveting kit, with the last two remaining Cleco fasteners still in position.*

LEFT: *Pneumatic riveter used for the clips that secure the front grille.*

RIGHT: *The rear badge, which Ben repainted for a 1948 80in restoration.*

New clips to mount a starting handle are added behind the seats.

painting the black background with enamel paint and a fine brush. Various badges and colour schemes were fitted throughout Series I production, so it is worth researching which one is appropriate for your Land Rover. The 1948 model year used a cast-alloy badge with green and red paint; in 1949 these changed to green with yellow lettering; and from the 1954 model year the badge was pressed rather than cast, with black paint. Series I pressed badges say 'Birmingham', while Series II and III badges say 'Solihull'.

CHOOSING A TILT

For all Series Is, the canvas hood or 'tilt' comes in one large piece, whatever the design. Two UK suppliers (Exmoor Trim and Undercover Covers) can provide the full range of canvas trim, including associated items such as hood sticks (supporting hoops), fume curtains, chain covers, tool rolls, rope sets and so on. Some larger brands have also entered this part of the market in recent years, and it is worth making enquiries with other Series I owners before choosing which type to buy, as there are many different variants.

A tilt has to be chosen carefully. There are many different styles of tilt for an 80, depending on model year, with different sizes of window and different methods for lacing them up at the back. The design of the galvanized supporting sticks changed in mid-1949, and again with the introduction of the 86 to allow for the weather seal. 80 tilts were all khaki, but later Series I hoods could also be sand, green and blue. Some other colours are now available.

The lifespan of a canvas tilt on a vehicle that is kept outdoors is rarely more than around six years, so buying one second-hand is unlikely to be worthwhile, unless you find one that has not been exposed to the elements for very long. Repairing a damaged tilt is rarely practical, because the canvas becomes brittle with age and too weak to sustain the tension caused by new stitches. Pulling the thread tight tends to break the material, and the stitches may also introduce a weakness that can spread. However, it is sometimes worth replacing a plastic window if it becomes cloudy or perishes before the canvas; this involves unstitching the original and stitching the new window into position.

New canvas will shrink, and will continue doing so for years. The better manufacturers account for this, so the new tilt will initially be baggy. It is recommended that the canvas is wetted soon after fitting, preferably on a warm and dry day, which helps it to shrink more accurately into the desired shape. (Tailgate flaps tend to continue shrinking more than the sides, as they spend less of their life under tension.)

11

Building the Rolling Chassis

The time has now come to start reassembling the Land Rover. The process begins by creating a 'rolling chassis' – that is, a chassis with the suspension, axles and wheels attached. In this chapter the bulkhead will also be added to the rolling chassis.

The 109's swivels and hubs have not been restored in this chapter, even though we described this process in Chapter 6, because this project vehicle wasn't restored and photographed in the same order as the chapters in this book. The axles were in fact rebuilt after they were attached to the restored chassis, and you may choose to do the same. Adding the axles to the chassis as soon as possible has the advantage of making the whole assembly more mobile, while taking up less space. The downside is that, if serious flaws are discovered in the axle while it is being dismantled, it may be necessary to remove it from the chassis (together with the suspension components) all over again.

ATTACHING THE AXLES AND SPRINGS

The project chassis has been shot-blasted, repaired and painted, so it must now be prepared to receive the suspension. The spring mounting

bushes were burned out with a blowtorch when the chassis was stripped in Chapter 2, but their steel sleeves still remain, so when painting the chassis, the inside of the tube remains clean and free of paint. These sleeves need to be cut out of the chassis before the new bushes can be added. This can be done by pushing a hacksaw blade through the hole and reattaching it to the saw on the other side, then cutting through the sleeve. Once they have been cut all the way through, they will contract and it will be possible to drift them.

The front chassis bushes are removed from the chassis rail in similar fashion. Note that a Series I uses two bushes side by side in the same tube.

A rare set of new-old stock spring bushes has been sourced for this restoration. When deciding which way round they go, their slightly longer protruding end needs to face inboard. To push them into their holes, a bush removal/installation tool supplied by Laser, part number 6193, can be used; the tool is supposedly designed for Range Rover Sports, but it is also well suited to this application. It is essentially a basic type of press, with a threaded bar that is passed all the way through the chassis. As the nut on the thread (protruding left in our pictures) is

tightened, the shaft is held firm by the spanner on the right, as the cup pushes the bearing into the tube. The tool has an integral bearing to prevent the nut from grinding against the bush, and it can also be used to push two bushes in from opposite sides, as is required for the front spring bushes.

A complete set of new leaf springs is being fitted to this vehicle, which is quite common. Be careful to select the correct type of springs, as their specification varies depending on wheelbase, engine, body style, model year, and their position on the vehicle. Thus springs for 80in Series Is up to 1950 were 1¾in wide all round. For the 1951 model year the front springs became 2½in, and for the 1954 model year onwards all models received 2½in springs all round.

There are two ways to attach the axles and springs to the chassis. The first method is to attach the shackles to the chassis, and the rear ends of the leaf springs to the swing shackles; the axles can then be rolled into place and attached to the middle of the springs, and finally the front of the springs are attached to the chassis. This is the approach taken with the rear axle of the demo vehicle. The rear of the chassis can be hung by a sling beneath a forklift to give plenty of clearance.

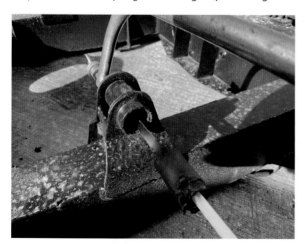

Using a hacksaw to cut the old bush sleeves out of the chassis.

Driving the sleeve out with a drift.

Failing a forklift the chassis will need to be propped up, but be sure to do this securely to prevent it from being jolted and falling as the axles are attached.

Note that the front springs on late model Series Is are offset beneath the chassis rails; they should be aligned so that they align with the outside edge of the chassis rail. This is achieved by orienting the shackles the correct way round: the one with the protruding boss goes on the inboard side, with the boss facing the spring (*see* picture). For all these suspension components it is important to use brand new fix- ings, especially for the locknuts, and to make sure they are done up securely.

The head of the bolt that runs through the middle of the springs acts as a dowel for correctly locating the axles on top of them – an important feature for ensuring correct alignment. Each dowel fits into a corresponding

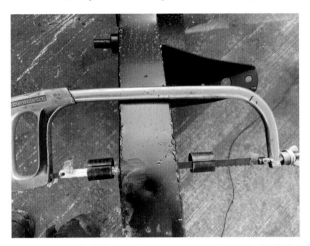

Front suspension bush sleeves – the two meet up against each other in the chassis.

New-old stock bushes for the front of the 109. The two bushes touch inside the chassis.

Bush tool being used on the rear spring bush.

The same tool pushing two bushes simultaneously for the front spring.

The correct position for the inner shackle boss for the front springs, which offsets the spring (prior to the addition of the shackle bolt).

The new rear springs are being mounted to the chassis rail, and the axle has been rolled into position ready to fit.

The rear spring shackles. The nuts and threaded shackle go on the inside, and the bolts go through from the outside.

The rolling chassis, ready to receive the shock absorbers.

The spring plate and U-bolts being fitted, with the new mounting plate for the brake pipe.

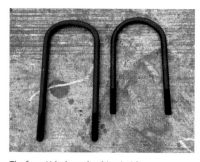

The front U-bolt on the driver's side.

hole in the spring saddle on the axle. The axle is fixed to the springs using new U-bolts and locknuts, and it is helpful to attach these before fixing the front of the springs to the chassis. The original bottom plates (cleaned and painted) are used here, but new brake-pipe mounting plates have been added, sandwiched between the spring and the axle. These plates attract mud and corrode easily, so anodized versions were bought, which were then painted black.

The rear U-bolts are all the same, but the U-bolts on the right-hand side of the front axle come in different lengths, and their curves follow slightly different contours to account for the taper of the axle casing. Be sure to order and fit the correct U-bolts for each position.

The alternative method of assembling the suspension is to mount the springs to the axle separately, with the axle upside down; this is the method used for the demo vehicle's front axle, purely for illustration purposes. Once complete, the assembly is flipped the correct way up, rolled under the chassis, and then bolted with its shackles to the chassis. It's a good idea to assemble the track rod at the same time, which enables the rolling chassis to be manually steered by pushing sideways on the front tyres. (The track rod and steering assembly will be discussed in Chapter 13.)

We now have the basics of a rolling chassis. The springs and axles are attached to the chassis, so they can all be rolled around together.

FINAL SUSPENSION COMPONENTS

With the springs and axles attached, now the remaining parts of the suspension need to be fitted, beginning with the new bump stops. Together with the check straps, these will limit the extremes of the suspension's travel. Bump stops help protect the chassis from damage from the axles during extreme suspension compression, and the check straps prevent the shock absorbers from attempting to rip the mounts out of the chassis during full rebound. (The fact that the 109's chassis top mounts had been damaged suggests that the vehicle had been driven off-road without check straps.)

The bump stops are notorious rust traps, so it is worth making extra sure that the chassis is rust protected in this area before adding them.

The front axle upside down, receiving its new suspension.

Next we fit the shock absorbers. (Technically these are dampers, but 'shock absorbers' is the more widely used term.) These are fitted with new bushes, and the top mounts also receive new mounting bolts.

The long bolts that secure the tops of the shock absorbers are fed through from the inside of the chassis rail, with their threaded ends pointing outwards. This is the way they were installed by Solihull, and it enables the shock absorbers to be replaced without the bolt being removed from the chassis – which will be useful if the bolt ever seizes into position.

Because there is very little weight compressing the springs at this stage, you might find that the shock absorbers will not extend far enough to reach the mounts – in which case you will need to compress the springs to bring the chassis and axles closer together. This can be achieved by wrapping a ratchet strap securely round the chassis rails and the bottom of the leaf springs, progressively tightening them until the bottom of the shock absorber can fit on to the mounting peg.

Once the bottoms of the shock absorbers are on, they are locked in place with a large washer and a new split pin. (80in and early 86in Series Is have a slightly different arrangement here involving a washer and a nut, as the mounting post for the bottom of the shock absorber is threaded.)

With the springs still compressed,

The new bump stops being added.

The top of a rear shock absorber being added.

The lower shock bushes come in two cone-shaped sections.

The ratchet strap compresses the spring so the shock absorber can be fitted.

The split pin is bent over to complete the lower shock bush assembly.

Check straps prevent the spring from articulating too far (80in Series I pictured).

Wheels and tyres.

'ROK Australia' stamped into the wheels of the demo 109.

the new check straps are bolted in place, and then the springs are decompressed by removing the ratchet straps.

One of the final stages is adding the check straps round the axles. These are often ignored, but they are important for preventing the shock absorbers from over-expanding when the leaf spring reaches full articulation (which usually only happens off-road). This could damage the shock absorbers and their mounting points.

There is also the option of fitting parabolic springs, which offer better ride quality and slightly more articulation than standard leaf springs. The process for installation is the same, but long-travel shock absorbers should be selected to go with them.

WHEELS AND TYRES

All Series I wheels are 16in in diameter, but there were three possible widths, and the width will determine which tyres can be fitted. The width of the earliest wheels in 1948 was 4.5in, which changed to 5in during the second year of production. Land Rover now offers genuine remakes of both of these (the part numbers are 217629 and 231601 respectively). Late long-wheelbase models such as the project vehicle used 5.5in wheels, offset on the inside; the wheels on early 107s were 5in wide.

Split rims, also known as 'combat'

rims, are designed for ease of tyre fitting, and were fitted mainly to military Series Is. They are bolted together rather than welded, so the tyre can be changed by undoing the ring of bolts that unite the two halves of the wheel.

If restoring an Australian Series I it is likely you will come across ROK-made wheels, which are the same as the UK's Dunlop version, but made in Australia from 1953 and stamped 'ROK Australia'.

For short-wheelbase models, the wheels are generally painted the same colour as the body, but there are complex variations – for example, 86s and 107s with grey bodywork would have had a blue chassis and blue wheels if built for the 1954 model year; from the 1955 model year onwards they were black.

According to the old system of measurement, tyres were assumed to have an aspect ratio of 1:1, meaning the height of the tyre is roughly the same as the nominal width (from sidewall to sidewall, rather than across the tread). Therefore the 6.00 tyres that were standard on 86in Land Rovers are 6in tall and 6in wide. Also available were 6.50 and 7.00 tyres, the latter being standard on all long-wheelbase Series Is.

The standard tyres of the period

were Avon TMs (Traction Mileage) or Dunlop RK3 or T28s. Other Dunlop treads were also offered.

The choice of tyre makes a significant aesthetic difference to the overall impression of the vehicle, but the intended usage should also be taken into consideration. Choosing an original tread pattern and tyre size (where available) will add authenticity to a restoration, but the most historically accurate parts will not result in the best drivability compared with more modern alternatives, and they won't offer the best possible traction (on-road or off-road).

7.50 tyres were chosen for the demo 109: these are more affordable than period sizes and are available in a wider range of treads and brands (these can't be fitted to the narrower rims used on short-wheelbase vehicles). Although 7.50s were never originally fitted to Series Is, Land Rover did use this size on 5.5in rims for later models. Being

All-terrain 7.50 tyres chosen for the 109.

radials, these tyres are more forgiving on the road than the original crossply type, and their taller dimensions give slightly higher gearing. It was felt that this added usability was appropriate given the style of restoration the vehicle was receiving.

Tyres that have been fitted to a Land Rover for more than ten years are usually on borrowed time, but this depends on how they have been looked after. If they are kept well topped up with air, and are on a vehicle that is kept indoors (away from sunlight, which causes degradation) and rarely used, or not fitted to a vehicle at all, they can last longer.

Modern 205/80 mud-terrain tyres (fitted to an 80). This is a practical choice if originality is less important than off-road performance.

ADDING THE BULKHEAD

Fitting the bare bulkhead to the rolling chassis is straightforward, but obviously a second pair of hands will be needed to lift it, or the use of a forklift. The bulkhead does not have to be fitted at this stage – for example, you may choose to add the engine and gearbox first while the bulkhead is out of the way. However, engine and gearbox can be added to the chassis with the bulkhead already in situ. If the bulkhead is added first it gives more flexibility for adding parts to it, as and when these become available.

Note that a fabricated Series I bulkhead such as the demo 109's sits in front of the bulkhead outriggers, whereas the earlier pressed bulkheads fitted to 80s sit behind the outriggers.

The first fixings to be attached are the long bolts that secure the bulkhead's 'feet' to the chassis outriggers. For Series Is these were always inserted from the rear, with the threads pointing forwards (but they were fitted the opposite way round for Series IIs). The precise forward/back position of the bulkhead may require adjustment later on, which is accomplished by adding or removing washers to these bolts between the bulkhead and the outrigger. The demo vehicle did not have spacer washers here, so it was reassembled without any. Your Land Rover may be different, and almost all 80in Series Is were built with one spacer per side. In any case, don't fully tighten the nut on the bolt at this stage, as it will have to be undone later if alignment tweaks are needed.

This bulkhead did not require any spacer washers between the bulkhead and outriggers…

… but almost all 80s left the factory with one spacer washer, as did this Australian vehicle (awaiting restoration).

The bulkhead brackets are also added to the chassis and bolted to the front of the bulkhead. These enable a certain amount of adjustment in the tilt of the bulkhead, which will probably be needed when finer adjustments have to be made later on, so the bolts are only loosely tightened. The pressed steel bulkhead of an 80in Series I does not have these separate brackets (they are effectively integral to the bulkhead), so less adjustment is possible.

At the bottom of the bulkhead brackets, the bolt at the front is unique, with a curved shape to prevent any damage to the tyre if it rubs against it.

New wiring harness bought from Autosparks, part number LR108L.

Bulkhead bracket – note that the bolt with the rounded head goes at the front.

The front-to-back harness is pulled out through this hole, just in front of the rear crossmember.

One of the lower bolts for the bulkhead's front brackets, cleaned and painted.

BASIC WIRING HARNESS INSTALLATION

In most cases it's sensible to budget for a complete new wiring harness (or 'loom') for the extra reliability, longevity and smartness it provides. Corrosion makes the wires brittle and impedes the flow of current, especially at the terminals, where some green crustiness might be noticed. There's no reason why the wires shouldn't be replaced one by one, but buying a ready-made loom is cost effective and

will save a lot of hassle. These are available from Autosparks with braided sheathing that replicates the look and feel of the original.

Most of the work involving the wiring loom is covered later in the rebuild process (*see* Chapter 17), but there is one initial phase that is much easier to do now, while the chassis is still exposed.

A front-to-back harness delivers power to the rear lights, and it needs to pass through the chassis, inside the chassis rails. The original harness was left inside the chassis during shotblasting and painting, because it can now be of help when threading the new harness through. This is done by securely taping the back of the new harness to the front of the old, and

gently pulling the old loom backwards through the chassis until the new harness emerges at the rear.

If a chassis is new, or doesn't already have any wires passing through it, a length of brake pipe can be used to feed the new harness into place. Push the pipe all the way down the inside of the chassis, with the new harness taped or hooked to its rear end. Extract the pipe at the rear, and the new wires should now be in place. New rubber grommets must now be fitted to the holes to prevent the cable sheath from chafing against the chassis. In all Series Land Rovers (and Defenders), the wiring enters the chassis in front of the bulkhead, runs down the right-hand chassis rail, and exits just before the rear crossmember.

12

Installing the Drivetrain

The engine and gearbox can now be added to the rolling chassis. In this chapter some associated tasks will also be addressed, such as adding the exhaust, propshafts and the fuel system.

INSTALLING THE GEARBOX AND ENGINE

New gearbox mounts are bolted to the chassis, then the gearbox, bellhousing, transfer box and handbrake drum assembly is lowered into them as a complete assembly. In our case a forklift did the heavy lifting, but an engine crane is a perfectly good alternative. The gearbox should not be bolted to its mounts yet, for reasons we will come to.

Before lowering the engine into the chassis and marrying it up to the bellhousing, part of the clutch mechanism ought to be fitted inside the bellhousing. Although this can be done with the engine attached (by reaching through the little aperture for the clutch arm) it is easier to do in advance.

Gather the clutch shaft with its two collars and pins ready for assembly. The shaft will not need to be attached yet, but laying it out – as pictured – with its associated components will help you work out which parts to fit into the bellhousing. The smaller collar goes on the smooth end of the shaft which enters the bell housing. The pins at this end are shorter than the single pin for the larger collar at the splined end of the shaft.

Clutch shaft and associated parts. The small collar is at the bellhousing end.

The main component to fit at this stage is the small collar that fits over the input shaft on the right-hand side of the gearbox. It's held in place with a pin, then the washer is added to the pin, followed by a new split pin to hold it together. Once fitted, add a new grommet to weatherproof the aperture. (The remainder of the clutch linkage assembly will be described in Chapter 14.)

The engine can now be put in. If the bulkhead is already mounted to the chassis (as the 109's is), the engine must be lowered into place and bolted to the bellhousing before the two engine mounts are added to the chassis. This is because the shape of the bulkhead requires the engine to be quite low before it will align with the gearbox – lower than the engine mounts will allow.

Once the engine is lowered into place, it is carefully lined up with the gearbox. This requires the splines on the first motion shaft to align with those on the clutch friction plate, which is achieved by putting the gearbox into gear to hold the first motion

shaft still, then rotating the crankshaft via the front pulley until the splines

View inside the bellhousing, showing the collar attached with its pin, washer and split pin.

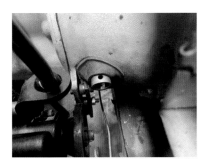

Collar protruding through the new grommet on the outside of the bellhousing.

The fully assembled engine is lowered into place prior to fitting the engine mounts.

can slot together. Once they are married, the gearbox's bellhousing can be bolted to the flywheel housing with new fixings (no gasket is involved).

Some space now needs to be created between the engine and the chassis, in order to slide the engine mounts into position. This requires the engine to be lifted just a few inches. It will bring the gearbox with it, which is why the gearbox must not yet be bolted to

its mounts. The 109's engine needed to be pushed slightly to one side using a length of wood, to provide clearance for the right-hand engine mount.

Once the mounts are in place, the engine is slowly lowered on to them – which takes careful precision. The mounts are secured using new locknuts, top and bottom, and the engine can then be released from its crane/forklift.

Engine mounts on an 80in are slightly different, as they aren't angled inwards, but the same issue applies to installation: if the bulkhead is already in place, the engine needs to be bolted to the gearbox first, then raised to allow clearance for the mounts to be added.

The main components of the drivetrain are all now in situ and ready to be filled with oil. The engine oil should

The two engine mounts are the same part number, but the right one has its own mount, while the other sits directly on a tab coming off the chassis.

The left-hand engine mount being attached to the chassis.

The right-hand mount on its bracket, ready to receive new locknuts.

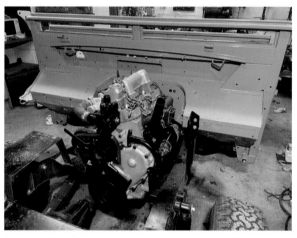

The refurbished engine attached, and released from the forklift – a satisfying milestone.

Engine mounts for an 80in are of this different design.

Fresh engine oil being added.

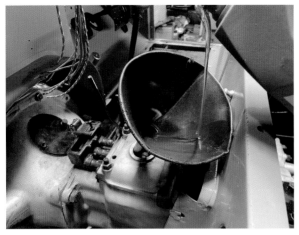

Oil being added through the top of the gearbox.

Adding fresh oil to the transfer box.

Transfer box oil is added through this plug on the rear side.

Adding fresh oil to the rear axle.

be 20w/50 mineral oil; any oil of this grade by a well-known manufacturer is likely to be appropriate, especially if it is branded as being a 'classic' oil.

The gearbox, transfer box and axle differentials all require GL4 EP90. Unlike later Series vehicles, the Series I gearbox has a dipstick to determine the correct oil level, and is filled with fresh oil through the top. However, the correct level of the transfer box oil is determined by the level plug behind the handbrake drum. The bung is removed while fresh oil is added from the top, and added as soon as the fresh oil starts to trickle through it.

The front axle oil is added through the level plug on the front of the differential, while the rear oil is filled through the plug on the nose of the differential.

PROPSHAFTS

A new rear propshaft needed to be sourced for the project 109 because the splines on the sliding joint were worn beyond economic repair. Series I propshafts are interchangeable with those fitted to later Series Land Rovers, so long as the chosen shaft is designed for a Rover axle rather than a Salisbury axle. In most cases, in all other Series Is, the propshafts are interchangeable with those specified for later Series Land Rovers, the length of the shaft being the governing factor.

◆ An 86in Series I has the same propshafts front and back, and these are equivalent to the rear propshaft of an 88in.
◆ A 107in rear propshaft is the same as a 109in rear.
◆ An 80in front propshaft is the same as an 88in rear.
◆ An 80in rear propshaft is the only propshaft that is unique. These are the most difficult to source, and may therefore need reconditioning by a specialist.

The shaft comes complete with new universal joints at either end, and it needs to be installed with the shorter section of the shaft oriented so the splined part of the shaft is positioned nearer the gearbox.

Each propshaft is attached with new

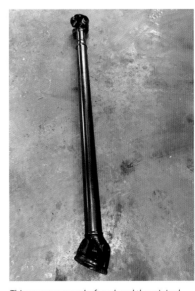

This new rear propshaft replaced the original, whose splines were excessively worn.

The propshaft bolted to the output flange of the transfer box.

locking nuts, and it is good practice to have the bolts pointing backwards, so the nut is on the back. Theoretically this means that the threaded end is less contaminated by road dirt and corrosion.

As described in Chapter 3, the clearance round the retaining nuts varies as the propshaft rotates, because the shaft does not sit exactly horizontal to the road. To make accessing the nuts easier, rotate the shaft about 90 degrees as you move from one nut to the next. Put the transmission in neutral, and if the rear wheels are already fitted, raise one of them off the ground to enable the propshaft to turn.

If any play is detected in the universal joints, these can be replaced cost effectively. Each joint has roller bearings contained in four cups at each end of the central 'spider', and water ingress coupled with inadequate lubrication causes these bearings to wear out. Removing the original UJ involves pulling out all four circlips and pushing the cup out of each yoke with a

press, or by tapping with a brass hammer. This process is repeated for all four sides, then the spider is removed. The yokes and the grooves in which the circlips sit then need to be thoroughly cleaned in preparation for the new joint.

To install the new UJ, place one new cup on a flat surface and rest one of the propshaft's yokes over the top, then gently tap the yoke down on to the cup. The spider can then be inserted, followed by the opposite cup. It is useful to push the first cup slightly further into the yoke than is necessary, because the spider will sit in a position that makes installation of the second cup easier. The most difficult aspect is making sure the needle roller bearings remain upright and do not fall over while the cup is being pushed into the yoke.

Once all the cups are in place and the UJ feels smooth, add new circlips in the ends of the yokes, and screw a new grease nipple into the spider. The UJ is now complete, and should be packed with grease via the nipple until

the excess is being forced out all round the joint.

EXHAUST ASSEMBLY

The exhaust for the project 109 is in three pieces: a front pipe, an intermediate section, and a silencer. The middle section varies according to the wheelbase of the vehicle.

When fitting a new exhaust, start at the front and work backwards. Obviously this can be done on a fully assembled vehicle, but it's much easier to do at this stage before the bodywork is attached.

First, the downpipe is attached to the exhaust manifold using the four $^5/_{16}$ BSF studs, together with a new gasket. Then the centre section is bolted to the downpipe, and hung from its bracket, then the rear section is added. New copper gaskets are used between each section.

The middle and rear sections hang from the chassis using the same design bracket. This consists of (in ascending order) a bottom clamp in two sections, one large pair of metal plates, a rubber, and a pair of smaller plates; these smaller plates are bolted to the bracket on the chassis. Modern versions of the rubbers wear out quickly, especially if the bracket isn't hanging straight down, so prevent the weight of the exhaust from twisting it by adjusting the lower clamp.

In all Series Is the exhaust needs to be routed so that it exits in the right-hand wheel arch, behind the wheel. The routing is sometimes slightly different for 107in vehicles compared to 109in ones, depending on the sup-

New fixings are used, including spring washers, and a new gasket between the downpipe and manifold.

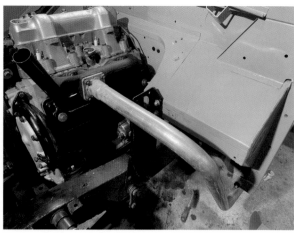

The new downpipe is bolted to the exhaust manifold.

The exhaust bracket broken down into its parts. The rubber is sandwiched between metal clamps, both top and bottom.

The symmetrical manifold on a restored engine in an 80.

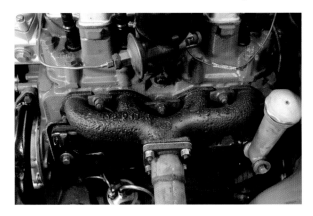

The long section being bolted to the rear silencer section, with another new gasket.

80in exhaust mounts are different – this is a rear mount for an 80in exhaust.

All 80in exhausts have heat shields to prevent the floor from becoming hot.

For 80in Series Is the exhaust is in only two sections, and the heat shield is slightly larger. Depending on the supplier of the exhaust, it may be that the heat shield is not included at all – our 109's exhaust does not come with a heat shield.

INSTALLING THE FUEL SYSTEM

It is likely that quite a few new parts will be required for the fuel system. Some of the components are difficult to source, and they can rapidly swallow a large chunk of a restorer's budget. For example, our 109 required nearly £100 worth of parts merely to connect the carburettor to the fuel pump. Those needing to budget for a complete fuel system, including fuel tank and

The complete exhaust, ready to receive the rear hanging bracket. Note the routing of the centre pipe, which is sometimes different for 107in Series Is.

intermediate section sometimes has to pass behind the left-hand spring shackle (above the spring) rather than passing in front of it – as has been done here.

In an 80 the exhaust downpipe attaches to the centre of the exhaust manifold, unlike later Series Is whose exhaust manifold is asymmetrical, and the downpipe aperture is offset.

plier of the new exhaust. This is due to the extra wheelbase inches, which effectively push the engine a couple of inches forward of the bulkhead. In a 107 without those extra inches, the

Beware of your budget being swallowed by small parts such as this little pipe, which cost about £25.

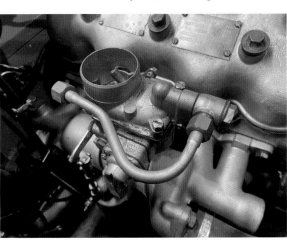

carburettor, will spend around £700 (at the time of writing).

With the engine and bulkhead installed, the rebuilt fuel pump can now be bolted to the mounting bracket on the bulkhead, along with the sedimenter, and the new carburettor can be bolted to the inlet manifold with a new gasket.

New steel pipes are available preformed. However, the restorer who prefers cunifer will need to make them himself, bending them into the required shape using the originals as templates, and forming the ends with a flaring tool.

The flexible metal pipe connecting the carb to the pump is not available on the aftermarket, so new-old stock will have to be purchased – but

The fuel tank now added to the chassis and plumbed in.

PROBLEMS WITH MODERN FUEL

E10 petrol is becoming standard in the UK at the time of writing, but it is already widespread in continental Europe, Australia, and even more so in the USA. Although Series Is are not at severe risk from E10 fuels (compared with later classics with high-pressure fuel systems), there are still some valid concerns that relate to the fuel system – and also the engine oil.

E10 petrol is up to 10 per cent renewable ethanol. Ethanol is a solvent that may cause degradation to old rubber components in a Series I's fuel system. The two areas of concern are the diaphragm in the SU fuel pump and the rubber pipe (with steel outer sheath) running across the top of the engine from the fuel pump to the carburettor.

Any new or rebuilt fuel pump will use ethanol-proof rubber. The pipe, however, is not available new, so if it is degraded a new-old stock or second-hand item will need to be sourced – and this may eventually degrade too. Until new remakes of these pipes are available, there is no easy solution to this problem, other than fitting a length of modern $^5/_{16}$in fuel pipe.

As for the carburettor, there are reports of E10 deteriorating solder, which may have ramifications for the fuel float. Gum and 'varnish' may build up inside the carb, caused by E10's sulphate and copper content. Various aftermarket corrosion inhibitors are available, formulated for E10 petrol, and some also aim to reduce the build-up of gum.

E10 also degrades slightly faster through oxidation, resulting in less complete combustion. Ethanol is hydroscopic, so the extra water content that E10 can absorb will slightly increase the rate of corrosion inside the fuel system, especially in fuel that is left sitting for a long time.

The higher ethanol content also introduces 'enleanment' to the fuel/air ratio, which can result in a small reduction in performance and slightly hotter running. To compensate, it may be necessary to run a slightly richer mixture than would be used for E5 petrol, although the difference is likely to be extremely small.

The engine oil also needs considering. E10 will result in the oil acquiring a higher water content over time, becoming more acidic and less viscous, therefore reducing its ability to lubricate efficiently. This will have less effect on oils formulated for modern engines than for classic oils.

Guy Lachlan, managing director of Classic Oils, has this advice:

We recommend that all classic drivers avoid E10 for as long as possible. All petrol engines create acids as part of the combustion cycle, and the additional impact of E10 is minor. Modern oils do have higher detergency to nullify the effects of the acidity, but are generally not suited to older cars, especially those without oil filters. We expect E10 issues to be limited to people using 'classic' monogrades in older (mostly pre-war) vehicles, and our recommendation is to change to one of the Penrite Shelsley range (www.penriteoil.com.au), which are designed for cars of that generation but have chemistry that is better able to deal with E10 combustion acids. Being an Australian product, it has more history with E10 fuels. We strongly recommend anyone who continues to run monograde oils with E10 fuel to engage with an oil analysis service such as our 'Insight' programme, which will identify issues with oil degradation before they become serious.

In summary, if and when you are obliged to use E10 petrol, it is advisable to use appropriate fuel additives, to upgrade any degradable rubber components in the fuel system, and to choose your engine oil carefully. E5 'super' grade (97+ octane) petrol will still be available from certain filling stations in the UK for the next few years, but its availability is likely to decline.

The fuel tank mounted in place with new fixings.

this will not be compatible with E10 fuel.

The fuel tank also needs adding to the rolling chassis, before the seat box can be installed. Fuel tanks on 80s are deeper than those on later Series Is and they have a steel guard underneath, which tends to be bashed from off-road use. All Series I tanks are filled directly into the top of the tank, under the seat, with no filler neck involved. They all also contain a removable sleeve, designed to make it easier to fill via a jerrycan.

Any tank that is leaking or considered to be weak should be swapped with a new tank as part of any full restoration. Leaks may occur round the welded seams, usually round the bottom. Tank sealer can be used to prolong temporarily the lifespan of a tank that has a minor weakness, but this should not be considered a long-term fix. Welding repairs into petrol tanks carries an extreme risk of explosion caused by igniting petrol vapours inside the tank. It is also not necessary, as new tanks are readily available.

BRAKE COMPONENTS

This is an appropriate stage to attach the reconditioned brake master cylinder to the chassis, along with a new master cylinder. These were connected up using new sets of copper brake hoses, fabricated from scratch using a pipe bender (*see* Chapter 7).

13

The Steering System

The main components of the steering system are the column, the steering box (at the base of the column), the steering relay (mounted in the front crossmember), and the linkages and balljoints. All these components can wear, giving Series Land Rovers their reputation for wayward steering, and any restoration project should involve a complete new set of balljoints. A thorough assessment of the steering box and relay is also required, and costs will soon mount up if either of these parts is found to be worn internally. As discussed previously, the relay can be very difficult to extract from the chassis.

Before dismantling, our initial inspection of the project 109 revealed some play in most of the balljoints, so they were all replaced. The steering box also felt normal, but an internal inspection is easy to achieve, and worth doing anyway. Furthermore no play was detected between the top and bottom sections of the steering relay, so this was left undisturbed in the chassis.

Dismantling of the steering relay can be very dangerous, due to highly compressed springs inside. The only recommended maintenance of the steering relay is to ensure that it is well lubricated, by removing one of the four small bolts around its circular upper part, and topping to the brim with EP90 gear oil.

Where we refer to components being 'upstream' or 'downstream' from each other, the furthest 'upstream' component is the steering wheel, and the furthest 'downstream' is the right-hand front wheel.

BALLJOINTS AND RODS

Fitting a complete new set of balljoints can have a very positive effect on the handling of an old Land Rover. These joints are found at either end of the trackrod and the two drag links – one long one leading to the left-hand wheel, and one shorter one running above the right-hand chassis rail. Because there are so many joints, it only takes a small amount of wear in each one for the steering to feel vague.

Fortunately balljoints are quite cheap, so there is no reason to preserve old ones. The rods are also cleaned and painted to help preserve them against corrosion. This work is straightforward, unless any of the joints are seized into place.

Each rod is clamped in a vice so the balljoints can be removed. They are likely to be stiff, and may need an overnight soak in penetrating fluid to help free them off. If this doesn't work, try applying heat from a blowtorch. In rare cases even this won't work, which is what happened with our trackrod. One of its joints took half an hour to remove. The second withstood our attack for another half-hour, but even-

These clamps, which grip the balljoint in its thread, will need to be undone.

A large ring spanner can be used to give enough leverage to unscrew the ball joint.

tually the thread inside the rod was sheared smooth. This rendered the whole rod useless, so we had to use a trackrod from another Series I (Series II/III trackrods are a different length to those on Series Is, due to the earlier vehicle's narrower track). Series I trackrods are not easy to source affordably, but fortunately they are interchangeable across all Series Is.

To give enough leverage to turn the trackrod end in its thread, use a strong ring spanner over the end of the balljoint as it is unscrewed from the trackrod. For this to work, the rod will need to be held very firmly in a vice. Once the balljoint begins to move, it will probably need to be wound out in small stages, going in a little before being unwound further, to help loosen the thread.

As each joint is removed, make a

Applying heat will usually release a stuck balljoint.

Rapid cooling was tried, but even then this joint would not budge.

Once the rod is cleaned and painted, the new joint is wound in, and locked by tightening the clamp.

The puller arms should be positioned against the lugs on the drop arm.

The steering-box mounting bracket being removed from the box.

note of the exact number of turns required, and when the new joints are installed, give each one the same number of turns as its predecessor. This will put them in roughly the right position (assuming the old ones were set up correctly) – but they will probably need further adjustment once the steering system has been built into the vehicle and the tracking adjusted. Note that the balljoints are handed with left-hand and right-hand threads (three of each), so make sure you order the correct parts.

Repeat this process for the six balljoints and three bars, and keep them together ready for installation.

STEERING BOX AND COLUMN

The steering box translates the rotation of the steering wheel through 90

degrees. There are two types fitted to Series Is: the 'worm-and-nut' type was used on earlier models, until the 'recirculating ball' type replaced it in 88/109in, although this later system was sometimes retro-fitted to earlier models as it can offer more precise steering.

The project 109 is the later type, and it needs to be assessed for any wear or corrosion inside, which can be a major contributor to the sloppy handling that Series Land Rovers are notorious for. The process begins with the steering box still assembled with the column, plus the drop and attached rod, and all

these parts have been shotblasted together.

Before dismantling, the first step is to check for play in the (obscured) bronze bush around the output shaft, by manipulating the drop arm and feeling for play. In our case none was detected, so this bush could be left alone.

To separate the steering box from its mounting bracket, the drop arm – sometimes known as the Pitman arm – needs to be removed. This is firmly located on the splined output shaft, so a gear puller (available for around £20) can be used to extract it. The

The steering box being held in a vice, with its cover plate being removed.

A puller is used to detach the drop arm from the steering box.

Lots of oil – good. But it's black – bad.

fixings securing the steering box to its mounting bracket are then removed: there are two bolts and two studs.

The box and steering column are held in a vice while the side plate is removed from the box. It is actually quite unusual to find the steering box full of oil, because of their tendency to leak, and many owners forget to check and top up the oil. Wear and corrosion then develop inside.

Our steering box is surprisingly full, which is good – but the oil is black, so something is not right. Oil will usually only acquire a dark colour like this in drivetrain components that become hot, but this should not have happened inside the steering box. We suspect this is actually used engine oil, repurposed for the steering box – a theory that was confirmed with a quick sniff test.

Fortunately it hasn't done any harm, and wrong oil is better than no oil at all. Once it was drained off, the ball guides (the channels around the screw) were revealed to be in perfect condition. If the worm has deteriorated a groove will be seen down each channel, and if the box is under-used or under-lubricated, there might also be some pitting (corrosion) round the ball guides. These are part of the steering column, so in extreme cases it might be necessary to replace the steering column with a good, used item (new columns are not available).

Once emptied out, this steering box can be thoroughly cleaned, greased, and refilled with the correct oil. Land Rover originally recommended using grease to lubricate the moving parts when reassembling from scratch, and topping up the box with oil once assembly is complete. The cover plate is then painted and replaced, using a new gasket. Be thorough when preparing the mating faces because there is a tendency for these to leak. A smear of gasket sealant on each side of the gasket is a good idea.

The bottom cover plate was also removed for repainting, and refitted with the same number of shims. These shims adjust the preload on the bearings at the top and bottom of the steering box, and the play in these bearings can be assessed by manipulating the column and looking through the side plate to detect movement.

Removing shims will tighten slackness in the bearings, but if you are at all uncertain – or if removing shims fails to eliminate play – we would recommend sending the steering box to a specialist for a full overhaul, including new bearings. Complete rebuild kits are available, including bearings and balls.

The reassembled box needs calibrating correctly, using the adjuster nut on the cover plate. Too slack and the steering will feel sloppy; too tight and the steering will be stiff and will fail to self-centre, and wear inside the box will be accelerated. Adjust it by slackening the external nut, tightening the inner adjuster screw to 14lb/in, and lock it in position by tightening the external nut again. This can compensate for wear in the mechanism, but only to a limited extent.

The demo 109's steering column was sanded, primed and sprayed black, along with the bracket that attaches the steering box to the chassis. The original UNC fixings were retained, along with the galvanized locktab – left unpainted, as it left the factory.

Earlier Series Is with worm-and-nut steering have the horn mounted in the middle of the wheel, rather than on this separate arm. The wiring runs down a stator tube that passes through the centre of the steering column, and there are no removable shims at the bottom of the steering box. If any end float is encountered in the central shaft at the top bearing, it can be compensated for by adjusting the preload on the thrust ball race to between 7lb/in and 9lb/in. This is done by slackening the top nut, tightening the adjuster nut beneath it with a torque wrench, and then tightening the top nut again.

The later recirculating ball type, such as ours, uses a bush at the top of

The cast-steel 80in worm-and-nut steering box.

Despite its terrible oil, this worm gear is in excellent condition.

Locknut and adjuster nut at the top of a rusty 80in steering column – different to our 109.

The arm for the horn button had a non-standard switch, but the hole could be repaired.

Arm with the hole repaired, before linishing.

Bakelite steering wheels eventually become cracked…

The wheel after receiving an initial etch primer, and mounted on a broomstick. Next comes grey high-build primer.

…This wheel is particularly bad round the back.

Finishing with a 'high solids' paint gives this excellent and glossy result.

the column rather than an adjustable bearing. It is rare to find severe weakness with this bush; ours was found to have no play, so disassembly was not required.

The horn-button mount for our 109in had a hole bored through it, in which a (non-standard) push-button start switch could be located. There is no reason to keep this feature, and a hole like this can easily be welded up. First a hole saw was used to cut a circle of steel that was almost the same size as the hole that needed filling, then it was MIG-welded into place. The initial result was obviously rough, but after linishing it back with an angle grinder, then skimming the imperfections with filler, a decent finish was achieved.

This is the kind of repair that does not always make sense if your time is priced by the hour, as we could have looked for a second-hand replacement, but there is satisfaction to be found in retaining as many original parts as possible.

STEERING-WHEEL REFURB

The 109's steering-wheel rim is made of Bakelite, which is tough and hard-wearing, but it does become brittle when very old. Many Series I steering wheels are cracked and faded, especially if they have come from a hot climate, and the ageing to be seen on this example is typical. It is quite badly cracked, especially round the rear.

There are two solutions. The wheel can be sent to a Bakelite specialist who can re-mould the wheel in fresh Bakelite; however, we've chosen to

repair this vehicle ourselves by filling the cracks with epoxy resin, to show how this can be achieved. The resin seals the steering wheel from water ingress, and can be sanded smooth to recreate the original profile. This is an affordable method that is capable of excellent results if done carefully, although any steering wheel receives a lot of close scrutiny so it is worth taking great care over the finish.

The Bakelite must be clean and bone dry before any resin is applied. First the cracks are scrubbed with a stiff brush to clear out any debris, then a matchstick is used to push the resin into all the crevices. The resin needs to fill the cracks fully, without leaving any craters below the level of the original Bakelite. Messiness at this stage does not matter, as any excess will be sanded off.

Epoxy resin being used to mend the cracks round the steering wheel.

Once the resin has been allowed to set, it is sanded down by hand to give a smooth finish. Begin with 80-grit paper to remove the larger imperfections, and work up to 150-grit, wrapping the paper round the rim and rubbing in a circular motion. Once the desired smoothness has been reached, the wheel is ready for painting.

To get good access all round the wheel for painting, it is screwed on to an old broom handle using a self-tapping screw and a large washer through the centre of the wheel. Then the spokes need to be masked off as accurately as possible.

The first coat is etch primer, followed by a grey high-build primer, which fills any remaining tiny imperfections. Once dry, this is gently flatted down by hand using 400-grit paper.

The wheel then receives a coat of high-pigment two-pack paint. A 'high solids' Super Black produced by Mipa is used here, which has a high pigmentation to ensure a deep black with a good gloss finish. Once the paint has been allowed to dry, the masking tape can be removed and the wheel is ready for installation.

STEERING-WHEEL REMOULDING

The method above is effective at recreating the look for the original wheel, but to replicate the way it feels in the

Series I wheel, after the old Bakelite has been broken off.

Custom-made mould, specifically for Series I steering wheels.

The wheel emerges from the press with some extra material.

Strips of ebonite being wound round the rim.

four lengths. Ebonite is a natural, tree-derived rubber that will set hard, and is more resistant against cracking than the original Bakelite. The ends of each length are tucked into the spokes, and then sliced off.

The wheel is placed in a special press, with a two-part mould that has been custom-made for the purpose. The wheel spends four hours in this machine under 115 tonnes of pressure, while simultaneously being heated to 140°C.

The wheel is then removed from the

hands it would need to be completely remoulded from scratch. This can only be accomplished by a specialist as it requires large machinery and a dedicated mould – something that very few businesses possess.

The photos show the recreation of a Series I steering wheel identical to our demo vehicle's at Charlesworth Mouldings in the West Midlands. (Charlesworth is a family business that was about to celebrate its centenary as we were writing this book. They also produce gear knobs and high-quality gaiters for Series Land Rovers, and have been able to remould Series I steering wheels since commissioning this mould in 2012.)

First, the old Bakelite is chipped off the wheel to expose the steel frame inside. Occasionally the frame is too rusty to salvage, but this is relatively rare.

Rough strips of raw ebonite are then wrapped tightly round the frame, in

The large old press bakes the rim under high pressure.

press and left to cool. The excess fragments of ebonite are scraped off using a knife with a ceramic blade, which tends not to dig into the main body of the rim as easily as a steel blade would. The wheel is then ready to be sent off to the paint shop for the final finish to be applied.

A ceramic blade scrapes off the excess.

Wrapped and ready for the press.

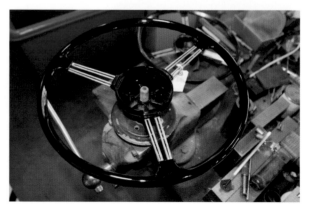

The finished wheel, back from the paint shop.

Charlesworth currently charges £295 plus VAT for this process, and they require a lead time of up to eight weeks: this is because the remoulded wheels must be sent for painting as a batch, rather than individually.

BUILDING THE STEERING SYSTEM

With the bulkhead attached to the chassis, the complete steering system can be assembled, and this is much easier when there is no bodywork in the way. As previously discussed, the demo 109's steering relay has remained mounted to the front cross-member.

Regardless of which model of Series I is being built, the process is essentially the same, although the different number of turns from lock to lock affects the steering-box centring procedure. It is helpful if the steering box is the first piece to be added, because calibration of the linkages requires the steering box to be properly centred, and the steering wheel attached.

The steering box is mounted to the bulkhead bracket (cleaned and painted black, as the original), which bolts to the chassis. The steering column is then passed through the bulkhead, and its four bolts are attached to the steering box.

The steering-column seal is a large grommet through which the steering column passes, and is attached to the rear face of the bulkhead (passenger compartment side) with a steel cover. The seal is obsolete, so a new one was created out of a piece of non-absorbent foam, using the cover as a template.

The seal and cover are then slid over the steering column and fixed to the bulkhead using dome-headed screws

The steering column seal being made bespoke, using the cover plate as a template.

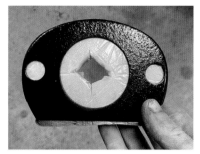

The freshly painted plate holds the seal against the bulkhead.

The seal and bracket fitted to the bulkhead, prior to the addition of screws and washers.

and the distinctive offset washers. The offset is to allow for adjustment, due to the size of the holes in the bracket and the seal clamp.

The column's support bracket can also be attached. This clamps round the column, with a thin strip of rubber inserted between the bracket and the column. The bracket's return flanges (top and bottom) are bolted to the bulkhead with new fixings, giving some much needed rigidity to the assembly.

Now the steering wheel can be added to the column. Our wheel was still drying at this stage, so we temporarily used another old wheel to align

the steering box. The alignment process involves centring the gear inside the box, which needs to be done before the attachment of the drop arm – this is why the steering column and wheel need to be in place first.

The steering box is centralized by counting the number of turns in each direction. This box has four complete turns from lock to lock (a 'worm-and-nut' type has fewer), so the centre point is achieved when the wheel has turned two complete turns from each extremity.

With the steering box centred, the steering wheel can then be lifted off its splines and replaced in the correct orientation, which means that one of its sets of spokes should be pointing straight upwards.

Then double check to ensure there

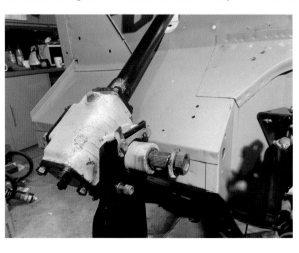

The steering box mounted on its bracket, ready to receive its drop arm.

Asymmetrical washers enable adjustment.

The steering-column bracket was cleaned with wire wool before fitting.

… which marry up to the corresponding gaps in the steering box's output shaft.

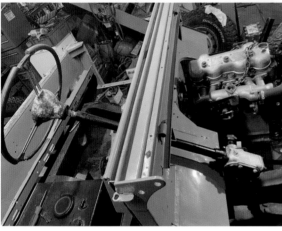

The column attached to the steering box, with the steering wheel (from a different vehicle) attached to enable centring of the worm gear.

is an equal number of turns each way. Any lack of travel in one direction will be mirrored by too much travel in the other direction – so for example, if the wheel stops at 3 o'clock when it is turned to the right, it will stop at 9 o'clock when turned to the left. To correct any error, return the worm to the central position, and then remove and reset the wheel.

The drop arm can now be added to the splines on the left-hand side of the steering box. With the steering wheel centred, the arm should be pointing straight downwards, and there are four 'master' splines that limit the potential for error. A large nut holds the arm in place, and is secured by a tab washer that is bent flat against the nut.

The arm can then be attached to the short drag link, which has been painted and fitted with new balljoints at either end. This rod runs along the top of the chassis rail, connecting the drop arm to the steering relay's top arm. Again, the rod and the top arm should meet at 90 degrees when the steering box is in the dead-ahead position.

Calibration consists of screwing the balljoints in or out of the steering rod to lengthen or shorten the distance between them. You may also need to reposition the top arm of the steering relay on its splines to ensure that the top arm and bottom arm (beneath the crossmember) are at 90 degrees from each other, with the top arm aligned with the crossmember and the bottom arm pointing forwards. Once you are confident that these angles are correct, the balljoints can be fixed in position by adding the castellated nuts and their split pins.

Next comes the long drag link that runs across the vehicle, connecting the steering relay's lower arm to the left hub. Again, the angle between the drag link and the arm should be

The drop arm bolted in place, with a locktab to secure the nut.

The steering box's drop arm, with yellow markers added to highlight the position of the master splines…

The steering relay's bottom arm has been correctly fitted at 90 degrees to the top arm.

90 degrees when the steering is in the dead-ahead position. You can ensure the left-hand wheel is dead ahead by running a long length of string from the front of the front tyre to the back of the rear tyre and pulling it tight: if the wheels are aligned, the string should touch the front and rear sections of both tyres.

Finally the track rod is added, connecting the right and left swivel housings. This rod determines the vehicle's tracking – that is, how accurately the front wheels roll parallel with each other. It is calibrated in much the same way as the drag links, by screwing the balljoints in or out to adjust the rod's length, with the steering box centred, and using a length of string to ensure the right-hand front wheel is perfectly aligned with the wheel behind it. For this method to work the same sized wheels and tyres will be needed.

Another technique for assessing the tracking is to measure the distances between the front rims, both in front of the axle and behind it. If the rims are exactly parallel, the two measure-

The steering rod running to the left-hand hub, with the drag link added behind it.

ments should be the same. (To ensure accuracy, measure between the wheel rims rather than the tyres.)

A professional garage will be able to achieve a more accurate alignment using specialist machinery, but the string method can give an adequate result.

After completing the assembly of the steering system, it requires a brief test by turning the steering wheel from lock to lock. It should give a smooth motion, with no play or clunking detectable in any of the joints, and no grinding from either the steering box or the steering relay.

14

Refurbishing Linkages

In this chapter the handbrake mechanism is inspected, and the clutch and brake pedal linkages refurbished, together with the throttle linkage – including the footwell pedals themselves.

These assemblies are comprised of many small parts that can be easily lost, and reassembly is very difficult without a detailed photographic record, a parts manual, or preferably both. Restoration is primarily a case of stripping, cleaning, painting where appropriate, and reassembling, using lubricant wherever any moving parts move against each other. In some cases

bronze pivot bushes will be found that require replacement, and replacing these will remove any slop from the mechanism (more on this later), making the vehicle considerably nicer to drive. Reassembly of these linkages will require some calibration, especially if new parts have been added, but this is all quite simple work, affordable, and easily achieved by a home mechanic.

THE HANDBRAKE MECHANISM

There is no adjustment that can be made in the ratchet mechanism of the handbrake, but it ought to be inspected for wear. This is most likely to be found on the paw (the small piece of pivoting metal that bites into the ratchet), although the teeth of the ratchet can also be worn smooth.

The demo 109's handbrake ratchet mechanism was in good condition, so all it needed was a thorough clean with degreaser to remove ingrained dirt. Greasing this mechanism may cause it to stick, so a light spray of silicone-based lubricant is ideal.

If the ratchet teeth are worn a sec-

ond-hand part will have to be sourced, as new ones are not available. Paws are available new, but a worn paw can sometimes be improved by filing it down to a point, and reassembling the mechanism with new split pins.

Fortunately the mechanism can be inspected without having to dismantle it completely, but if any worn components are spotted and it needs to be taken apart, be careful not to lose the many small washers and pins. The ratchet should always be tested repeatedly after final assembly, because this should be considered a safety-critical component: if it lets go, the vehicle could roll.

In the project vehicle the lower relay arm that pivots on the chassis was very rusty and stiff, but salvageable. The mechanism here sometimes has a tendency to seize gradually, so dismantling and lubrication is required. The circlip was removed, and the arm was removed from its pivot to reveal that the bronze bush inside needed replacing, so the original was pushed out with a press and replaced. After cleaning and painting, the parts were reas-

The paw and teeth of this handbrake ratchet are in good condition.

The base of the rod that pulls on the ratchet mechanism.

The handbrake's lower relay and adjuster rod, being dismantled.

The circlip being added to complete the refurbishment.

Shaft housing, with the return spring's anchor plate.

The assembly refitted to the vehicle, viewed from above.

sembled with fresh grease and a new circlip. The adjuster rod was corroded enough for the threads to become weak, which would have caused problems for the adjuster nuts, so a good replacement was sourced from another vehicle, and cleaned and lubricated thoroughly.

Our handbrake lever could then be reinstalled on the chassis, along with the relay arm beneath, with the adjustable rod connected to it. Note the angle of the handbrake lever and the pivot relative to the chassis rail in our photo taken from above – the mechanism is designed to sit at a slight angle, and not parallel to the chassis rail.

THROTTLE LINKAGE

The throttle pedal and its linkages need connecting up to the carburettor mechanism, which is screwed to the inlet manifold. The throttle pedal and shafts have been primed and painted, with the exception of the cast aluminium housing on the front of the bulkhead, which was originally unpainted. Take care to retain all these numerous small components, as it is easy to lose track of which part is which.

First, the small bracket that secures the cross-shaft is bolted to the inside of the footwell, together with the cross-shaft and pedal. The cross-shaft exits through a housing that sandwiches the anchor plate for the throttle return spring against the bulkhead in the engine bay.

Another bracket for the small cross-shaft is then added to the bulkhead, followed by the shaft and the two levers, which should be oriented so that the two balljoints are not pointing towards

Throttle pedal with the cross-shaft mounted in the driver's footwell.

Small cross-shaft on its bracket, with two levers attached.

each other. The angle between these two levers will need calibrating shortly, so they do not need to be fully tightened to the cross-shaft yet.

The two control rods are then attached to these two levers. In Chapter 9 the carburettor linkage was rebuilt, and some bronze bushes that can wear were described. However, it is more common to find wear in the small balljoints at the ends of the throttle linkage rods; unfortunately some of

These balljoints need lubricating, as they can wear out.

The two main control rods connecting the throttle levers.

these balljoints are obsolete, in which case new-old stock replacements will need to be sourced. They will benefit from thorough and frequent lubrication.

The small rod assembly then connects the carburettor to its refurbished linkage on the manifold.

The two return springs are the last to be attached. These are the throttle return spring (which connects the base of the throttle arm on the carb linkage to the sedimenter mounting bracket), and the throttle pedal return spring (which connects to the anchor plate where the pedal's cross-shaft exits the footwell).

Calibrating this complex system of

The rod assembly attached to the carburettor.

rods and levers is an inexact science, as there are so many points that can be adjusted. Loosely fit the levers and connecting rods, and make sure the throttle butterfly at the carburettor is fully closed. A good starting point is to set the arms on the small cross-shaft so they are pointing upwards at roughly 45 degrees. The at-rest position of the throttle position is then set by raising the pedal to the desired height and tightening its clamp on the main cross-shaft. To check the full travel of the throttle mechanism on the carburettor, the throttle pedal can now be pushed to the floor while making sure that the throttle butterfly in the carburettor is fully open. Once the at-rest and fully depressed positions of the throttle are calibrated, and the pedal has a smooth action from one extremity to the other, the linkages can be fully tightened.

Finally, the choke cable can be mounted to the bulkhead, and the inner cable added to the choke lever – but only fastened once you are confident that the mechanism is not engaging the choke inside the carburettor when the knob is pushed all the way in.

REFURBISHING THE BRAKE AND CLUTCH MECHANISM

The clutch arm and the brake arm both pivot on the same shaft, which runs through the chassis, and this shaft can remain in the chassis throughout if it is not worn. (If the shaft has wear and needs to be replaced there is a nut and a lock tab on the inside of the chassis rail; the pivot will then need to be pressed out of the tube.)

Each lever has its own phosphor-bronze bush, which it pivots around. If the shaft is not properly lubricated via the grease nipple, these bushes will wear prematurely, and as was discovered when the vehicle was stripped,

Clutch release arm.

the shaft showed no signs of lubrication. No wonder, therefore, that these bushes are significantly worn, creating a very sloppy and imprecise mechanism. Replacing them will significantly improve pedal feel.

This is the kind of job that should be considered standard procedure for a high-quality restoration but will often be overlooked during a quick rebuild, even though it is not expensive to do.

A press was used to extract the worn bushes from both the clutch and brake arms, but this could also be done by cutting the bush with a hacksaw and tapping it out (as shown for the spring shackles in Chapter 11), taking care to avoid damaging the inner face of the tubes. The arms were also thoroughly cleaned and refreshed with some black paint.

Placing the new and old bushes for the clutch lever alongside each other highlights how much wear there was in the old bush. In extreme cases of wear and poor adjustment, the pedal may be pushed nearly to the floor before the mechanism actually does any work.

Note that the bushes for the clutch lever and brake lever are not the same size, and the pivot shaft protruding from the chassis rail is stepped to allow for this.

The old bronze bush at the bottom of the clutch arm.

Old and new bushes for the clutch arm.

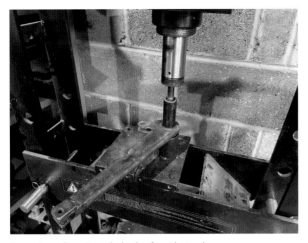

A press is used to extract the bushes from the two levers.

Cross-shaft installed with collars at both ends.

A finished lever, with fresh paint and a new bush pushed into it.

Careful spots of weld can restore the tread pattern.

It is common to find wear in the pivot holes where the adjuster rod attaches to the clutch arm. The only way to refurbish this would be to cut away the entire hole, replace it with a new segment of metal, and drill a new

The clutch relay pivot bush, next to a non-worn one.

The demo 109's clutch relay mechanism prior to cleaning.

hole, having taken measurements to ensure the new hole is in precisely the same location as the original. In our case, this was not required.

Two additional bronze bushes were required in the chassis for the clutch relay to pass through, as the originals were severely worn. These were tapped out using a drift, and new ones were driven in using a copper hammer, with a little lubrication to help them slot in.

The relay itself was given a thorough clean and a coat of fresh paint, and new grease nipples were screwed into the clutch relay shaft as well as the pedal pivot. The originals were unlikely to be able to deliver an easy flow of grease.

Before cleaning and painting the pedals, it was decided to restore some life back into them by renewing the metal treads. This is done by dropping a little puddle of weld on to each of the dimples, and grinding off any excess.

ASSEMBLING THE BRAKE AND CLUTCH MECHANISM

Most of these parts are vulnerable to being splashed with mud, so it is worth

making sure they are well protected from rust and properly lubricated. All the bronze bushes should be smeared with grease before reassembly.

The cross-shaft is first to be added. Our clutch's input shaft has already received the collar that protrudes from the bellhousing (*see* Chapter 12), so now we can attach the cross-shaft to it, using the original pin.

The cross-shaft is then ready to be attached to the relay shaft, but it helps to have the relay assembled with the adjuster and arm before adding them to the chassis, so that the toothed end of the cross-shaft can be calibrated properly. Before the cross-shaft and relay are connected, with the relay at rest, the cross-shaft should be rotated clockwise by hand until it stops. Then the splined collar is offered up so the cross-shaft and relay can be joined by the addition of the two pins. Fine adjustment can then be carried out using the adjustment rod between the clutch relay and the arm.

The adjuster rod needs two nuts on either side of where it passes through the pedal: the outer nuts lock the inner nuts in place.

The stop nut for the clutch relay arm is added to the outrigger, then the relay shaft is pushed into the chassis

Assembled clutch linkage components.

The two nuts either side of the pin for the clutch arm. After adjustment, they will be locked together.

and connected to the cross-shaft with the second collar. This collar is toothed to allow for calibration, and the mechanism is aligned so that the pin securing the collar is vertical when the top of the relay arm is resting against its stop nut.

A new bronze spacer washer is then pushed on to the pivot shaft, to sit between the clutch arm and the brake arm, and then the brake arm is added.

The large springs that attach to the base of the brake arm and the lowest point of the clutch linkage were in reasonable condition so they were simply cleaned and painted to help preserve them, but it is often necessary to replace these, and doing so will also improve the pedal feel.

The bottom of the brake arm is attached to the master cylinder's input rod using a pin, which is held in place with a split pin and washer, not forgetting the small mounting plate for the spring, which actuates the brake switch. This smaller spring is only

The threaded adjuster rod in place, in between the clutch relay (left) and the base of the pedal (right).

Bronze spacer being fitted to the pivot.

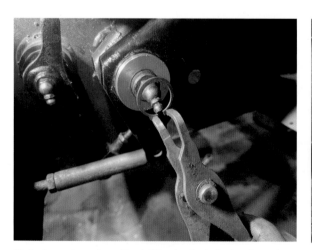

The brake arm is now in position, held in place by the final washer and a new circlip.

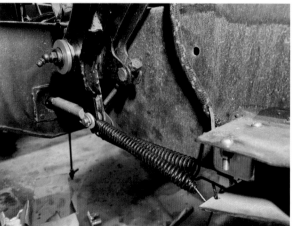

Brake master-cylinder rod connected, and new springs added to both pedals. The brake light switch is at right, beneath the plinth.

Painted pedal, with a new felt washer and rubber grommet.

Pedals installed.

loosely assembled at this stage – it will be calibrated more precisely when the rest of the electrical system is installed later.

New rubber grommets, together with new felt washers, are fitted where the brake and clutch pedals enter the bulkhead. These must be fitted the correct way up, otherwise they can prevent the pedals from being fully depressed. The pedals themselves are handed, so they must be fitted the correct way round (*see* photo). They pass through the felt washers and are clamped into the tops of the pedal arms using new bolts.

The rod from the front of the brake master cylinder is then connected to the base of the brake pedal, and secured with a new washer and split pin. New return springs are connected between the bracket protruding from the chassis, and the clutch and brake pedals. The two springs are different, the clutch spring being the stiffer of the two. These tend to wear out round the hook and can be difficult to source; in this case a good second-hand clutch spring is fitted, and the brake spring is new.

Finally, the clutch's adjuster rod and stop bolt should be adjusted so that the clutch pedal and brake pedal are at the same height when at rest.

Now that the brake arm is connected to the master cylinder via the horizontal adjuster rod, the rod needs to be calibrated. All the nuts need to be free to enable the position to be finely adjusted, before nipping them up. Adjust the thread so that, with the brake pedal at rest, you can pull the arm down slightly before you feel it engage with the master cylinder piston. This small amount of free play is important for allowing the master cylinder to return to rest – otherwise the brake system will be continuously pressurized.

15

Bodywork Assembly

Now that the bulkhead and the majority of the mechanical components are fitted to the rolling chassis, we are ready to start assembling the bodywork. This has been left to a late stage of the proceedings so there is plenty of access to mechanical components – particularly in the engine bay, which is easiest to access with the wings off, and under the cab.

Adding the bodywork is straightforward and no special tools are needed, but it is useful to have someone available to help lift the larger sections. The complexity lies in aligning the parts properly, and for this reason all panels should be loosely fitted at first to allow for adjustment. Their fixings are then tightened progressively, with shims being added where appropriate.

Series Land Rover bodies are known for their large tolerances with plenty of possible adjustment. However, the margin for error during these early years is less than it would be in later decades, and the range of possible adjustment is generally not so extreme. We will cover this in more detail later this chapter.

Some specialists will sometimes have ready-made wooden templates that help align panels by acting as a jig or spacer of a known width – particularly for the door apertures.

All seals should be renewed, and all are available to buy. Attention must be paid to the correct orientation of certain seals (use the photos as a guide), and it pays to take time to ensure they are seated correctly, as they may otherwise become misaligned or pinched, allowing water ingress. Some rebuilds have used sealing compound instead

---

RUSTY FIXINGS

Many of the small nuts and bolts around the bodywork will be reusable, especially if they are original fixings that were all sherardized from new. (Sherardizing is a method of galvanizing, using zinc powder to apply a highly durable, corrosion-proof coating to ferrous metals such as steel.) Various products are available to help rid components of dirt and corrosion, ranging from degreasers and ultrasonic cleaning baths to acids and electro-plating devices. Used in combination, these will improve the look and longevity of old fixings, although the effort of doing this is rarely worthwhile for a restorer who is charging by the hour.

One easy option for dissolving rust is a product such as Evaporust, which uses a chemical process called chelation to remove rust. The components need to be submerged in the product overnight, or for a couple of days for deeper rust, then rinsed with water and dried. An application of paint will then add a little protection and smartness, at least in the short term.

A concours restoration will typically involve many of the original fixings being sent away to be zinc-coated or sherardized by a specialist, and any severely rusty items would be replaced with identical sherardized items that offer excellent longevity and add authenticity to a restoration. Also, unlike stainless steel, they won't increase the rate of galvanic corrosion surrounding the fixings.

Unfortunately a significant premium must be paid for sherardized fixings, and not many suppliers can provide them, so new zinc-coated fixings have been used in most places on this vehicle, to help keep the restoration attainable. These offer a fair compromise, lasting longer than uncoated steel, but saving some expenditure. We also spray painted many of the reusable original fixings.

Soaking fixings overnight in a fluid such as this will dissolve surface rust.

Rusty fixing, before and after soaking in a chelation product.

Sherardized fixings can be distinguished by their matte, almost gritty texture.

of seals in certain places, but this is not required, and it will also make future disassembly difficult. A well-positioned seal that hasn't degraded with age will do its job perfectly well.

Galvanic corrosion is also to be considered when assembling bodywork, wherever aluminium panels meet the structural steel sections (as discussed in Chapter 10). These areas need to be monitored on an ongoing basis for white powder forming on the Birmabright sections.

REAR BULKHEAD AND DOOR ALIGNMENT

When aligning the bodywork, the main focus needs to be the apertures round the doors. The objective is to enable them to close properly, without any large or uneven gaps, and without them fouling against the surrounding bodywork. Achieving this may take a lot of subtle adjustment, and you may need to make different adjustments at each side of the vehicle. Throughout this process the fixings are kept as slack as possible but as tight as necessary so that the panels don't slip out of calibration. Only when the panels and doors on both sides align properly should fixings be fully tightened.

The process of alignment is slightly different on long-wheelbase 'Regular' body styles such as ours. On short-wheelbased models the rear tub is a non-adjustable fixture, so once it is bolted to the rear crossmember the main bulkhead has to be adjusted until the door apertures are correct. With a long-wheelbase such as ours, the rear bulkhead panel is adjusted on the rear mountings, and the tub (or tray in our case) is separate. This means that both the front and rear bulkheads can be adjusted together until the door aperture is correct. The door hinges may also be adjusted slightly.

With the demo vehicle, adjustment of the rear bulkhead must be done before the seat box is added. The first step is to add the rear bulkhead and the sills, with the sills bolted firmly to the rear bulkhead but only loosely at the front to enable some adjustment. Don't forget to slide the captive plate between the fuel tank and the outrigger, and to push its threads backwards into mounting tabs on the chassis

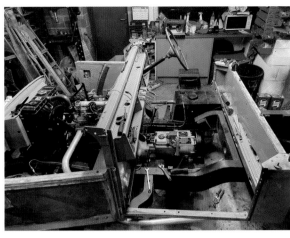

Rear bulkhead and sills loosely fitted.

Passenger door dropped into place to aid alignment.

Spacers being added between the rear bulkhead and the mounting tab on the chassis.

Galvanized cappings are perfectly level and the door gap is even all the way down. This is looking good.

– tricky because it has to be done by feel.

The door bottoms are then dropped on to their hinges so the door gaps can be assessed. Attention is paid to where the top of the door marries up to the capping on the rear bulkhead to make sure they sit level with each other and don't collide. The gap on both doors also needs to be even down both sides. (The rear gap is more difficult to align on 80in Series Is due to the diagonal angle of the rear edge of the doors, which tends to magnify any problems caused by even a small misalignment.)

If required, shims can be added between the bulkhead and its mounts on the chassis, pushing the bottom of the rear bulkhead forwards. This will shrink the lower half of the door gap, and affect the distance between the striker and the latch. There is also a small amount of up/down movement possible for the rear bulkhead, as the mounting holes are slotted. Adjust the height so that the capping at the top of the rear bulkhead is precisely level with the door capping, then tighten the fixings.

Adjusting the forward–back position of the main bulkhead is achieved by slackening off the long bolts that pass through the bulkhead outriggers, and adding or removing spacer washers between the outriggers and the bulkhead. In our case no spacers were required here. The angle of the bulkhead can also be adjusted by slackening the bolts on the front brackets on the inside of the chassis rails, pushing the top of the bulkhead into the desired position, and retightening the bracket. Angling the bulkhead forwards will raise the rear of the doors, and vice versa.

Handbrake and brake master cylinder are present and correct by this stage.

To a limited extent, warping in the bulkhead or chassis (caused by accident damage or galvanizing) may be ironed out by twisting each side of the bulkhead in different directions, then retightening the bolts on the front mounting brackets. Although this isn't ideal, it is fairly common.

The pressed bulkhead of an 80in Series I does not have separate mounting brackets. Instead, the mount is integral to the bulkhead, and the bulkhead's angle is much less adjustable (although the holes are very slightly oversized). If it's not sitting perfectly upright, it is usually a sign that something is out of alignment.

ADDING THE SEAT BOX

Adding the seat box impedes access to the fuel tank, gearbox, handbrake, brake master cylinder and clutch linkage, so it makes sense to have all these areas sorted before proceeding. Once the rear bulkhead, sills, doors and main bulkhead are properly aligned, it is usually easy to jiggle the seat box so that its bolt holes align, as they offer quite a lot of front-to-back adjustment along the sills.

One way to reduce the risk of galvanic corrosion, causing future problems where the seat box meets the sill, is to mount the box on a thin strip of foam tape, which prevents the Birmabright and steel from touching. However, this is not something that was ever done by Solihull, and corrosion along this point is less common on Series Is than it is on later Series Land Rovers. It was therefore decided not to use it on this vehicle.

Our seat-box assembly was laid on

Original hinges are pop riveted to the lids using correct aero rivets.

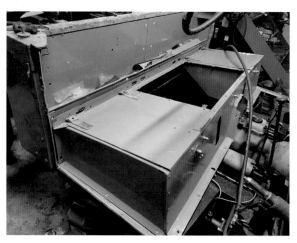

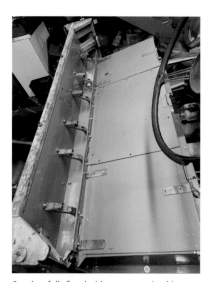

Aligning the seat box with the holes in the bulkhead.

Seat box fully fitted with seat mounting hinges bolted to the bulkhead.

to the sills as an almost complete unit, slotting round the handbrake handle, and was carefully aligned with the holes in the sills and the rear bulkhead. The freshly painted lids and their hinges were also fixed in place; the back section of the hinges bolt to the front lip of the rear bulkhead, and the long ends are riveted to the lids using aero rivets to replicate the original specification.

Note that the lids are right/left-handed, and the curved lips on the tops (which locate the seat bases) determine which side the lids go. The lip needs to be on the inboard side, so the lid with the lip on its left is for the right-hand side of the vehicle.

The galvanized brackets behind the seats are then bolted to the rear bulkhead, along with the door strikers. The refurbished parts were methodically replaced and all the parts bolted back where they came from, whilst being careful to protect the new paint and taking care to align the holes before securing anything in place.

Once the seat box is installed, the handbrake lever mechanism needs to be calibrated by turning the nuts at the top and bottom of the threaded rod to adjust its effective length. With the lever down, the handbrake expander should be fully at rest. The adjuster rod also needs to be short enough to restrict the upward motion of the handle when fully applying the handbrake.

ADDING THE WINDSCREEN AND CAB

On the demo 109 a little money was saved by choosing a generic foam rub-

ber strip for the seal along the top of the rear bulkhead, prior to adding the rear section of the cab on top of it. Shorter sections running longitudinally were cut for fit at each end (right up against the outer edge of the capping), with one long foam section running along the top of the rear wall – this long piece required two large holes to be drilled for the mounting threads to pass through. New clips for the starting handle were also riveted to the front of the rear bulkhead.

New seals need to be added to the bulkhead, in preparation for the bulkhead vents to be attached. The seals are in four sections for each vent, and they must be fitted the right way round. Adhesive is used to hold them in place, so the surfaces need to be clean before application, but it is worth doing a trial fit first so that you are confident about the correct orientation before applying the adhesive.

The top pieces are slightly chamfered, and their pointed corners need to be pointing upwards and back, so that they fit snugly inside the shape created by the top rail.

Once the adhesive has been given time to dry, the vent flaps are added.

Pop riveting the starter handle mounting clips.

New bulkhead seals, showing the pointed edge, which needs to point upwards.

Bulkhead seals stuck in place with adhesive.

Foam seal in three sections added to the rear bulkhead wall.

The bulkhead vents are now secured in position.

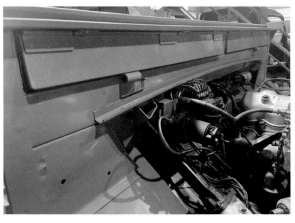

These levers are added after the flaps and their hinges have been attached.

Each of the three hinges on each flap is secured to the top rail of the bulkhead with a dome-headed 2BA set screw.

The levers for the vent flaps are then bolted in place with new fixings: two bolts attaching to each flap and two bolts into the top rail. (On the demo vehicle no restoration of these mechanisms was required, beyond cleaning.) The levers are adjustable using the round knob: screwing it clockwise will tighten the flap against the bulkhead when in the closed position. The hinges and pivot points of the lever mechanism were then all given a spray of silicone lubricant to keep them moving freely.

A new windscreen seal was rested along the top of the bulkhead, then the windscreen was added. It is advisable to have a second pair of hands at this stage, as the windscreen is fairly heavy and there is a risk of scratching the bulkhead. The threads at the front of the windscreen, and the wingnuts behind it, were only loosely fitted to allow for some slight adjustment of the angle of the screen.

Installing the cab roof will also require two people. For the project vehicle, the roof and the rear of the cab were bolted together, then the two sections together were added to the vehicle. The rear panel was rested on the new seal along the rear bulkhead, then

New rubber seal sandwiched between the windscreen and bulkhead – note its orientation.

Our first trial fit of the cab on the rolling chassis.

Tightening the bolts securing the cab to the rear bulkhead.

Cab glazing channels being put in place.

the leading edge of the roof was married up to the top of the windscreen.

Long vertical studs hold the corners of the bodywork's middle and lower sections together. These are interchangeable with the equivalent parts for a Series II or III, but the later versions will have UNF threads, whereas the originals are BSF (Whitworth).

Adding the roof will reveal whether the angle of the windscreen requires adjustment. With the windscreen's lower mounts slack, the screen may be slightly tilted to ensure that the bolt holes line up with the brackets in the corners of the roof section. Before any bolts are tightened, the doors (bottom and top sections complete) are added to their hinges to ensure a comfortable fit round the entire door aperture. The

New perspex window added.

long studs in the rear corners are then tightened down, along with the two nuts along the top of the rear bulkhead, and the roof bolts.

With the cab in place, the lower full-width window channel (with its new felt inner section) can be screwed to the rear wall. For the rear window new sheets of perspex were chosen, rather than the glass we used for the doors, and these were cut to size by the supplier. The vertical metal pieces (which had been scrubbed and repainted grey) were riveted to the outside edges of each sheet, and the sheets were secured in place by the addition of the upper window channel.

DOORS AND REGLAZING

Series I doors are longer lasting that those fitted to later Series Land Rovers. The lower sections of doors for 80in vehicles were all aluminium and

Our driver's side door, ready for restoration.

The old seal, prior to removal.

The new seal requires holes to be drilled for the new rivets.

rarely have any corrosion issues, but they do tend to suffer from fatigue and cracking in the frame around the door latch. Lower doors for later models that combine steel with aluminium may suffer galvanic corrosion of the skin – in which case reskinning is generally viable – but a door that is in reasonable condition will usually simply require its dents to be straightened out.

Fortunately reskinning was not required on the demo 109 as there was no serious corrosion in the door skins, and they did not have any serious dents. Also the door-lock mechanisms were in perfect working order, although there was room for improvement. Each one was dismantled into its four main component parts and thoroughly degreased, and a coat of matt black paint was applied to the C-shaped bracket and the outer handle – not the inner handle, for the sake of originality. The lock assemblies were then bolted back on to the doors with new fixings.

At the time of restoring, the C-shaped bracket was available to buy, along with the mounting plate, which is often found to be cracked – but the spring-loaded latch mechanism is obsolete, so the demo 109's were well lubricated internally and in good working order. Note that the latch mechanisms and the handles themselves are handed (different on the right and left sides), but the other two pieces are identical for both sides.

New seals were also required be-tween the top and bottom sections of each door. Later spec door seals from a Series II/III were used, which are just as functional as the Series I variant; they need to be riveted into the door top. Holes need to be drilled into the rubber strip to match the spacing of the holes in the metal. When adding the rivets, always start with those in the middle and work outwards to ensure that the seal stays flat without pinching.

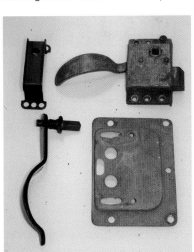

Dismantled door lock and handle assembly, with the outside handle painted.

Riveting the new seal in places, starting in the middle.

Reassembled with new fixings.

Trimming off the door seal with a diagonal cut to match the contour of the frame.

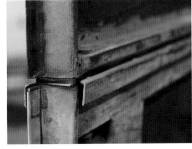

The finished door seal – notice the orientation of the lip.

The rusty window catch was removed and derusted.

The two sections of the doors were then bolted together using the original nuts, and the ends of the seals were trimmed off with a knife, with a diagonal cut at the rear end to match the angle of the metal.

Series Is have spring-loaded window catches that are obsolete, so they are often replaced with Series II items if the originals are too badly corroded. The Series I version looks to be a similar design to the thinner Series II version, but the mechanism is different inside, using a thread rather than a pegged cam. Ours were quite rusty but functioning, so they were unscrewed and soaked overnight in a chelation product before being refitted.

Next the glazing and the window channels were addressed. Each window runs in felt sliders, which sit inside galvanized channels top and bottom. The felt part can be removed on its own, retaining the original channel; sometimes these will need replacing, but the demo 109's are in good condition. (In Series II-onwards Land Rovers, the channel and the felt are integral

The old felt being pulled out of the top channel.

to each other and the ungalvanized steel corrodes easily.) The channels are unscrewed from the door and the original perspex is removed, then the insert is pulled out and replaced with a new strip.

The perspex eventually degrades in sunlight, becoming translucent and brittle, so it was decided to replace the side windows with automotive laminated glass instead. Glass also tends to run more smoothly in the channels, and will give a higher quality feel.

The window channels are similar for the majority of Series Is, although for approximately the first nine months of production Solihull used a different design with a stainless-steel channel carried over from Rover saloons, and these are much better at resisting rust. For the demo 109, the felt part can be bought on a roll, cut to the desired length and pushed into the original channel. The channels are then screwed back into the door frame, along with the new glass.

In some rare cases it may be found that the upper door frame is becom-

Unscrewing the bottom channel.

The bottom channel with its old insert being removed.

ing delaminated – as was the case with the project 109. There is not much that can be done about this, and the gap is unlikely to be very big, but it is worth inserting some rustproofing wax or silicone compound into it to prevent water ingress, which could cause corrosion inside and push the gap wider.

If a door requires a new skin, the following is an example of what can be achieved. This is the right-hand front

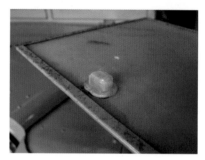

The opaque old perspex that needed replacing.

The new window channel insert has a specific shape and can be bought as a roll.

Early 80in window channels, pictured at CKD Shop.

Screwing the top channel in place, with the new glass in situ.

The new felt runner in the original bottom channel.

Delaminating the door frame – a rare and minor issue if caught early.

Example of an 80in door, showing the different lock mechanism and canvas.

door of a 107in Station Wagon that has been successfully reskinned. The first step was to remove the door top, and drill out the rivets holding the capping to the door bottom: solid rivets along the top of the capping, and pop rivets down its side. The solid rivets holding the lock mechanism in place were drilled out, and then a pair of grips was used to peel the folded edges of the skin away from the frame. The frame could then be separated and cleaned. In some cases a restorer may wish to have the steel frame regalvanized, although this is rarely required.

The new skin does not include rivet holes, so it has to be offered up to the frame squarely and precisely before the new rivet holes are added. This requires care, and the alignment of the panel must be checked after each of the first holes are added. After the addition of each of the first few holes, temporary Cleco fasteners are added to the panel to hold its position while the remaining holes are drilled. Once the holes

A reskinned front door on a project 107in Station Wagon.

are drilled and the capping is riveted in place, the edges of the new skin are tapped over gently using a peening hammer, with a dolly held against the outer face.

Note the use of domed and pop rivets.

For doors on 80in vehicles, the final stage will involve adding the necessary canvas sections, paying attention to the correct arrangement of the solid rivets and aero-style pop rivets.

FRONT BODYWORK

Moving to the front of the vehicle, the battery tray can now be bolted to the chassis. This is also a good time to attend to any pressing issues around the engine bay, as access is partially hindered by the addition of the wings. (For example, you may choose to install some elements of the wiring loom at this stage, although this topic will be addressed in Chapter 17.)

The demo 109 radiator has returned from being reconditioned, which involved a new core being installed, followed by repainting of the whole unit. It is easiest to assemble the front panel, radiator and cowl together before bolting them to the chassis, rather than adding them individually. Care needs to be taken when handling any radiator, as the fins can be very easily damaged.

New glass in place.

The battery tray installed.

The radiator and front panel assembly mounted in place.

The top rail is attached to the back of the refurbished radiator.

The first step is to attach the top rail to the radiator. This is the only bracket required, as the sides of the radiator have flanges, enabling it to be bolted directly to the front panel. The front panel is then laid face down on to a soft surface, the radiator is lowered on to it, and the two are bolted together with four bolts down each side and four along the top.

The cowl can then be fitted, using slot-headed screws. There are different designs of cowl, so if a cowl needs replacing, take care to source the correct one. The main difference is in the depth of the round part that protrudes round the fan blade; this section protrudes further on vehicles from 1956 onwards to account for the longer engine bay. Solihull created this extension using an extra piece of metal, but the demo 109's cowl is of a much rarer pressed-steel design, made in Australia (because it is a CKD vehicle).

The assembly is then ready to be attached to the chassis. Three bolts hold it in place, and at each mounting point a small rubber buffer should be inserted under the mounting points. These reduce metal fatigue from vibration, but they are often lost over the years, and omitted from rebuilds. Once mounted, the radiator's top and bottom hoses are added with new hose clips.

Before the wings can be fitted to the body, their galvanized mounting brackets need to be added to the bulkhead. The original brackets are given a good clean, and, as Solihull did, are left unpainted.

For each of the front wings there are four fixings attaching it to the bulkhead, plus three for the bulkhead

The radiator laid on the front panel, ready to be bolted down.

80in/86in radiator cowl (left), and the later type for the demo 109in (right)

A line of slot-headed screws secures the freshly painted cowl to the radiator.

The rubber buffer sits between the front panel and the chassis.

The radiator is connected to the engine with the top and bottom hoses.

Wing support brackets are added to the bulkhead, above the footwells.

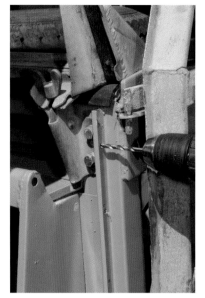

The wings are loosely bolted into place.

The old rivets securing the door seal to the bulkhead are drilled out.

The door seal's inner strip is cut to length.

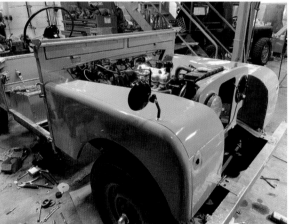

New wing mirror in place.

The metal strip is held against the door aperture, and rivet holes are marked with a pen.

bracket and three for the front panel. A little up/down adjustment is possible in these holes, excluding those in the bulkhead, and the final alignment can't happen until the bonnet is in situ, so initially the bolts are only done up finger-tight.

With the bonnet added to the bulkhead, the front panel is aligned with the leading edge of the bonnet, taking advantage of the oversize mounting holes at the base of the front panel and the slotted (left/right) holes in the chassis. The wings are then set to the correct position, sliding them up or down the slotted holes on the front panel until they are level, with an even gap between the side edges of the bonnet and the wing tops.

DOOR SEALS

The 109's refurbished doors are among the last items to be added to the cab, where they receive their new channels and new window glass (in place of the original perspex). The new perspex for the rear of the cab was also added, along with the channels they run in.

Fitting new door seals to a Series I is a little more complicated than it is for later Series Land Rovers, because the seal and its internal metal strip are separate parts that have to be assembled first and cut to length.

The strip being inserted into the rubber seal.

All the demo vehicle's original seal rubbers had perished, leaving just the internal metal strips still riveted round the door frame, so the first step was to remove these strips by drilling out the rivets.

Then a length of metal strip is cut to length, replicating the length of the original seal. (The example photographed is the vertical seal at the lower front of the right-hand door aperture.) This is then held up against the original rivet holes in the door aperture, and the position of the holes is marked on the new metal using a permanent marker. The metal is then placed on to a wooden block, and the holes are drilled out.

The metal strip is then fed into the rubber strip (quite a time-consuming task) and the rubber strip is cut to length. It is then held against the door aperture with the lip of the seal on the inside, and holes are drilled in the rubber, using the rivet holes in the door aperture as a guide for the positioning of the drill bit. Once the holes are drilled, the seal can then be riveted to the door. Repeat this process for all six seals on each door.

For ease, ordinary pop rivets were used for these seals, but to replicate the original spec semi-tubular rivets with a shallow dome should be used.

For those who live in a cold climate where there is a risk of sub-zero temperatures freezing the door against its seals, a thin smear of silicone grease along the seals will prevent this from happening, and will not degrade the rubber.

INTERIOR TRIM

A Series I such as the demo 109 has very little trim – in fact the only trim items that this vehicle requires are its seats. Virtually every common piece of trim is available new, although certain rare items – such as door cards and seats for Tickford Station Wagons – are not held in stock and would need to be commissioned to order.

If new seats are purchased they usually come with M6 metric threads for attaching the hinged bracket to the backrest (correct at the time of writing, but do check this with the supplier). Those who wish to retain the original BSF threads will need to have the original seat backs retrimmed – but this service is likely to cost more, and will take longer. For the 109 restoration it was therefore decided to purchase new seats from Exmoor Trim.

The colour of the interior trim in Series Is usually depended on the colour of the bodywork. Blue was chosen for the demo 109 because it was felt it complemented the grey paint, and early 86in and 107in Land Rovers that were painted grey were fitted with blue seats. However, this is technically incorrect for the model year of this particular vehicle: from 1957, 'Elephant Hide' was the correct seat trim for Series Is with grey bodywork, and this also became an option in Bronze Green Series Is.

The new seats do not come supplied with the metal brackets for the rear of the seat backs, so the originals have to be transferred from the old seats. In our case, one of these had become weak through corrosion, so an identical piece was cut and folded from a sheet of steel, with the other brackets used as a template to position the holes in exactly the right locations. The new

Door seal being pop riveted to the bulkhead.

The finished seal – note the orientation of the rubber lip.

Hinge brackets with central split pins and spring washers were transferred from the old seats.

A new seat with two original brackets, and a new leather strap.

Replacement bracket (right), made from scratch.

Door card in 'Elephant Hide', fitted to a left-hand-drive 107in Station Wagon

metal was etch primed and painted grey to protect it and help it blend in with the other three brackets.

Although it was decided not to add door trim to the 109in, to help retain its pared-back and utilitarian feel, new door cards are available in period-style trim. For example, the door on the 107in Station Wagon above has trim (bought from Undercover Covers) finished in grey 'Elephant Hide' vinyl – also available in green and RAF blue – with a wooden frame backing, as the original. (The kit also includes a shoulder rest and trim for the upper section of the door, not fitted here.)

The new door card is ready-made to fit, and only requires screwing into position round the galvanized frame using self-tapping screws. First, holes will need to be drilled round the edges of the card to match any pre-existing holes in the frame, or – if the frame does not already have screw holes – equally spaced holes drilled through the door card and the frame together. The holes drilled should be smaller than the self-tapping screws.

16

Rebuilding the Tray

The trayback body style is synonymous with Australian 'utes' (short for 'utility vehicles') and has been fitted to many types of 4×4 from various manufacturers. It was never officially offered by Land Rover, so there were no plans or parts catalogues to guide us through the process of rebuilding this one. The work in this chapter therefore involved more creativity than might normally be associated with vehicle restoration.

The tray needed to be rebuilt mostly from scratch as it was extremely battered all round, but care was taken to retain some of the original structure. We believe it originates from the 1970/80s rather than the 1950s, owing to its all-steel construction (later trays would start incorporating aluminium), so old photos of Australian trayback

Land Rovers were researched in order to come up with a design that was more typical of the 1950s. (Although this is a utility vehicle, aesthetics have a role to play.) Essentially this meant changing the steel base for a wooden one, and omitting the side panels.

For the floorboards, reclaimed 8×2in pitch pine was used, which has the double benefit of giving an almost 'patina' look – though not too pristine to use – while saving a little money. It was therefore perfectly appropriate for the approach with this restoration. The planks had already been chemically treated, making them durable against rot. This is another reason for replacing metal with wood: a steel loadbed in the UK would rapidly rust as soon as any coating was scratched away.

Different species of wood all have different properties when it comes to rot resistance, hardness, the amount they swell when wet, and their ability to resist warping, so it is worth thinking about the timber you use. (A useful little book summarizing the properties of timbers is *Wood Identifier* by Aidan Walker.) If a floor is liable to be damaged, make sure the design enables the boards to be easily removed and replaced. A simpler alternative is simply to use strong plywood (ideally resin-impregnated) as found in many trailers, but use wooden planks if a more accurate recreation of the original style is wanted.

In total, this tray took roughly forty hours to build, and required about £500 of materials. A lot of the time was spent cutting and welding, as there were many welds involved.

The tray is very heavy, so a forklift was used to lift the original trayback on to axle stands so it could be dismantled and cut down. Otherwise it would have required four people to lift it.

The original metal floor and the horizontal rails that supported it were all welded together, so removal required a lot of cutting with an angle grinder. This left the rear crossmember and main longitudinal chassis rails and the front headboard (detached) – these were the only sections being retained. They were rested on to the chassis of the vehicle so that continual checks could be made, before any new parts were welded together.

A trial fit involved laying the horizontal rails and boards on top so the final measurements could be decided. It was important that the boards should not fit too snugly because the wood needs a little room to expand and contract, so it was decided there would be a 20mm gap at each side of the tray.

We replaced the original horizonal rails with new 20 × 20mm box-section steel, which was welded to the main

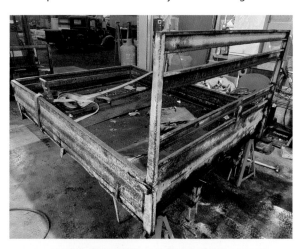

The original trayback, ready to be stripped.

The underneath view shows the extent of the corrosion, especially round the back.

The rear crossmember and main longitudinal legs, after removal of the floor and rails. This is what the new parts will be built on to.

Trial fit of the new and horizontal rails.

legs. Before each weld, an angle grinder was used to remove the rust off the old metal, and checks were made to ensure the alignment of the new horizontals in relation to the trayback's main rails.

The new horizontals prior to being welded on to the main rails to act as cross-bracing for the floorboards.

THE HEADBOARD

Unlike the original design for the head-board, this 109's needed to be unbolt-able, for two reasons: to allow the floorboards to be slotted into place, and to allow them to be replaced at a

The headboard laid flat, with the new C-section being welded to the bottom.

Grinding the original metal clean so the new panel can be lapped over and welded to it.

later date, if or when they were to deteriorate.

The lower section of the headboard was badly rusted, so it was necessary to recreate the bottom part of the front wall, and make a new horizonal channel for the floorboards to slot into. The rotten section of wall was cut out and replaced with a replica section made from 2.5mm steel sheet, slightly overlapping the original upper section, so they could be welded together. A continual line of weld would cause the metal to warp very easily, so instead a series of 2in stitch welds were made, spaced 5in apart.

To hold the front of the floorboards, a new C-shaped channel was fabricated out of two pieces of 2 × 2in angle, welded back to back.

THE SIDE RAILS

The side rails were replaced using 2 × 3in angle. Along the rear crossmember, the wood tucks under a 1in return lip that holds them in place, so a matching 1in lip needs to be added, running along the length of each side rail for the wood to slot underneath. The head-

The new front wall section is added, using a series of small welds to avoid warping.

board was standing on the chassis at this stage, to make sure that the side rails could be cut to the right length.

At each end of the rear crossmember a small section was sliced out of the top, and at the rear end of each rail a section was cut out of the side. This made them slot neatly into each other, with the weld being on three axes (left/right, up/down and front/back), which

The side sections being added. Note the cutaway round the rear crossmember.

The lashdown bar is welded in place.

A trial fit to work out the new way of mounting the headboard to the main rails.

Vertical tubes, one per horizontal rail, add some much needed rigidity.

The complete frame, minus the headboard and floor. Note the horizontal sections front and rear for mounting to the chassis.

created a much stronger joint than if the rails had simply been butted up against the crossmember and welded on two axes (left/right and up/down).

At the front of each side rail, the

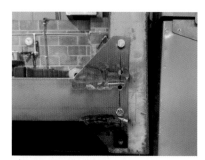

The right-hand side, front, showing how the braces counteract stress created by any rocking motion from the headboard.

This return lip was welded in to fill the gap and give the wood a tighter groove to slot into.

join with the headboard is liable to come under a lot of stress during driving, as the headboard rocks back and forth. Therefore the joints were braced by making fins out of 3mm plate and welding them on each side of the join, top and bottom, to spread the load. Five bolt holes were then drilled through the new metal and the headboard, to maximize rigidity.

The tray was originally attached to the chassis using U-bolts at each of the tray's mounting feet. Our revised version involved a long section of steel angle along the front of the tray, and a shorter section of 4 × 2in box section across the back; holes were drilled in both of these, enabling them to be bolted to the pre-existing mounting tabs on the chassis. This design should be significantly more secure than the original.

LASHDOWN BARS

The main structure of the tray was now complete, but it lacked any means of securing a load, so the final stage of fabrication involved adding lashdown bars down each side. The originals were badly broken, so new ones had to

be devised. These were initially given one weld at each end, securing them at the rear crossmember and the headboard, and then small vertical posts were welded along their length to give the required strength (this is slightly different from the original design).

These posts were cut from the same metal as the lashdown bars, with each one corresponding to the end of one of the horizontal rails. The posts were welded top and bottom, as well as against the horizontal rails, adding strength. This was a long process, but these bars do need to be rigid and strong.

The lamps were trial fitted to ensure there were no unforeseen problems, and that the new wiring loom was long enough to reach them without any extension being required. Then the

The tray is complete, ready for stripping and painting.

The tray and headboard removed and moved to the shipping container for blasting.

whole tray was removed and dismantled for blasting and painting.

It is important to blast all surfaces, new and old, to ensure a good key for the paint, but the blasting was mainly focused on the original rusty metal – especially in the crevices around the main rails where dirt and corrosion accumulate.

Once the tray and headboard were returned to the workshop, they received two coats of primer, two further coats of high-build primer, and then two coats of Dove Grey – the same paint that was used for the rest of the bodywork.

When the paint was dry the tray was then returned to the vehicle, reassem-

The tray and headboard receive their first coat of primer.

bled, and bolted to the chassis across the front and rear.

If the floorboards ever need removing in future, for replacement or for access to the chassis underneath, this can be done by unbolting the front headboard and sliding it forwards, exposing the front ends of the planks.

Each plank can then be pulled forwards a little, so it's no longer tucked under the rear crossmember, and the side planks can be slid inwards – then they will simply lift out.

The finished tray. The glossy finish is rain, not varnish! (The doors are yet to be restored at this stage.)

The unboltable headboard will enable planks to be removed when required.

17

The Electrical System

With the bulkhead and bodywork assembled you can start to complete the installation of the electrical system, which is as simple as will be found on any vehicle of this era. Restoration will usually require an entirely new wiring loom, along with various lamps and switches, installed with the help of the appropriate wiring diagrams (found in Rover's workshop manual) to tell you which wires go where.

Installing the wiring for a whole vehicle can seem daunting, so this chapter will guide you through some basic principles that make this work achievable by anyone with a basic knowledge of electrics. No expensive equipment is

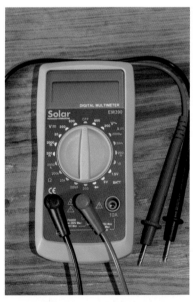

The multimeter is a versatile and essential tool.

Crimping tool designed for bullet connectors.

required, although a wire stripper and a crimping tool may be needed for replacing certain terminals, including a crimper that is designed for bullet connectors. A basic multimeter will also be useful for diagnosing any faults that may occur.

At this stage in the demo 109's restoration, the main front-to-rear section of the new loom had already been installed in the chassis rails. The headlamp cables had also been run through the front panel, but all the electrical equipment still had to be inspected, refurbished in some cases, and installed.

The types of electrical equipment evolved continuously, partly in response to changing regulations. Determining which parts to use can therefore be complex. The full topic is too large for this book, but a few of the key differences will be described here.

POSITIVE VERSUS NEGATIVE EARTH

All Series Is were originally positive earth, meaning the battery is earthed from its positive terminal, while the feeds to the lights and other equipment are all negative. From the 1960s this was replaced by negative earth systems – a decision that was made across the vehicle industry. There is some debate over the precise reasons for the change, but a key factor seems to have been the way in which galvanic corrosion attacks the wiring in vehicles with negative earth, but in vehicles with positive earth it primarily attacks the earthing points to which the terminals attach (and replacing the wiring is a cheaper solution than repairing rusted earth points).

Another downside of a positive earth system is that it is incompatible with modern cigarette lighters and the accessories that typically run from them. If you intend to drive long

journeys in your Series I, a negative earth system might therefore be more appropriate.

If you wish to convert to negative earth but retain the dynamo, it will be necessary to change its polarity – a process that is sometimes referred to as 'flashing' the dynamo, and achieved with the dynamo out of the vehicle. A pair of jump leads is attached to a 12-volt battery, and the negative lead is clamped to the dynamo's casing. The positive lead is then touched against the main output terminal for around five seconds, twice in a row. You will know that the process has worked if the charge light on the dash is properly extinguished when the vehicle is running.

Switching from a dynamo to an alternator will also require a change to negative earth, and remove the need for a voltage regulator (sometimes known as the voltage control box). However, the regulator can be retained as a junction box for the original wiring to the charge light and the ammeter.

THE INSTRUMENT PANEL

Before the wiring loom is installed, there are some aesthetic improvements to be made.

The restoration of dials and gauges is complex work that is best handled by a specialist, of which there are few. Parts can be sourced for the later gauges, as used in our 109in, and a specialist will charge around £300 per gauge – assuming the gauge can be salvaged. Parts supply is not so good for the earlier style of gauges fitted to 80in models, so a specialist is less likely to be able to fix one that is non-functioning.

Whatever the style of gauge, if it is faulty, the most affordable solution will be to find a working second-hand unit and give it a visual overhaul or transfer parts between the two – the kind of work that anyone can do. This was the

The reassembled gauge, after cleaning and spraying, and looking a million times better.

The demo 109's dash panel instruments and lights were shabby, and the speedometer was broken.

Dirty instruments and panel, ready for restoration.

Rotate the bezel until its tabs align with the gaps in the casing.

Glass and bezel removed, revealing rust that will be rubbed away.

The instrument casing cleans up nicely. Be careful to avoid scratching the black face of the dial.

The bezel is scrubbed clean prior to painting.

The broken speedometer (left) with the functioning unit that replaced it (right).

option chosen with the demo vehicle's speedometer.

The instruments tend to corrode round the bezels, and the glass goes cloudy with the build-up of rust and dirt on both sides. The affected areas can be taken apart quite easily for cleaning and repainting, which has a very positive effect on the overall appearance of a shabby-looking dash panel.

To remove the bezel, it needs to be turned until the tabs on its back line up with the cutouts in the lip round the casing – then it should pull off, and the glass will come away with it.

Wire wool is ideal for cleaning dirt from the bezel and the glass, and the rim of the instrument's housing. If you are gentle with the wool there is no significant risk of scratching the glass, and glass-cleaning fluid can be used to finish off if the glass is particularly grimy. The bezel is then ready to be sprayed with gloss black paint, and when fully dry the unit can be reassembled – which is the opposite procedure to dismantling.

Our 109's speedometer was missing its glass, and its needle and internal mechanism were clearly broken. A shabby but working second-hand unit was sourced, and smartened up by using the better condition bezel and

The lightly refurbished speedo – cleaned, painted and lubricated.

These obsolete parts hold the lamps into the instrument panel.

Our reassembled warning light, back in position.

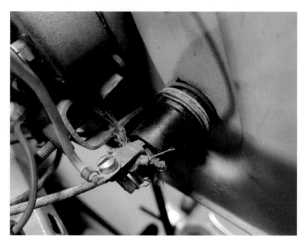

The refurbished lamp, looking as new.

rear mounting clamp from the original unit. The bezel and glass received the same treatment that was given to the other gauges, and the needle was repainted with white enamel paint. Undoing the two screws at the rear enabled a visual inspection of the mechanism, and a little 3-in-1 oil was applied to the gears. The two gauges were then returned to the instrument panel (which by now had been stripped and painted separately).

The bulb holders in the instrument panel can also be effectively renovated – this is worth doing because replacements would have cost around £40 each.

First they were stripped down to their component parts. Then the bezels were scrubbed and spray painted with matt black to restore the original finish, and the coloured glass was cleaned on both sides. The terminals were cleaned with a bench-mounted wire wheel, and wire wool was used to clean the Bakelite and ensure that the electrical connections were rust free.

A fragment of cloth insulates the earth post (positive) with the small brass screw from the centre post (negative). The cloth insulation is an original part of the lamp.

Try not to lose the springs and C-shaped clips that secure the lamps into the panel, as new replacements are not available. Each set has three parts: the C-clip that is pushed into the outer casing of the bulb holder, the washer that sits on top of it, and the spring that sits on the washer.

The lamp is pushed into the panel from the front, then the spring is added from the behind. The cup is then added to the back, and the C-clip holds it in place.

The central ignition switch was replaced with a new unit, then the instrument panel was complete and ready to be wired in.

The new speedometer cable was also added to the back of the gauge and run out through a hole in the bulkhead, down behind the engine, past the

The original dash warning lamp units, with their bezels and glass removed.

SAFETY PREPARATIONS

Once you are ready to connect the battery, make sure there are no shorts to ground, or uninsulated cables that could cause a spark. It is important there is no flammable material or spilled fluids such as petrol within the vicinity of the vehicle. Sparks may be caused by (for example) carelessly shorting the battery terminals by resting a spanner on the battery, or accidentally touching a feed wire against any earthed component.

The restored instrument panel with refurbished instruments and lights.

left-hand side of the gear lever, round the left side of the gearbox to the housing at the back of the transfer box, and mounted to the clip at the back of the gearbox. A separate clamping ring must be fitted over the cable first; this attaches the cable at the transfer box, where it is secured with three screws.

EXTERIOR LAMPS

Many different types of exterior lamp were fitted to Series Is, and trafficators remained an option until quite late in production. Fitting the correct type will add authenticity to a restoration, but will not necessarily be the most practical, or the safest, so the intended use for the vehicle should be taken into consideration.

All lamp units are available to buy, although some can be expensive – especially rear D-lamps (Lucas part number ST51) that were fitted to 80s and also early 86/107s. New-old stock trafficators are also extremely rare and sell for hundreds of pounds each.

The rear D-light, as fitted to 80s.

The Lucas SE62 trafficator was optional on 80s. It is pictured here fitted on a 1948 model, with the original spec wiring sheath.

An early 5in Lucas headlamp, as found in 'lights behind the grille' 80s.

With the exception of the earliest 'lights behind the grille' models, all Series Is use 7in Lucas F700 lamps – part number 553935 (a common fitment in vehicles of this era) – nested in steel bowls, rather than the plastic equivalents found on later Series vehicles. They are simple to assemble and adjust, and use two 'pre-focus' 36/36w bulbs, meaning that each bulb draws the same current for dipped and high beam. These bulbs can be replaced in seconds without any tools, simply by twisting the whole unit to dismount the bezel from the spring-loaded screws, pulling the lamp out, disconnecting

the plug and removing the bulb – then refitting. A notch in the bulb's mounting plate prevents the bulb from being fitted the wrong way up.

Confusion can arise over the term 'bezel', as it tends to be used interchangeably to describe the steel ring that mounts to the spring-loaded adjuster screws, or (on later Series Land Rovers) the aluminium trim piece that surrounds the light. Series Is don't have this trim piece so the confusion is less likely to occur, but when ordering parts, make it clear that you are referring to the inner mounting ring with its slotted holes.

The original bowl with the new wiring passing through.

The Lucas 488 sidelight in position.

The original Lucas F700 lamp attached, with the bezel resting on it.

Constituent parts of a Lucas 488 sidelight.

The Wipac stop lamp and Lucas indicator give a period look.

The sidelight is wired like this.

Installing the headlamp into the front panel.

The original headlamp bowls of the project 109 were in good condition, as is usually the case with Australian vehicles – this is much less likely in UK vehicles, where they often accumulate water. This 109's were sanded down and painted black before reinstallation. Any deterioration of the internal reflective surface in the headlamp units themselves will mean that they need replacing, as was the case with ours.

After installing the headlamps, the beam pattern needed adjusting. An MoT station will have the equipment to test this accurately, but a basic set-up can be achieved without it – this is most easily successful in dim light. The Land Rover needs to be parked on level ground, facing a wall about 8m (25ft) away. Then a measurement is taken to determine the height of the headlamp bulbs from the ground, and this height is marked on the wall. The headlamps are switched on to main beam, and the spring-loaded screws are adjusted so that the top of each beam pattern comes up just a few inches below the mark, with each side level.

As for the flashers, Lucas 488 front sidelights are being fitted with glass lenses; they take twin-element bulbs, and are slightly larger than the single-element Lucas 489 lights that would originally have been fitted. By the time our vehicle was made in 1957, Lucas 488s were standard on 88in Station Wagons and optional on other models.

Our stop lamps are new-old stock Wipac S3588 lamps, a type often fitted to trucks in the late 1950s and early 1960s, so they give a period look and suit the trayback body style – although they were never fitted by Solihull. In its original form, this vehicle would have had Lucas 518 'pork pie' stop lamps, or (because it is a late model) either Della Red Beacon or Sparto rear lamps. Earlier models would have had D-lamps. The rear indicators are also Lucas 488s with single filament bulbs, and amber glass instead of clear.

INSTALLING THE LOOM AND OTHER ELECTRICAL COMPONENTS

After taking the new wiring loom out of its bag, spread it out on the ground to separate the different wires and arrange them in the same layout that they will be in when fitted to the vehicle. The kit will comprise various smaller harnesses and some individual

Dash wiring being fed through.

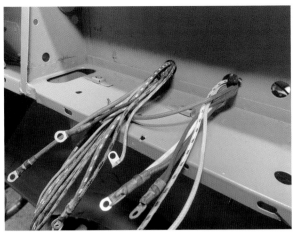

View of the rear side of the bulkhead. The left-hand bundle contains wires for the fuel gauge, ammeter, main-beam light and indicators. The wires on the right are for the ignition and light switch, plus warning lights for the choke temperature and the dynamo charging light.

wires, and their colours should match those of the original. Certain colours changed over the decades, but in a new loom the colours should replicate the originals, so an original wiring diagram can be used. For example, earth wires in our loom are black, as was standard in British vehicles up to the 1990s.

There is one single 35amp fuse for the whole vehicle, and not all the circuits round the vehicle use it – for example, there is no fuse for the headlights, sidelights, coil or fuel pump. It is therefore particularly important to make sure that none of the wiring is able to chafe against the bodywork, as a damaged sheath will enable a short to ground, which could blow a switch or bulb, and potentially cause the loom to overheat and catch fire.

The two bundles of the bulkhead loom can now be inserted through the two holes in the bulkhead, after adding grommets over them. Check the colours with the wiring diagram to determine which group of wires is which. In our case, the wires for the regulator, fuel pump and ignition/light switch go to the right-hand side (the driver's side) of the vehicle; those for the horn, coil, fuel gauge, ammeter, indicators, main beam light, choke light and oil-pressure light should be on the left.

It is important to use rubber grommets of the correct size wherever wires pass through a panel, to prevent the wires from chafing and then shorting against the bodywork. The bulkhead loom's two large washers were left loose until the final test-drive phase, in case the harness needed any adjustment.

Single bullet connectors: one wire in, one wire out…

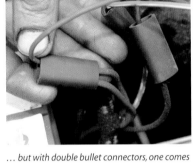

… but with double bullet connectors, one comes in, two go out – commonly misunderstood.

All the wiring uses Lucas bullet connectors and terminals, in both single and double format. The doubles are often confused, in the assumption that two wires can come in and two wires can come out. In reality, these connectors are designed to split a single feed off into multiple directions – a similar concept to a T-piece.

The demo 109's fuse holder is a very rare item. It was dirty but in good condition. To ensure clean connections the contact points were rubbed gently with emery paper, before being added to the reconditioned mounting plinth,

The fusebox, before being cleaned up, with the manufacture date of August 1957 stamped in the side.

Brake-light switch, where water and mud can cause problems.

LEFT TO RIGHT: *Reconditioned fuel pump, regulator and fuse holder, mounted on the freshly painted plinth.*

New flasher relay.

If the dynamo is being replaced with an alternator, the voltage regulator becomes redundant – although some people choose to keep it in place (disconnected) for aesthetic reasons. The demo vehicle was missing its regulator, but fortunately the RB105 is available to buy new.

Mounted to the back of this plinth is the three-pin flasher unit, Lucas part number SFB100. (On an 80 the flasher is located behind the instrument panel.) New-old stock versions use a bi-metallic strip inside (this is what makes the clicking sound), whereas modern versions use a diode. Experience has shown that modern Lucas-branded versions will work with positive earth, but cheaper versions will only work with negative earth. The flasher unit sends out two feeds: one to the dash-mounted switch, which determines which lights to flash, and one to the green light above the switch – which is the same as the oil-pressure light, but with different coloured glass.

This is the type of flasher set-up that was used for Station Wagons fitted with Lucas 488 sidelamps (described earlier in this chapter). In earlier models fitted

which was repainted separately from the bulkhead.

The gauges, fuel tank sender, indicators, horn and wiper motor all share the same 35amp fuse, which will typically only fail as a result of water ingress in the brake-light switch.

The fuel pump, voltage regulator and fuel holder are fixed to a separate plinth. Once the plinth has been sanded and painted, these parts are all assembled together, and the plinth is bolted to the front of the bulkhead.

The Lucas RB105 regulator is an electromechanical device that stabilizes the voltage from the dynamo. (Various different regulators were fitted to 80s.)

Auxiliary switch panel for the indicator switch and lamp.

The assembly has been returned to the bulkhead, and the wires connected. The wire from the dynamo to the middle of the regulator box is the next to be fitted.

with indicators, a Lucas switch interrupts the brake light and front sidelight circuits. These switches are rare and difficult to source, but a dedicated indicator circuit will not be needed.

The mounting plinth can now be fixed to the bulkhead, and the new wires from the bulkhead loom are attached. The two wires connecting the voltage regulator and dynamo (yellow, and yellow with green) are bundled together separately from the main harness. When connecting the fuel pump, it is important to use a lead washer on the main terminal, to ensure a good connection between the post and the armature wiring.

The new loom is designed for an original dynamo that would require a ring terminal secured by a nut, but our modern equivalent needed a spade connector instead, so this part of the loom had to be adapted accordingly. A similar change was required for the terminal on the oil-pressure switch.

The very corroded headlamp dipswitch in the driver's footwell was replaced with this modern remake. It cost more than the later Series IIA type, which is often used instead, but the later version is smaller, incorrect for the period, and usually not as robust. These Series I switches were only fitted to 88s and 109s, but they also carried over into Series II production; they can be distinguished from the later type by the diamond-shaped back. The three wires are connected to the terminal on its underside, then the switch is screwed into position using slot-headed screws, with locknuts on the back. These switch units have extra mounting holes because they were fitted to a variety of vehicles, but only two of them need be used.

This wiring that connects the regulator to the dynamo (with the original ring terminals) is separate from the main part of the loom.

The dynamo connected to the loom with new spade terminals.

New headlamp dipswitch, identifiable by the triangular plate on the underside.

The starter-motor cable attached, plus the wire for the oil-pressure switch, whose terminal also required a change to a spade connector.

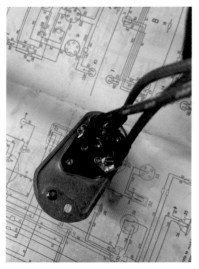

The wiper motor was dismantled but was found to be in good working order.

Wire orientation on the underside of the dipswitch.

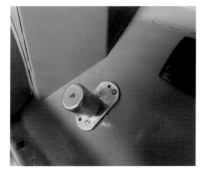

The dipswitch wired up and screwed into position.

There were two types of wiper motor fitted to Series Is, and the one pictured is the Lucas model that was fitted to all Series Is from 1953. It was found to be in good working condition, but we removed its cover and inspected and cleaned its internals to be sure. The armature was scrubbed with a wire wheel to restore some shine, then reassembled and bolted to the bulkhead with a new wiper arm and blade. One common weak point is the spindle shaft to which the wiper arm attaches, but this part is available to buy new, as is the manual override handles. (80in Series Is use a Lucas CW1 wiper motor which is smaller, and the arm has a slightly smaller swept area.) A second wiper motor was an optional extra, not fitted to our vehicle.

New versus old earth strap.

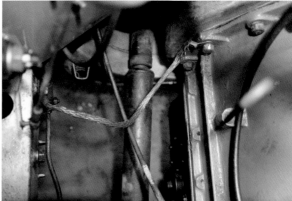

ABOVE: *Earth strap in situ.*

LEFT: *The junction box on the front of the driver's footwell.*

A new earth strap is fitted between the gearbox and the chassis. This is critical but easily overlooked, and is always worth replacing with a new part, as a poor earth will result in poor starting.

New battery leads (to run from the battery to the start switch, and from there to the starter motor) are also made from 16mm battery cable. For maximum durability these have a soldered terminal on the end, finished with heat shrink to help shield the terminal from arcing against misplaced spanners; this is more important on live feed wires than ground wires, but still worth adding.

The ignition system was completed by bolting a new coil to the bulkhead, and connecting it to the ignition switch and the distributor.

Technically the horn should be a Clearhooter type, mounted on the left-hand bonnet hinge, but a more attainable version was fitted, as it was felt that the £100+ cost of an original model was difficult to justify for a non-concours restoration of this type.

Once all the electrical components are installed and found to be working, the final step is to revisit the entire system to ensure no grommets have been left out, and that any loose cables are tied up using cable ties to prevent them flapping and chafing.

New battery lead with soldered terminal and heat-shrunk end.

18

Fine Tuning and Test Drives

The demo vehicle is now fully assembled and ready for its first test drive. This concluding chapter will finish a few final calibrations, outline the road-test procedure, and describe a few common tweaks that may be required for your own restoration.

All vehicles over forty years old in the UK are exempt from requiring an MoT pass certificate. However, the MoT is a useful opportunity for a qualified 'second pair of eyes' to check that your vehicle is safe and legal, and we strongly advise that you have the test performed. The Federation of British History Vehicle Clubs publishes a list of 'Historic Friendly MoT Stations' on their website (www.fbhvc.co.uk), whose mechanics should be familiar with the testing requirements of vehicles

such as these, and not have unrealistic demands of them.

It should be noted that the MoT exemption does not apply to vehicles that have received 'substantial changes' within the last thirty years. Most modifications that are typically applied to Series Is will not count as 'substantial', but if you are uncertain, check the guidelines on the government website: search for 'historic classic vehicles MoT exemption criteria' at www.gov.uk.

All vehicles must be taxed and insured, and have valid V5 documentation before being used on the road in the UK for the first time, even for a test drive. Once your vehicle reaches forty years old (so this applies to all Series I Land Rovers) it is eligible for road tax exemption – and you must apply for

this from the DVLA before using the vehicle on the road. Even without an MoT, the law requires that the vehicle is roadworthy, so your restoration must be safe and complete, including details such as number plate and functioning lights. In our case we had access to some private roads surrounding the workshop, so we did not have to jump through these bureaucratic hoops before road testing the vehicle (hence the lack of number plates in the photos).

TEST-DRIVE PROCEDURE

Each drive lasts a few miles and should involve some periods of fully open throttle and heavy braking (where it is safe to do so), in order to allow

The finished vehicle.

Articulating the rear suspension by parking one wheel on a mound.

the engine and transmission oils to reach a high temperature, and to test the strength of all gaskets, bearings, pipework unions, hose clips and so on. Meanwhile you should be feeling carefully for any slackness through the steering wheel, ensuring all the pedals and gearchange operate smoothly, and listening for any unusual noises from around the engine, transmission, axles and suspension.

Taking the vehicle off-road will put extra strain on the wheels, suspension and steering components, giving you good peace of mind that they are (hopefully) functioning well. Driving along a rough track will also reveal any loose electrical terminals or bodywork fixings, and it is better for you to discover any such issues now, rather than at speed on the open road. However, for safety's sake it is important not to drive the vehicle over difficult terrain until you have tested it on more gentle ground first.

Find an empty space where you can drive in a figure-of-eight, testing the steering at full lock in each direction. You want to make sure that you have the same number of turns from lock to lock, and also that the tyres do not rub against the arches.

One useful exercise is to articulate the suspension to its furthest extent, to check there is no snagging of tyres, exhaust or brake lines. This can be done by jacking up one corner of the vehicle at a time, or by parking with one wheel higher than the other.

For anyone restoring a Series I for the first time, it is not easy to keep all the necessary checks in mind, so a printed list is a useful aid (even though an experienced expert will rarely need to use one). The checklist can be referred to after a series of test drives, with any issue being marked with a cross and then addressed in the workshop. Each test drive begins with a clean checklist, and hopefully the number of issues noted after time will gradually reduce to zero with each successive drive.

The 'Defect Location' sections of Rover's original Workshop Manual provide a useful reference for diagnosing a large number of symptoms, with lists of possible causes to investigate.

ENGINE AND DRIVETRAIN

After driving the vehicle and assessing its performance, it is likely that you will need to make adjustments to the carburettor's mixture and idle speed. The idle should be adjusted to between 700 and 850rpm when the engine is warm, but without a rev counter you need to judge this by ear. The mixture can be assessed while driving and putting the engine under heavy load; black smoke from the exhaust (signifying unburnt fuel) suggests that the mixture is too rich and the screw needs to be wound in slightly; no black smoke but faltering acceleration suggests the mixture is too lean.

Oil seepage from either of the rocker covers or the sump may require a gasket to be replaced, and expansion of the radiator hoses may reveal coolant leaks. Small seepages can sometimes evaporate before you spot them, but they tend to leave a tell-tale stain. If your hoses are new and the metal they join to is clean, any seepage can usually be stopped by simply tightening the hose clip or repositioning the hose.

After 100 miles (160km) the tightness of the cylinder-head bolts will need to be rechecked with a torque wrench, and a new gasket will be required when refitting the inlet rocker-cover gasket.

Driving puts the vehicle's various flu-

The engine bay.

ids under higher pressure and temperature, making them more likely to leak. Check for signs of dripping oil round the base of the engine, steering box and relay, gearbox, transfer box and axles, and round the drive flanges on the wheels. Over longer distances, leaking oil will cause a greasy spatter up the rear tailgate, but you should spot and rectify any drips before they reach this stage. Generally speaking, minor seepage is acceptable, but drips are not.

STEERING, HANDLING AND BRAKING

If you are confident that all the components are in good condition but the

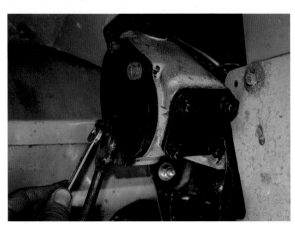

Adjusting the steering box.

steering still feels vague or slack, the steering box probably needs tightening slightly. By contrast, if the steering feels tight, the box is probably too tight, and this will normally be accompanied by a reluctance for the steering to self-centre as you drive along.

For the 'recirculating ball' steering box, adjustment is made using a couple of spanners. With the steering wheel centred, slacken off the outer nut on the right-hand side of the steering box, then wind or unwind the inner thread, and lock it in place by tightening the outer thread. This process will take up any slackness round the gear and the balls. Use small increments of change in

between test drives to help you zero in on the correct calibration. Rover did not recommend a torque setting for this adjuster nut, but suggested tightening 'until resistance is felt', then tightening a further tenth of a turn.

With all the balljoints replaced, the linkages properly calibrated and the steering box and relay in good condition, the steering should be free of play. Do not expect the handling of a sports car or even a basic saloon – but you should feel in direct control of the wheels, and capable of at least 50mph (80km/h) cruising without 'sawing at the wheel'.

The first test of the brakes should be with the vehicle stationary. Simply push the pedal and make sure it feels firm, doesn't sink to the floor, and feels the same every time you push it – without significantly increasing in firmness with each pump.

After doing this, the whole system needs be to be checked for hydraulic fluid leaks before you attempt to drive anywhere. This topic is addressed in Chapter 7, but to recap, the final stage of the brake bleeding procedure is to have someone press firmly and repeatedly on the brake pedal while you inspect the entire system from the master cylinder down to each wheel cylinder, looking for any seeping fluid.

To test the brakes while driving, you will need to make sure there is no one behind you, and also that there are no obstacles on either side that you could swerve into – which can happen if the brakes are imbalanced. From about 20mph, put the gearbox into neutral, return both hands to the wheel and press firmly on the brakes. Notice whether the car tries to pull to either side, and whether the rear wheels are trying to lock up. Pulling to one side means that the brake shoes on one or more of the opposite wheels are not gripping effectively. On a newly restored vehicle this is usually due to poorly adjusted shoes, but it could also result from an oil or fluid leak that has contaminated the inner face of the brake drum. If the rear brakes lock up during heavy braking, this will be caused by poorly adjusted shoes at the front, or air in the brake lines, indicating that more thorough bleeding of the system is required.

Land Rovers were designed to carry and tow heavy loads, so they should brake reasonably well when unladen. Don't be too forgiving if the brakes feel unsafe, but bear in mind that any new brake linings will 'bed in', and require the adjusters to be recalibrated after they have been used a few times.

OUR 109'S TEST DRIVES

Our vehicle received three vigorous test drives of about 5 to 10 miles (8 to 16km) each. These revealed a small number of issues that are typical of those that might be found on any newly restored Series I.

Test Drive One

This was a short drive of a few miles back and forth along a smooth road, and included testing of all the electrical items.

It was determined that the throttle linkage needed some fine adjustment to ensure the accelerator arm was able to open fully. To cure the problem, one of the arms in the engine bay was slackened on the bulkhead-mounted cross-

Road Test Checklist

Vehicle: 1957 109 TRAYBACK

Test number: 1   Date:

Odometer start: 82,011   Odometer finish: 82,019

	Ok?	Notes	Done
Engine			
Idle	◯	Too high	
Acceleration	◯	Adjust linkage	
Temperature	✓		
Electrics			
Lights	✓		
Gauges	✓		
Horn	✓		
Wiper(s)	◯	Adjust sweep	
Transmission			
Clutch pedal feel	✓		
Gear selection	✓		
Holding gears	✓		
High/low ratio selection	✓		
4WD selection	✓		
Steering			
Holding a straight light	✓		
Play	◯	Steering box	
Vibrations	✓		
Handbrake			
Roll test	✓		
Lever travel	✓		
Bodywork			
Weatherproof	✓		
Nothing loose	✓		
Brakes			
Pedal feel	✓		
Emergency stop	✓		
Leaks			
Oils	✓		
Hydraulic	✓		
Coolant	◯	Top hose	

Other observations

Test drive one.

Adjusting the idle screw.

The wiper arm needed slight adjustment.

shaft, then repositioned and retightened. The idle speed was also found to be slightly too high, so the carburettor's idle screw was wound in by about a quarter-turn.

The steering box also felt a little slack, so the adjuster nut was tightened by about an eighth of a turn. We then made a visual inspection for any leaking fluid, checking the wheel cylinders, master cylinder, transmission, axles and all round the engine bay. The only seepage we found was in the top radiator hose, so this was adjusted and retightened.

Some fine calibration was also required to the sweep of the wiper arm, by repositioning the arm on its spindle by a few degrees – then the vehicle was ready for its next test drive.

Test Drive Two

This test drive was a similar distance along the same smooth road, but incorporating some heavier braking and acceleration, plus some extra pot-holes.

By now the new shoes had started to bed in, resulting in slightly too much travel at the brake pedal. Each wheel therefore had to be raised from the ground so that the adjusters could be reassessed, and tightened very slightly where required.

It was also felt that the top end of the engine was noisier than it should have been. The inlet rocker cover was removed and the tappet clearances checked, and a couple of them were found to be slightly too large, so they were readjusted to the specified .010in (when cold) and reassembled. While in the workshop waiting for the engine to cool down, another visual inspection underneath revealed that the rear differential's pinion seal was weeping oil (a common issue), so this had to be replaced.

It was also spotted that the nearside front wing had come to rest gently on one of the brake pipes, and over time this would have chafed against the pipe and caused it to fail – precisely the kind of subtle issue that could have severe safety implications later on. The problem was fixed by slackening the bolts that secure the wing to the front panel, raising the wing, and tightening the bolts again.

Road Test Checklist

Vehicle: 1957   109   TRAYBACK

Test number:	2		Date:		
Odometer start: 82,019			Odometer finish: 82,025		

	Ok?	Notes			Done
Engine					
Idle	✓				
Acceleration	✓				
Temperature	✓				
Electrics					
Lights	✓				
Gauges	✓				
Horn	✓				
Wiper(s)	✓				
Transmission					
Clutch pedal feel	✓				
Gear selection	✓				
Holding gears	✓				
High/low ratio selection	✓				
4WD selection	✓				
Steering					
Holding a straight light	✓				
Play	✓				
Vibrations	✓				
Handbrake					
Roll test	✓				
Lever travel	✓				
Bodywork					
Weatherproof	✓				
Nothing loose	Ⓧ	NSF wing resting on brake pipe			
Brakes					
Pedal feel	Ⓧ	Too much travel			
Emergency stop	✓				
Leaks					
Oils	Ⓧ	Rear pinion seal			
Hydraulic					
Coolant					

Other observations

Top end noisy — check tappets

Test drive two.

Beware of bodywork settling against brake pipes like this.

Test Drive Three

This drive was a repetition of the second test drive, with the addition of a couple of miles along a rough track, including an opportunity to flex the suspension. After re-adjusting the brakes we also performed another brake test (described earlier in this chapter) to ensure they were balanced correctly. Finally we found an open space to drive in a figure of eight, in order to put some strain on the wheel bearings at full steering lock.

The engine was sounding better, and no further issues were detected. Back at the workshop, the vehicle was jacked up and each wheel rocked up and down to check whether any of the wheel bearings needed tightening, but no play was detected. With the vehicle raised on the ramp, all the bolts for the suspension, body mounts, engine and gearbox mounts, propshafts, wheel cylinders, exhaust and steering components were checked to make sure nothing had come loose. The wiring loom was also inspected for any loose wires or chafing, and (now that the cables had had a chance to settle) the two main grommets were inserted into the bulkhead.

To round off the restoration, all the fluid levels were checked again, and all the grease nipples round the entire

Road Test Checklist

Vehicle: 1957 109 TRAYBACK

Test number: 3   Date:

Odometer start: 82,025   Odometer finish: 82,033

	Ok?	Notes	Done
Engine			
Idle	✓		
Acceleration	✓		
Temperature	✓		
Electrics			
Lights	✓		
Gauges	✓		
Horn	✓		
Wiper(s)	✓		
Transmission			
Clutch pedal feel	✓		
Gear selection	✓		
Holding gears	✓		
High/low ratio selection	✓		
4WD selection	✓		
Steering			
Holding a straight light	✓		
Play	✓		
Vibrations	✓		
Handbrake			
Roll test	✓		
Lever travel	✓		
Bodywork			
Weatherproof	✓		
Nothing loose	✓		
Brakes			
Pedal feel	✓		
Emergency stop	✓		
Leaks			
Oils	✓		
Hydraulic	✓		
Coolant	✓		

Other observations

Test drive three: a clean sheet.

These grommets could now be pushed into the bulkhead.

The wing getting a final polish.

vehicle were checked to make sure they were fully packed with fresh grease.

Finally, all the demo 109 needed was a good polish, fresh numberplates… and it was ready for its MoT.

FINISHED!

Our work is now complete. The result is a practical and characterful Series I, ideal for use around a farm, estate or other business. And because this is such a pared-back example, it will be an ideal blank slate if any future owner wishes to adapt it to more specialist use. Perhaps its next keeper will install a Fairey overdrive for better cruising ability, coupled with a Smiths heater and interior trim for a more civilized ride. Perhaps free-wheeling hubs might be installed for (marginally) better fuel efficiency, and perhaps a rear power take-off might be fitted (together with an oil cooler and temperature gauge) to operate a circular saw or other machinery. The range of possibilities is extensive.

A Series I can be put to any number of practical uses, and offers decades of enjoyment in the process. Giving this one a new lease of life has been a hugely satisfying experience, worth the hundreds of hours and thousands of pounds that have been invested in it.

The finished restoration.

OPPOSITE AND ABOVE: *The finished restoration continued.*

The finished restoration continued.

The finished restoration continued.

Appendix

PARTS SUPPLIERS

Autosparks
Nottinghamshire
0115 949 7211
www.autosparks.co.uk

Black Paw 4× 4
East Riding of Yorkshire
01430 861077
www.blackpaw4x4.co.uk

Carburetter Exchange
Bedfordshire
01525 371369
www.carburetterexchange.co.uk

Charlesworth & Son Ltd
West Midlands
01675 470382
www.charlesworthmouldings.co.uk

CKD Shop
Warwickshire
01926 911352
www.ckdshop.co.uk

Cross Channel Classics (Australian 109 supplied by)
West Sussex
07849 979105
www.crosschannelclassics.com

Design & Development Engineering
Hampshire
01730 827121
www.designdevelopmenteng.co.uk

Europa Spares
Staffordshire
01283 815609
www.europaspares.com

Exmoor Trim
Somerset
01984 635060
www.exmoortrim.co.uk

Flannery Speedometer Repair
Gloucestershire
01594 861095
www.magnetic-speedometer-repair.com

Holden Vintage & Classic
Herefordshire
01885 488488
www.holden.co.uk

HDS Engineering (machined our flywheel)
East Riding of Yorkshire
01430 860510

John Wearing (Rover P4 specialist)
Lancashire
01254 386935
www.johnwearingp4parts.co.uk

L.R. Optional Equipment
Leicestershire
07575 986344
www.lroe.co.uk

Northern Radiators (recored our radiator)
West Yorkshire
0113 243 5051
www.northernradiators.co.uk

P.A. Blanchard (supplied our short rear halfshaft)
East Riding of Yorkshire
01430 872765
www.pablanchard.co.uk

Parrys (supplied our paint)
Greater Manchester
01942 244669
www.parrysgroup.co.uk

Past Parts (reconditioned our rear-wheel cylinders and master cylinder)
Suffolk
01284 750729
www.pastparts.co.uk

Pegasus Parts
Surrey
01737 764377
www.pegasusparts.co.uk

Radford Bulkheads
Aberdeenshire
01346 531062
www.radfordbulkheads.lrsoc.com

Stephen A Brear Gearboxes Ltd (rebuilt our gearbox)
Leeds
01132 632073
www.stephenbreargearboxes.co.uk

Series I Club Shop
www.lrsoc.com
email clubshop@lrsoc.co.uk

Tom Pickford
www.wwspares.co.uk

Undercover Covers
West Midlands
0121 622 5562
www.undercovercovers.co.uk

WHERE TO LEARN MORE

Perhaps the best way to learn about Series I restoration is to see as many restored and original Series Is as you can in person, and to talk to their owners, so club meets and Land Rover shows are worth making the effort to attend. Much can also be learned from studying your own vehicle, which is why making a close photographic record before dismantling the car will be a great help when you come to put it back together.

The Series One Club's online forum (www.lrsoc.com) is generally considered to be the largest and most useful source of information relating to these vehicles, benefitting from a large number of knowledgeable contributors. The Club has over 4,000 members worldwide and can supply a wide range of parts. It also holds a significant archive of useful articles and period photography, all available online. For 80in Series Is in particular, The Land Rover Register 1948–53 is another valuable resource. Both the Register and the Series One Club produce well respected magazines: *Full Grille* and *The Legend,* respectively.

As for other magazines, the three main titles in the UK are *Land Rover Owner*, *Land Rover Monthly* and *Classic Land Rover*. The latter naturally contains the highest proportion of material related to these vehicles, but Series Is feature in all three. Period magazine articles featuring road tests of Series Is can also be as instructive

as they are entertaining. Various books have been written about the evolution of the Series I, but the vehicle came in so many forms, and changed so much (especially during its formative years), that the reader should not expect any one source to provide comprehensive details about their particular model.

Learn from other Series Is and their owners by attending Land Rover shows.

Index

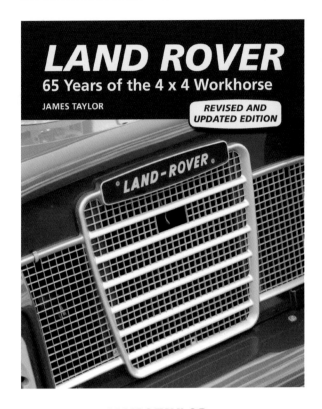

JAMES TAYLOR
ISBN: 9781847974594

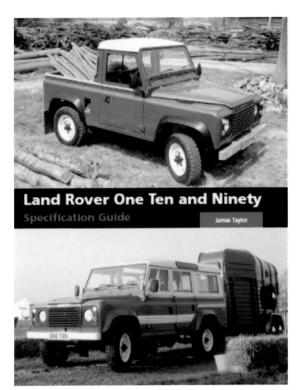

JAMES TAYLOR
ISBN: 9781785007736

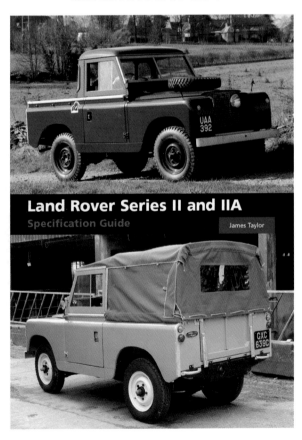

JAMES TAYLOR
ISBN: 9781847971609

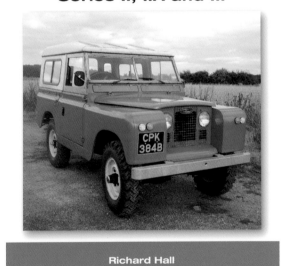

RICHARD HALL
ISBN: 9781785001352